THE EXTERNALIZATION
OF CONSCIOUSNESS
AND THE
PSYCHOPATHOLOGY
OF
EVERYDAY LIFE

**Recent Titles in
Contributions in Psychology**

Sexuality: New Perspectives
Zira DeFries, Richard C. Friedman, and Ruth Corn, editors

Portrait and Story: Dramaturgical Approaches to the Study of Persons
Larry Cochran

The Meaning of Grief: A Dramaturgical Approach to Understanding Emotion
Larry Cochran and Emily Claspell

New Ideas in Therapy: Introduction to an Interdisciplinary Approach
Douglas H. Ruben and Dennis J. Delprato, editors

Human Consciousness and Its Evolution: A Multidimensional View
Richard W. Coan

From AI to Zeitgeist: A Philosophical Guide for the Skeptical Psychologist
N. H. Pronko

Inevitability: Determinism, Fatalism, and Destiny
Leonard W. Doob

The Psychology of Writing: The Affective Experience
Alice Glarden Brand

Medieval Psychology
Simon Kemp

Hesitation: Impulsivity and Reflection
Leonard W. Doob

Culture and the Restructuring of Community Mental Health
William A. Vega and John W. Murphy

THE EXTERNALIZATION OF CONSCIOUSNESS AND THE PSYCHOPATHOLOGY OF EVERYDAY LIFE

Stephen T. DeBerry

CONTRIBUTIONS IN PSYCHOLOGY, NUMBER 17

GREENWOOD PRESS

New York • Westport, Connecticut • London

Library of Congress Cataloging-in-Publication Data

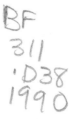

DeBerry, Stephen.
 The externalization of consciousness and the psychopathology of
everyday life / Stephen T. DeBerry.
    p.   cm. — (Contributions in psychology, ISSN 0736–2714 ; no.
17)
 Includes bibliographical references and index.
 ISBN 0–313–27280–8 (lib. bdg. : alk. paper)
 1. Consciousness—Social aspects. 2. Civilization, Modern—1950– —
Psychological aspects. I. Title. II. Series.
BF311.D38   1991
153—dc20   90–36638

British Library Cataloguing in Publication Data is available.

Library of Congress Catalog Card Number: 90–36638
ISBN: 0–313–27280–8
ISSN: 0736–2714

First published in 1991

Greenwood Press, 88 Post Road West, Westport, CT 06881
An imprint of Greenwood Publishing Group, Inc.

Printed in the United States of America

This book is dedicated to Linda, without whose love it could never have been written, and to Julian, whose newborn consciousness is beyond reproach.

Contents

Preface

This book is about human consciousness, ordinary, everyday, garden-variety consciousness. Yet, there is nothing at all ordinary about consciousness. In contrast, it is truly extraordinary, a fact to which technological progress has made people oblivious. They are as jaded to the gift of consciousness as they are blinded to a universe that endlessly reveals itself in infinite forms, shapes, and patterns of existence.

The purpose of this book is to present a new model of human consciousness. The model is not a radical one, but rather an original synthesis of existing information. From the perspective of general systems theory, the text first describes human consciousness and then discusses its shift into the impersonal dimension, where only the material world matters.

The constriction of the vibrancy, passion, and life of intuitive and emotional personal experiences not only reduces consciousness of the world but easily manipulates it. With concern about this constriction, this work represents a rather penetrating look at one of the most subtle, yet serious cultural changes of contemporary life.

The proposed model explores the relationship of consciousness to the accelerating technology of the television-video universe in terms of the quality of people's daily lives. As Fritjof Capra states, there is a vast and crucial difference between the concept of quality of life and the more familiar and popular yardstick, standard of living. To their detriment, most people measure their lives by the latter dimension, a matter of no small importance that will be explored later.

Regarding the accelerating and all too pervasive video universe, for the first time in human history entire generations are being raised from infancy in a predominantly visual world, yet there is little knowledge as to how this will affect future generations. The dominant paradigms in psychology and psychiatry do not, as a rule, place very much emphasis on the relationship between technology and consciousness. With few exceptions, as in, for example, John Condry's book on the psychology of television (which will be discussed in chapter 9), there is a paucity of empirical and experimental literature on the relationship between technology and consciousness. In fact, the research literature on television is polemical and equivocal. It seems that people either love or hate technology, especially the technology of television. Yet, by reintegrating the concept of consciousness into mainstream psychology, one can begin to study holistically the effects of technology on people. However, ecological psychology, which is what a holistic approach is all about, is not a favorite son of the predominant psychological paradigm.

Writing this book has been a rewarding as well as an illuminating experience. The topic of consciousness does not easily lend itself to precise scientific inquiry. This difficulty is partially why psychology has virtually abandoned it as an area of serious study. To write about consciousness and its relation to culture, I have had to investigate a remarkably diverse body of literature and research ranging from anthropology to quantum physics and Zen Buddhism. Writing a book about consciousness has actually changed by own consciousness. I have been literally forced to think—to reexamine my old, cherished, and often erroneous assumptions concerning the nature of reality. (For an excellent and scholarly in-depth exploration of consciousness and culture, see O. B. Hardison's recent book, *Disappearing through the Skylight: Culture and Technology in the Twentieth Century.* His work provides a thorough and eclectic introduction to the relationship of art and culture.)

This book, about "ordinary consciousness," which can be connected to just about everything, will of necessity have to maintain a generalist approach. The generalist approach—one not currently popular in the behavioral sciences—is a legitimate, fundamental tactic of the natural sciences, phenomenology, and empirical research (Lorenz, 1950). There are at least three basic reasons for objecting to the immediate dismissal of ideas suspected of belonging to his unpopular genre. First, in clinical work ideas about a patient shift over time from a general to a specific nature. In the beginning of psychotherapy, psychotherapists have a cluster of ideas, postulates, hypotheses, and theories regarding the patient. As psychotherapy proceeds, some of these beginning impressions change, some are further validated, and others are completely discarded. They are all, however, initially worthy of exploration. Second, in delusional or paranoid patients or even in ordinary stereotypes, for that matter, there is always a kernel of truth; additional exploration for this possible truth is called for. Finally, almost all psychotherapists learn to look for an intense reaction of denial as a confirming possibility that a personal truth has been touched. The second half of the book explores cultural institutions of perhaps a strong personal nature from a very particular and, at times, unflattering perspective that might be painful.

This approach to consciousness does merit certain qualifications, the first being that the intent is not to be right or wrong, but rather to provoke thought, dialogue, and questioning, to provoke the reader to think about consciousness and its relationship to everyday life. Perhaps the admonition of the neuropsychologist Karl Pribram (1986) is applicable here: "I will provide one caveat: The approach taken here is new and must therefore of necessity be inadequate and even 'wrong' in detail. The important consideration is that the approach is a viable one and that it can be progressively sharpened by recourse to experimental disconfirmation. The approach is essentially scientific but heeds the questions so carefully honed by philosophic inquiry" (p. 509). As Charles Tart (1975), the pioneer researcher and theoretician of consciousness, states, all work on consciousness is by its very nature transitory.

Second, the presentation in this book is *a* model and not *the* model of consciousness. Psychologists, especially those of an academic or theoretical persuasion, are so often involved in polemics and theoretical territoriality that they miss the basic point. One basic point, and certainly not *the* point, is the need to develop an integrative, comprehensive, and pragmatically useful science of existence, a science that can help people live their lives in a useful fashion. Although the precise formulation of such a science has not yet developed, it is time at least to begin heading in that direction (Capra, 1982; Ornstein & Erlich, 1989; Pagels, 1989; Tart, 1975). The postulates in this book concerning consciousness must be viewed primarily as an invitation to experimental verification and only secondly as a new way of "looking at the world." Pop science has suggested too many new ways of looking at the world; part of the problem is that humankind is now drowning in a whirlpool of ambiguity.

Third, since this work derives from the framework of a clinical psychologist, the book must be considered somewhat elemental in terms of providing a solid background in physics, especially in the area of quantum mechanics. For a solid introduction to these areas, see the authors from whom I borrow, especially Heinz Pagels, Paul Davies, Nick Herbert, and Fritjof Capra.

Another qualification is that this model of the mind is concerned with the consciousness of higher cortical processes as reflected by their expression in terms of language. Consciousness should be distinguished from reactivity, in that reacting to an object does not necessarily imply consciousness (Pearce, 1974). Because they do not employ language, subcortical, animal, or unconscious processes are deliberately being ignored.

Finally, although this book for the most part avoids jargon and metatheoretical constructs, it assumes, with the exception of the chapter on general systems theory, at least a basic working knowledge of psychology, philosophy, and science. Although the book is geared toward those in the mental health profession, it is not just another "psychology book" and includes case studies only as a way of illustrating the key points of each chapter, keeping these clinical examples to a relevant minimum.

The first six chapters are somewhat theoretical in that they concern themselves mainly with the construction of a model of consciousness. The remainder of the book is less theoretical and represents the attempt at understanding the problems of daily existence through the eyes of the model. The perspective, therefore, shifts as the text progresses. Seven postulates concerning consciousness are explored. These postulates represent the linkage between an individual and a community model of consciousness. The tone of the text must shift from a specific (individual consciousness) to a more general perspective (community or cultural consciousness).

Since the book has been written in a building-block fashion that proceeds from the molecular to the molar, it should be read in a serial fashion, as each chapter depends in part on its predecessor. For those more interested in larger issues, like culture, community, consciousness, and the psychopathology of everyday life, it is possible, however, to start with chapter 10 and work backward. Any questions that arise through this reverse method should be answered by the time the reader finishes chapter 1.

The following is a brief synopsis of the text's progression:

- Chapter 1. Explores the relationship of scientific paradigms to the ability to investigate and understand consciousness.
- Chapter 2. Provides a scientific and philosophical background relevant to theories of consciousness, especially as they are related to the introduction of several new concepts.

- Chapter 3. Introduces a general systems theory of consciousness and presents the concepts of perspective and focus.
- Chapter 4. Describes how consciousness can be transformed over time and space, especially in terms of intrapersonal, interpersonal, and impersonal factors.
- Chapter 5. Depicts how values and reality assumptions affect the system of consciousness.
- Chapter 6. Relates how language is one fundamental building block of consciousness that is intertwined with perspective, focus, values, and reality assumptions.
- Chapter 7. Summarizes how distortions in perspective, focus, values, reality assumptions, and language have led to an "externalized consciousness" in which the impersonal dimension predominates.
- Chapter 8. Proposes the ideas that the individual construction of consciousness described in the preceding chapters is directly related to issues of contemporary culture and community. Examples of law and government are employed as illustrations.
- Chapter 9. Begins to explore how technology, especially visual technologies, contributes to the distortions in consciousness described in the previous chapters.
- Chapter 10. Compares how distortions in individual and community consciousness are related to what is described as the contemporary psychopathology of everyday life.

The model itself is always framed within the boundaries of general systems theory. Although this transformation may be a bit disconcerting to the casual reader, it is nevertheless part of the process inherent in the inductive process of shifting from an individual to a community perspective. A common theme that might be helpful to remember is that both individual consciousness and community consciousness are interdependent parts of the same general system. What happens to one part is connected to what happens to the other. I have, perhaps because the topic itself is so fluid, tried to maintain both a consistent internal logic and a solid scientific basis.

This book is written for those professionals who not only want to enhance the scope of their particular discipline but desire to have a beneficial impact on human relations and, therefore, the future of the planet itself. The book raises some important questions of interest to psychologists, yet it is not intended for psychologists or mental health professionals alone. The text is directed as much toward anthropologists, teachers, and politicians as toward those already familiar with the psychological sciences. It is intended for those who think critically, reflect, and feel that life has more potential and purpose than they allow it.

One additional issue with respect to this book's reading audience concerns the use of masculine pronouns. The consistent use of the masculine pronoun when referring to abstract persons should not be interpreted as exclusionary, for no implication with respect to gender is intended.

An essential question that this book attempts to address is: Why does it increasingly seem, on a personal, community, national, and international level, that what my patients are sometimes conscious of, I am also conscious of? The bridge from individual consciousness to national and international community is a matter of no small importance. Ashley Montagu and Floyd Matson (1983) rightly state that "neither in the person nor in the nation are mind and body disconnected; the realm of ideas and the world of affairs are joined in continuous reciprocal interaction, and neither can be understood without reference to the other" (p. xii). Obviously, such a broad area of inquiry could not be restricted to psychology alone but, rather, must include an integration of several disciplines.

But it is to the scientists and experimentalists that I put forth my dilemma and address this book. Anyone can write a mystical book on consciousness. Heinz Pagels has eloquently demonstrated that certain epistemological positions like monism or categorical dualism are beyond practical verification. Hopefully the postulates in this book concerning the nature of ordinary consciousness are to some extent experimentally verifiable and, therefore, pragmatically useful. This book may be attempting to place operational behaviorism within a philosophical value system. Perhaps that attempt is just what behaviorism needs. Therefore, this model must be viewed not as an attempt to replace the biopsychosocial or cognitive behavioral models but as an attempt to integrate and perhaps transform the prevailing models into a less reductionistic and more holistic-ecological paradigm of operational definitions. In any event, hopefully these ideas will be tested and confirmed or discarded.

In *The Closing of the American Mind*, Alan Bloom (1988) has correctly pointed out that American methods of education have deteriorated to the point that knowledge has lost its value base and thus has lost its pragmatic usefulness not only as a guiding force but as a solution to everyday life. Therefore, values are reintroduced as a central theme of this book; values should be a more recognized area of science. According to Schwartz (1990), "science does have, and indeed should have a prominent role in an inquiry into values. It is just not quite the role that most scientists expect or assume it to have. What science in general, and experimentation in particular, does is provide vivid examples or demonstrations. What the scientist must then do is embed these examples in a narrative, or argument, that attempts to identify their particular historical or cultural significance" (p. 15). This book represents such an attempt.

Those recently trained in psychology, science, and psychotherapy were taught that their work should be value-free. This idea is patent nonsense and has resulted in much of the current intellectual, spiritual, and practical confusion. To reintroduce the concept of values in a scientifically meaningful way, this book must explore what may seem like rather unconnected topics. Yet, the book will show what quantum mechanics teaches, that not only are these concepts connected and interdependent, but that they are directly related to the notion that it is the mind or, more precisely, consciousness that connects and, in essence, constructs reality. Therefore, this book's roundabout approach is essential because psychology and the human sciences have gone so far astray that it becomes necessary to start from scratch regarding the nature of ordinary consciousness. This book attempts to demonstrate that consciousness is the common denominator for all people and that the components of consciousness can be identified, understood, studied, and improved. The present model conceptualizes consciousness as an evolutionary structure that historically has been shifting from an internal, metaphorical matrix of intrapersonal, interpersonal, and impersonal meaning to an external locus of predominantly impersonal meaning. This evolutionary shift is directly involved in the complicated interactions of everyday life, human consciousness, and psychopathology.

Introduction

CONSCIOUSNESS AND SCIENCE

Consciousness now seems to be the province of physicists rather than psychologists. Physical scientists such as David Bohm (1980), Fritjof Capra (1977, 1982), Paul Davies (1983), Heinz Pagels (1989), Rudy Rucker (1982), and Fred Alan Wolf (1982, 1989) have started to apply the incredible mathematical world of quantum mechanics to consciousness and the mind. The implications of quantum physics to the psychology of mind and consciousness are of profound importance and have literally begun to rewrite psychological and psychoanalytic theory. Even more important is that these recent advances in what might be considered the most esoteric of theoretical sciences have incredible applicability to everyday life.

Yet, mainstream psychology has remained painfully, but perhaps deliberately, unaware of the implications of quantum mechanics. This situation has led to the rather puzzling and ironic result that in some ways physicists now have more of an advanced understanding of consciousness than do psychologists, psychiatrists, or psychoanalysts. The traditional psychological sciences have responded to the discoveries of the physical sciences by moving in several different and rather limited directions, three of the most prominent being cognitive-behavioral psychology, transpersonal psychology, and biological psychiatry. All of these subdisciplines are of value. Problems arise, however, when any one of them, to the exclusion of other perspectives, is employed as the only way in which to understand or assist humanity.

Transpersonal psychology is the subspecialty that purports to understand the connections between humanity and the universe. It is a valuable area of inquiry that has resulted in new information concerning the spiritual, existential, and teleological nature of being. Yet, transpersonal psychology is especially vulnerable to becoming an escapist solution prone to quasi-mystical distortions. It too easily allows for the abandonment of problems related to everyday consciousness in the present and instead explores extraordinary forms of consciousness such as people's relationship with the universe, God, spirits, or past lives. Although some of the research and literature of transpersonal psychology, especially as evident in the works of C. T. Tart and Robert Ornstein, both of whom are quoted extensively in this book, is very practical, valuable, and scientific, a large portion of it remains speculative. At its worst, transpersonal psychology seduces one into abdicating an empirical approach to reality for the sanctuary of unproven popular speculation. Transpersonal psychology has aligned itself with mysticism, the occult, channeling ESP, altered states of consciousness, and extraordinary phenomena. This direction is partially responsible for the current neglect of ordinary consciousness and for the preoccupation with mystical consciousness and esoteric philosophies and methods of healing. At its best, however, transpersonal psychology reminds people that it is essential to understand the nature of their connection to the universe in which they live.

Cognitive-behavioral psychology and biological psychiatry are currently the dominant paradigms and, although not the cause, are nevertheless partially responsible for the current reductionistic approach of Western psychology and psychiatry. Again, however, there is a paradox. The subdisciplines of cognitive-behavioral psychology and biological psychiatry have been responsible for some of the most important changes in contemporary mental health care. Behavior modification, classical and instrumental conditioning, assertiveness training, therapeutic blood monitoring, and pharmacological therapy are but a few examples of beneficial effects. The problem then, becomes one of basic paradigms and elemental assumptions. The underlying elemental assumption of both biological psychiatry and cognitive-behavioral psychology is that human behavior can be reduced to a series of basic chemical, genetic, or stimulus-response factors. At their best, such underlying paradigmatic assumptions allow for a more thorough understanding of how elemental forces affect people's lives "from the bottom up." At their worst, such paradigms deny not only the developmental implications but the ecological connectedness of existence itself.

Yet, there has been some movement in the right direction. Behaviorists like Donald Meichenbaum (1974) have introduced concepts such as "internal dialogue," Arnold Lazarus (1972) speaks of the basic id and multimodal therapy, cognitivists like Victor Guidano (1987) are developing cognitive-emotional models of development, and psychiatrists like George Engels (1987) are constructing "biopsychosocial" models of treatment. But, the underlying reductive paradigm remains the same, and as the physician-philosopher Richard Chessick (1985) states, too often scientists simply give these ideas "lip service," pretending to study people when in reality they are looking only at synapses and stimuli.

REDUCTIVE TREATMENT APPROACHES

The practical overflow of these paradigms is evident in the plethora of simplistic, mechanistic self-help books, "pop" psychological theories, and recipe cookbook cures that are so predominant today. Such formula approaches represent the negative side of the cognitive/behavioral/biological paradigms, that is, reductive distortions of an already reductionistic model. These quick-fix, pharmacological, and behavioral attempts at change rarely work or rarely last because they are based on outdated and incomplete conceptions of the brain, the mind, consciousness, the self, and reality in general. The quick-fix philosophies and techniques are popular because they preserve the traditional, orderly sense of a predictable and purposeful universe that is consistent with both the senses and the sense of self. They promote an outdated but safe and mechanical understanding of problems that lend themselves to being fixed or cured by an ever-growing professional army of healers, doctors, technicians, and psychotherapists.

As an illustration, let me describe my impression of the now faddish Optifast and Medifast weight loss programs. These programs, which are an excellent example of the quick-fix philosophy, in 1988 earned for the Sandoz Pharmaceutical Corporation in excess of $700 million, despite the fact that over 95 percent of people who initially lose weight on Optifast/Medifast programs regain all or more of the weight back. Yet, the programs continue to attract millions of people so that most centers now have waiting lists of people begging to part with their money. But for what?

Clearly the empirical evidence scientifically demonstrates that these programs, although initially effective, do not provide lasting results. How can one explain this seemingly paradoxical phenomenon? In brief, I have come to realize that what my Medifast patients want is not so much to lose weight (although on one level this is important) but to have their worldview confirmed. That is, in an age of ever-increasing uncertainty, anxiety, and potential ecological or nuclear catastrophe, they are looking for reassurances that there are simplistic, mechanical solutions to an ever-increasing complex and interrelated range of problems. I have found this need for simplicity and certainty so great that many patients are willing to pay money and continue to fail and blame themselves if only to preserve their notion of reality. In other words, it is more important for these people to sustain their sense of the world (and theories, for example, of why they were overweight) than to accept a new version of reality and thus the possibility of true change.

Any type of lasting change must be accompanied by a change in consciousness. Yet, most people are not even aware of how their ordinary consciousness affects their lives. They might be concerned with improving their spiritual, religious, or extraordinary consciousness, but they have little understanding of what is happening to them on a day-to-day basis. This lack of understanding is manifest most clearly in language and behavior as evidenced by how they act and what they talk about.

LANGUAGE AND CONSCIOUSNESS

One of the most accepted phenomena of everyday life is language. A central theme of this book is that language is a direct reflection of both behavior and consciousness and that disturbances in both consciousness and behavior can be measured by linguistic analysis. The connection of consciousness with language has a solid history established in part by linguistic experts such as Noam Chomsky (1968, 1989), Howard Pollio (1977, 1982, 1990), Benjamin Whorf (1957), and others. As an expressive mechanism, language can either expand or reduce consciousness. All too often individuals settle for the constrictive effects.

A typical dinner party can illustrate this point. When not everyone knows each other, at first the conversation is a bit stifled. Eventually, however, a common ground is discovered, and the conversation takes off. This common ground usually consists of impersonal topics such as money, real estate, movies, television shows, sports, music, celebrities, or everyday news and politics. People talk almost always about things outside themselves, that is, the talk is external.

In brief, this example illustrates the externalization of consciousness. People are becoming more aware of and involved in the materialistic external world of things and abstractions at the expense of their rich interpersonal and personal world of emotions and experience. The psychopathology of everyday life is reflected in this external shift and is evidenced everywhere, for example, in the breakdown of community, the increasing chaos of family life, relationship difficulties, and problems with closeness and intimacy (Bellah, 1987). Psychotherapists are noticing that patients with an ever-increasing frequency are in a "demoralized state," with combinations of narcissistic and other borderline character problems that not only severely impede the ability to relate but are incredibly hard to detect (Frank, 1978; Fromm, 1956, 1973, 1976; May, 1953, 1986). This situation means that pathology is often culturally disguised as normality. As Thoreau stated, "things are in the saddle and ride mankind" (Foucault, 1973; Lasch, 1979, 1984; Marcuse, 1955, 1964).

The way people see the world is reflected in language. They tend to talk about things external to themselves as if the things were part of them. Most people, as Rollo May has pointed out, are more comfortable talking about things rather than about their feelings, themselves, or others. More recently, because of the media explosion, people have now begun to talk about others with whom they have no direct contact as if they know them. Conversation at the dinner party mentioned earlier may revolve around celebrities and stars about whom everyone has a tremendous wealth of knowledge. Yet, the ultimate paradox is that these are people that no one really knows directly. Thus, there is the illusion of intimacy without any real intimacy at all. At no time do guests talk about inner feelings concerning themselves, each other, or what is going on in the present moment, that is, the experience of the dinner party. The dinner party is an everyday common experience considered too boring or mundane in comparison to the rarefied atmosphere of Michael Jackson, "Dynasty," and the latest French import.

The problem, of course, is that nothing in the conversation is real. It is all derived from the media technology of television, movies, and video. Although people seem to be interacting and chatting merrily, in reality they might as well be reading scripts. Real intimacy requires, among other things, the risk of direct personal involvement. Has the technological age with its proliferation of electronic intimacy made direct personal involvement obsolete?

Before beginning to answer this question, one must first ask, What is direct personal involvement and why is it such a risk? Concepts such as direct personal involvement, risk, intimacy, and consciousness can be empirically understood and operationally identified. Operationally defining these terms is crucial in that not only does it allow identification of the behaviors necessary to change consciousness or create intimacy, but it likewise helps to avoid abstract "psychobabble," metatheory, and fuzzy euphemistic jargon.

A main contention of this book is that the predominant mode of consciousness is a highly distorted illusion so powerful that it seems real, a pseudo-intimacy that is not really intimacy at all. It is a form of relating and a form of consciousness that are incomplete, that leave people unsettled, empty, and ever searching for the mystical philosophy, transpersonal experience, drug, acquisition, success, power, or cognitive-behavioral strategy to feel whole again.

This feeling of wholeness or well-being will never happen unless the quality of consciousness is allowed to become more complete. People are losing the ability to understand and communicate feelings about themselves and others. They have retreated from the sharing of inner experiences that are of necessity irrational, intuitive, or illogical because they do not fit the commonsense, mechanistic, and traditional notions of reality. This inability to communicate with each other is reflective of the growing inability to engage in dialogue that is meaningful, real, and productive. It has led to the overuse of bureaucratic jargon and fuzzy euphemisms as a replacement for reality (Bellah, 1987; Deikman, 1971; Lasch, 1984).

A CLINICAL ANALOGY: THE DIAGNOSTIC PROCESS

A clinical and perhaps a personal analogy may illustrate a basic point. This book intends not only to place my life and the problems of my patients into a more comprehensive perspective, but also to offer heuristic possibilities. Psychology, along with medicine and the behavioral sciences, has for too long been caught in a paradigm trap of Cartesian reductionism. The practical implications of being caught in this trap have unfortunately spilled over into treatment of patients. Most modern paradigms of psychopathology reflect an inability to account adequately for clinical observations. As long as a therapist chooses a specific model, for example, biomedical, cognitive-behavioral, or psychoanalytic, he can safely place his patients' symptoms within an epistemological framework that provides an explanation (diagnosis). Once a diagnosis is made, as, for example, in schizophrenia, there is no further need to deal with the person, only with the disease. Therefore, the clinician has no further reason to deal with or listen to the content of what the patient is saying. After all, she is schizophrenic, so she could not possibly be making any sense.

However, once I step beyond the safety of my theoretical net, I begin to notice that, increasingly, the observations my patients (these diagnosed, objectified others) are making about the world match my own. Thus, although I am presumably symptom-free, I find myself in the paradoxical position of agreeing with their observations, that is, their consciousness of the world, and yet disagreeing with their behavioral resolutions, that is, their symptoms. The classical way out of this dilemma is, of course, to ignore consciousness and concentrate on symptoms (Feldstein, 1978; Needleman, 1979). Hence, there is the contemporary preoccupation with nosology and diagnoses, synapse and symptom. The traditional reductionistic solution, however, begs the question and leaves a rather nasty moral aftertaste.

Even more troublesome if the fact that the problem about consciousness is not solely limited to patients but affects everyone. In fact, I have more problems with the limited consciousness of my colleagues than I do with that of my patients. Their consciousness problem becomes most evident in the language that they use, in this case, the professional jargon.

The intention in bringing forth yet another model in a field already drowning in models is basically selfish. That is, from both a clinical and a personal perspective, the existing biological/behavioral models that are currently predominant in psychiatry and psychology are woefully wanting in terms of providing an understanding of the present human (in this case my own) condition. Obviously, there are numerous problems in attempting this synthesis, one of them being the numbing triteness into which the phrase *human condition* has fallen (Montagu & Matson, 1983). People live in an age that in attempting to understand itself has unleashed a proliferation of metatheory and pseudoscience. The dogma and delusions to which people have succumbed are, of course, the products of their own fears. The applied human sciences have retreated into biological/behavioral reductionism while philosophy has fled into the positivistic safety net of semantics and semiotics. Yet, such a retreat was probably necessary, a healthy reaction to the obscure musings of the existentialists and secular humanists and the gothic preoccupations of the psychoanalysts, who have yet to accept that the outside world exists. The time has arrived to end the reductionistic retreat and reintegrate a scientific philosophy into a new paradigm of "the person."

To reiterate an essential point, in no way should it be misunderstood that these arguments are against cognitive-behavioral psychology or biological psychiatry per se. A renunciation of the teachings of these specialties is not advocated. The objection is to the dogmatic and unidimensional interpretations and applications of these paradigms so that, at the exclusion of all others, they become the paradigm of the person. For example, during my graduate training the predominant paradigm in psychology and psychiatry was psychoanalytic. By the 1970s the psychoanalytic paradigm was abandoned in favor of the biological/behavioral/cognitive paradigm. The problem with both these paradigms is that they eventually became exclusive, a process that precluded alternate ways of understanding. Such restrictions are not just a matter of theoretical or academic interest, for they affect the way people listen, think, and treat other people. Most psychiatric services now place priority on biological and behavioral treatment approaches. Although such approaches cannot be faulted, they become inadequate when used alone. Meaning, content, and consciousness become lost in the shadow of absolute reductionism. So do economic, social, cultural, historical, and political factors, all of which play an important role in human development. As some authors have noted, reliance on one paradigm has resulted in many treatment centers shifting to a pharmacological and social-support-maintenance model of care (DeBerry & Baskin, 1989; Udell & Hornstra, 1977).

Psychology or any human science requires a reintegration of various specialties into a general and holistic understanding of humanity. The physicist Heinz Pagels calls this process a horizontal integration of subdisciplines. In this sense, this book is, I hope, a step in that direction.

POSTMODERNISM AND CONSTRUCTIVISM

Unable to align myself with the psychoanalytic school's arcane mythology and finding humanistic and transpersonal psychologists too eclectic and vague, the behaviorists myopic and metaphysical, and the cognitive psychologists (with certain notable exceptions) behaviorists in disguise, I have developed another model, which owes its debt to a great many people. This approach is characteristic of a general movement called postmodern constructivism. Postmodernism and constructivism are really two different entities with separate origins. The postmodern movement, which first began in architecture and the arts, has now spread to philosophy and psychology. Although no one really agrees what the term *postmodern* means, it seems at best to refer to the evolution of the modern period into a transitional phase that is, in essence, becoming the future. The term represents a temporal distinction between the beginning and middle phases of the modern period in comparison to the later, postmodern period in which humans are now immersed. The term is not without its merits in that it suggests that consciousness is in a period of transition. The way in which people perceive their world is changing because the predominant mode of being is changing from a postindustrial, centralized base to an information-processing, global, and decentralized base. A highly complex and reciprocal relationship exists between this base and consciousness. Postmodernism will be explored in depth in chapter 8.

In reality, there is nothing new or modern about constructivism; in many different scientific, philosophical, and religious disguises it has existed for centuries. Simply put, the basic thrust of constructivism is that people selectively construct their own reality, a claim mystics have been making for centuries. Nevertheless, inventing new terminology is part of the process of academic and scientific advancement, a process certainly in operation here. The neuropsychologist Karl Pribram (1986) is perhaps one of the principal proponents of a constructivist model of consciousness. What does make constructivism presently important is that its proposition that consciousness is an active constructor of reality is very much in accord with recent developments in both neurology and physics. These developments will be discussed in more depth in chapter 2.

Couldn't scientists, therefore, simply look to what the quantum physicists have learned as a way of improving humankind or changing its condition? The answer to this question can only be an emphatic no. Before one begins to apply the revelations of quantum physics, they must be distilled down to everyday reality. Physicists do not deal with people on an everyday basis; they deal with mathematical equations and theoretical formulas that must be translated into everyday life. Or, perhaps because their work is so removed from everyday life, in their attempts to explain the world they often lapse into metaphysics and mythology. According to the physicist Paul Davies (1983): "Physics, in my opinion, makes its chief contribution through reductionism. The holistic aspects fall more appropriately into the cognitive sciences and subjects like systems theory, games theory, sociology and politics. . . . I don't believe that physics can tackle questions about, for example, purpose or morality" (p. 227). The practical implications of certain principles of physics are at times so obscure and pragmatically untestable that they can be used to justify almost any metaphysical belief, for example, in the use of the principle of quantum uncertainty to verify the existence of the spirit world.

On the other hand, as an observer of society, the clinical psychologist occupies a rather unique position in that he understands that individual symptoms are always rooted in a social context. Thus, one is afforded a rather unique opportunity to examine cultural phenomena, which are, after all, a major catalyst for psychopathology. As a clinical psychologist I see people who desperately need a new way of living. I am talking not just about the patients I see, who often have very specific complaints such as depressions, psychoses, phobias, or anxiety, but about almost everyone, my students, other teachers, my colleagues, my friends, and myself. In short, before any true transformation of human life can occur, it is normal, not abnormal, consciousness that needs to be first understood and then altered.

In Western Europe, during the latter part of the Victorian era, Freud

(1978) identified repressed instinctuality (sexual and aggressive) as the prime determinant of the daily neuroses of his era. In contrast, this book examines the contemporary externalized consciousness in a very general sense as the psychopathological breeding ground for the global psychological ills of this era, namely, alienation, despair, chronic anxiety, emptiness, pervasive depression, and narcissism.

This book begins with the question, What is consciousness? In agreement with Felman (1985), "the answer here can but disseminate the question."

THE EXTERNALIZATION
OF CONSCIOUSNESS
AND THE
PSYCHOPATHOLOGY
OF
EVERYDAY LIFE

1 *Paradigms of Science*

If the only tool you have is a hammer, you tend to treat everything as if it were a nail.

—Abraham Maslow

Before consciousness is explored, it will be necessary to understand first why psychology, the mental health profession, and the behavioral sciences have so carefully avoided the topic. They have been dancing about consciousness for years, afraid somehow that in embracing it, they would destroy themselves. In a sense, this description is partially true, for in order to study consciousness scientifically, their model or basic paradigm must be altered. The biases and preconceptions that accompany the basic paradigms of psychology and psychiatry are so insidious and pervasive that a brief exploration is necessary.

With few exceptions, in traditional Western psychology, ordinary consciousness since the time of William James has been virtually ignored. In fact, behaviorism, the predominant model in twentieth-century American psychology, considers consciousness to be an epiphenomenon not worthy of scientific investigation (Matson, 1974; Skinner, 1987). Whatever interest that has been generated has been devoted to extraordinary and altered states of consciousness such as hypnosis and ESP (Goleman & Davidson, 1979). Unfortunately, in terms of understanding consciousness, the psychologist as well as the average person is left with a strange amalgam of science and mysticism (Ornstein, 1977; Tart, 1983). Fortunately, parallel advances in the science of theoretical quantum physics, cognitive psychology, cybernetics, information theory, and general systems theory, as well as new perspectives in neurophysiology and neuropsychology, are beginning at least to restore the study of consciousness to an arena of respectability (Guidano, 1987; Pollio, 1990; Pribram, 1977; Rapoport, 1974; Von Bertalanaffy, 1973, 1974).

It is both necessary and essential to explore consciousness from a scientific perspective. In addition to experimental research, psychology requires global constructs that might necessitate the study of phenomena not directly observable. It must be remembered that physicists study and employ gravity as a useful construct, though it is not directly observable and barely measurable (Bornstein, 1988; Tart, 1983).

THE CHOICE OF PARADIGMS

Every branch of science has an epistemological paradigm complete with assumptions, values, methods and theories (Kuhn, 1970; Lakatos, 1974; Popper, 1959, 1972; Weimer, 1982; Youngdale, 1988). Paradigms determine and validate what a particular scientific discipline might consider legitimate areas of investigation.

Psychology, in its necessary but shortsighted attempt to model itself after the hard sciences of physics and chemistry, has always stressed the experimental method, as reflected by the quantification of techniques and results, as the mainstay of science. The strict logic and rules of experimentalism have led to the establishment of psychology as a solid, scientific discipline. However, this bias has likewise resulted in the exclusion of data that do not fit the method of inquiry, an unfortunate fact that has relegated consciousness to esoteric back burners of psychological investigation, for example, parapsychology and altered states. According to Davies (1983), "the main thrust of Western scientific thinking over the last three centuries has been reductionistic. Indeed the use of the word 'analysis' in the broadest context nicely illustrates the scientist's almost unquestioning habit of taking a problem apart to solve it" (p. 61). Huston Smith (1976) states that this bias of reductionism is damaging because it excludes not only consciousness, but anything that cannot be measured: "Values, life meanings, purposes and qualities slip through science like sea slips through the nets of fishermen. Yet, man swims in this sea so he cannot exclude it from his purview. That is what was meant when we noted earlier that a scientific worldview is in principle impossible" (p. 16). Clinical scientists working with people must develop healthy and ecologically pragmatic ways of dealing with reality. Science is one way of dealing with human experience. As the anthropologist L. A. White (1949) points out: "The word may be appropriately used as a verb: one sciences, i.e., deals with experience according to certain assumptions and with certain techniques." Values, meaning, purpose, and quality of life must be included in psychology and certainly have to be a part of any psychotherapeutic approach. Yet, in the reductionistic model of biological psychiatry or behavioral psychology these entities do not fit and are therefore ignored. The exclusion of what would seem the most valuable issues from the human applied sciences is a matter that deserves further attention.

First, is the choice of model or paradigm really that important? Wouldn't clinicians, scientists, and self-aware people take such matters into account and include a patient's sense of life meaning or values in their paradigm? In other words, as the question of a patient's purpose in life arises in treatment, wouldn't the therapist deal with it? Unfortunately the answer is "not necessarily so." In most cases it is one's model of the world or basic paradigm that determines reality. Reality is selectively constructed based upon one's chosen paradigms, and for most people these paradigms remain unconscious. That is, individuals are not even conscious that they are allowing a priori, unconscious assumptions to determine their reality. "The bias that arises from unrecognized personal attitudes, interests, and preconceptions is the most treacherous of all the subversive enemies of sound, scientific progress. The vital germ of untrammeled, imaginative thinking is discarded, and too often people seem quite content with the dead husk that is so easily weighed, measured, classified, and then stowed away in the warehouse" (Herick, 1949).

Perhaps a personal illustration is the best way to convey that unconscious paradigms are not just a matter of academic interest. For the past year I have suffered from a very disturbing skin rash. During the course of the year I consulted several dermatologists, who diagnosed my problem as ectopic eczema and idiopathic vasodilation. I was treated with a variety of antihistamines and steroids, but to no avail. The rash persisted and grew worse. Perhaps my biggest problem was that the rash intensified whenever I perspired or was excited, and it severely restricted the range of my activities. Finally, I decided to try an alternate route and consulted an allergist. Fortunately, I know the faculty of a major medical college so all I had to do was call the Department of Immunology. I was lucky enough to reach a friendly fellow in immunology who had just finished medical school and was beginning her specialization in allergic reactions. However, at this point she was still a general practitioner, that is, that nearly extinct breed of new medical doctors who do not specialize. She listened to my complaints for a few minutes, told me that I had what she thought was a cholinergic problem, and suggested that I come to the allergy clinic for a thorough evaluation. I thanked her for her time and advice and began to think about what she said: "A cholinergic problem. That made sense since the cholinergic nervous system is involved in the activation of the sweat glands. I wonder what would happen if I took an anticholinergic drug; perhaps it would alleviate the problem." I promptly called my dermatologist, who, after patiently listening to me, told me that in dermatology they don't use the word *cholinergic*; it's too general. "It doesn't mean anything, Steve." I finally convinced him, despite the fact that he did not like the word, to place me on a trial of anticholinergic medicine. The results were incredible! I felt as if an eraser were removing the rash from my body like chalk powder from a blackboard. I couldn't wait to keep my appointment at the allergy clinic.

The day of my appointment came, and I was quite excited abut telling the fellow the good news, that her diagnosis had been correct and that I was, for the first time in a year, both rash- and medication-free. Since she was in training, first I had to see her superior, the head of the entire Division of Allergy and Immunology. He, in his best head doctor manner, asked me what my problem was, and I told him the entire story from beginning to end. (The beginning was when by mistake I jumped into my father-in-law's overly chlorinated swimming pool, damaging my skin and sweat glands. The end, of course, was my present state of remission, thanks to this astute fellow.)

What happened next was astounding. The head of the Division of Allergy and Immunology of this major medical center turned beet red, stood up, and slammed his fist into the desk. "We do not, Dr. DeBerry, as allergists use the word *cholinergic*. It is a meaningless word, an empty concept." I protested that despite the apparent uselessness of the term, I was under the naive impression that curing my symptoms was part of the treatment, a protest that was immediately brushed aside as irrelevant. The fellow was then called in and berated for using such a meaningless term as *cholinergic*. In other words, she was being criticized for curing my symptoms because her employment of the concept *cholinergic* did not fit the paradigm under which allergists work. I was then put on the same antihistamine that for the past year had been useless and was told never to take anticholinergic medication again. I can still remember the look of benign resignation on the fellow's face as she listened to her superior. She was in a real catch-22 situation and had no choice but to go along with her superior's prescriptions; after all, her medical career was at stake. I left shaken but somewhat more aware that if this situation could happen in medicine, where the parameters of treatment are somewhat well defined, what then could possibly be happening in psychiatric practice, where the course of an illness or its treatment is much less clear and certainly more complex? In what ways could therapists be doing the same thing to their patients?

This example illustrates that one's underlying assumptions, paradigms, models, and maps of reality determine what he sees. This position is basically Thomas Kuhn's position, that the paradigm precedes and partially determines reality (Kuhn, 1970).

The fellow's paradigm was still that of a generalist, not of a specialist. Her observation had no place within the specialist paradigm of immunology or dermatology. After all, specialization is the hallmark of professionalism, and as the educator Vartan Gregorian (1989) says, "We're sub-sub-sub-sub-specializing." It is not that one model is better than another or that generality is superior to specialism but that each alone is inadequate.

A true science of people must be able to incorporate both specialist and generalist principles. Even more important is to be conscious of underlying assumptions regarding reality. It is necessary to be aware of as many paradigms as possible and thus to be able to apply those most applicable to the problem at hand. Alfred North Whitehead (1925) made these points over sixty years ago. In fact, the call for a holistic science is probably as old as science itself. Later chapters will explore reasons for this seemingly eternal rift.

PRAGMATIC ECLECTICISM

The contemporary practice of psychotherapy is a good place to examine the effects that paradigms have on treatment. The integrative approach to psychotherapy is an example of a clinical movement that attempts to combine seemingly disparate models into a larger, more inclusive paradigm. The integrative approach has as its philosophical basis a type of pragmatic eclecticism. Pragmatic eclecticism involves the application of psychotherapeutic procedures independent of any one theoretical base.

If a person consults with me, I see my primary goal as doing whatever it takes to help professionally. Whether the person's problems or symptoms can be placed within my favorite paradigm has to be secondary to their alleviation. Too many people spend valuable time and money languishing in rigid and dogmatic treatment approaches. The clinical research clearly indicates that the quality of the patient-therapist relationship is more important than matters of theoretical orientation, that is, the therapist's paradigm (DeBerry, 1987, 1989b). This finding is one of the reasons why patients of Freudians sound like Freudians, Jungian patients sound like Jungians, and patients of biological psychiatrists sound like pharmacists.

The quality of the psychotherapeutic relationship as well as the conceptualization of the patient's problem is directly related to the psychotherapist's basic paradigm.

How psychotherapists think about a problem is extremely important, as it has a direct relationship to the treatment. The conceptualization is always based on an underlying paradigm or model of reality. For example, psychotherapy has been conceptualized as "a biological treatment that acts through biological mechanisms (interneuronal synaptic facilitation, provision of external physiological regulation, exploration of hippocampal memory processing) on biological problems" (Mohl, 1987, p. 325). Likewise, "For practical purposes our definition of what constitutes a mental illness is simply a medical illness with major emotional and behavioral aspects" (Winokur & Clayton, 1986, p. iv).

Several well-respected clinicians have pointed out that current diagnostic categories, as exemplified in the above passages, are reductionistic, unidimensional, and in "bad faith," that is, totally detached from any concept of the mind, consciousness, the person, or the human condition (Marmor, 1985). The following passage from the philosopher-psychoanalyst Richard Chessick (1985) quite succinctly and eloquently clarifies this contemporary difficulty:

The problem of every physician, whether he is a psychiatrist or in any other specialty, is how to deal with the human self of each patient. In psychiatry this problem is so clear that it intrudes into every aspect of psychiatric practice, and only with the advent of pharmacological agents has it been possible to disavow it, to push it into the background. The rest of the medical profession relies heavily on a reductionistic biomedical model of the human being with molecular biology as its basic scientific discipline, a mode which leaves no room for the social, psychological and behavioral dimensions of illness. . . .

Even Engel's "biopsychosocial model" will not suffice, because it is too easy to pay it lip service while practicing on the biomedical model—more "bad faith." . . .

Whether we like it or not, we are forced in the practice of psychiatry to make certain philosophical assumptions and to form certain preconceptions. . . . The choice of the biological paradigm in psychiatry . . . is an inauthentic choice. It is an act of bad faith that enables psychiatrists temporarily to avoid facing the problems that are really troubling their patients. (pp. 372–81)

It seems, then, that there is a desperate need of a humanistic, yet scientific philosophical framework in which to place ideas and patients. The current paradigm, the reductionistic model of biology and behaviorism, which is sometimes called the "biopsychosocial model," has culminated in both the vacuous *Revised Diagnostic and Statistical Manual III*, as well as the 3,000-page, four-volume *Treatment of Psychiatric Disorders* of the American Psychiatric Association. What is implied here is not that the biopsychosocial model be replaced but, rather, that it be augmented by a more holistic paradigm. Such a paradigm would have to include the serious study of ordinary consciousness.

Holistic or ecological paradigms are dynamic, fluid, and, of course, potentially chaotic. Yet, the study of chaos suggests that the process is an integral and ubiquitous part of existence. One of the problems with using only reductionistic models is that they are too easily distorted into simple and elegant explanations and guidelines for therapeutic treatments. The problem with biobehavioral and biological models is not that they do not work but that they work too well. Because they possess great explanatory power, reductionistic models often end up replacing the processes that they were originally designed to explain. That is, the model becomes mistaken for the reality. In comparison to helping a person change, it becomes easier to eliminate a symptom, modify a behavior, or increase a neurotransmitter. Somewhere in this equation, the person is lost.

As Chessick states, the biopsychosocial model is the biomedical model in disguise. This diagnostic model reflects the experimentally based biobehavioral bias of American psychiatric thinking and is a reflection of what Chessick calls the shift from mind to brain in theoretical formulations. This shift is the logical outcome of the long history of moving away from a true science of the person to a science of classifiable parts, for example, ego, brain, or synapse. This bias has a long history and can be traced, at least contemporarily, back to the original translations of Freud's writings. Yet Freud is not to blame, for he was only following a scientific legacy whose history stretches from the Renaissance back to ancient Greece. Democritus, Pythagoras, and Plato and, later, Sir Francis Bacon, Newton, and René Descartes are all involved (Briggs & Peat, 1984; DeBerry, 1989b).

Before exploring their influence, this discussion will take a very brief look at Freud. It has often been stated that Freud's original writings in German were very warm, human, and person-oriented. His works were modified in translation to fit the then current mechanistic-behavioral orientation of American psychiatry. The difference in choice of words, though seemingly subtle, has had a profound effect on the way psychotherapists treat patients. The former provides a process-oriented, less precise, person-centered perspective; the latter, a sterile, static, symptom-oriented, reductionistic approach. This transformation was, however, inevitable, as Freud's model of the conscious and unconscious was quite amenable to being described in the Cartesian mechanical terms of the classical nineteenth-century physics on which the reductionistic, biomedical model was basing its science. Partially, this bias has been a result of the tendency to model psychological theory after the so-called hard sciences such as physics and chemistry. Psychiatry's and psychology's admiration and emulation of the quantifiable and measurable methods of these disciplines have led to a skewed picture of humanity that is not only incomplete in philosophical terms but out of step with the latest discoveries in the hard sciences as well.

Up until the twentieth century, the cornerstone of Western science could be summed up in Descartes's famous sentence, "Cogito ergo sum"—I think, therefore, I am. This so-called dualist position of mind and body is so entrenched that it has been called an unspoken "official doctrine" of language and culture (Davies, 1983). As a consequence of this Cartesian division of the self, consciousness has been equated not with the complex network of the whole self, but nearly totally with the language-oriented, analytic left hemisphere of the brain. Descartes's postulations, occurring as they did in the seventeenth century along with Newton's discovery of the principles of classical physics, inexorably paved the way in the social sciences for a singular, mechanistic view of the mind, in which each person sees himself as an isolated ego existing in a mind, quite separate from the body. This view in turn has led to the belief that the mind has the task of controlling the baser instincts of the body, resulting in the apparent conflict between conscious will and involuntary instincts and emotions.

This worldview provided a perfect doctrinaire vehicle for the ideas of most major religions and governments, whose basic existence depends on a simplistic perception not only of the person but of the world as well. Classical psychoanalysis, for example, with its mechanistic view of the mind and consciousness, formulated in the language of classical physics, was the twentieth century's attempt at understanding this Cartesian conflict of the person. However, the discovery of the principles of quantum mechanics has indeed complicated this simplistic worldview and has rendered classical intrapersonal psychoanalytic theory obsolete. Perhaps one of the most important outgrowths of quantum physics is that it has returned the observer, and thus consciousness, to being a critical part of the reality equation.

The twentieth century has seen a significant shift away from the traditional, mechanistic, Newtonian universe of determinism to the quantum universe of indeterminacy, infinite possibilities, parallel universes, and multiple possibilities. On humankind's level of existence, the laws of Newtonian physics work quite well. On the subatomic and cosmic levels, however, new models of understanding the universe are being developed.

The mechanistic worldview, still advocated by subdisciplines such as behavioral psychology, psychobiology, and biological psychiatry, is now known to physicists to be a limited point of view that applies best and perhaps only to certain aspects of the macroscopic world. Thus, the emulation that the humanistic and behavioral sciences have accorded the hard sciences is rather out of step with the current formulations of modern physics. In fact, several physicists have postulated eloquent mathematical models describing the reciprocal nature of consciousness and reality and have tied these mathematical concepts to philosophical notions of humanity (Bohm, 1980; Bohr, 1958). In all fairness, this trend is not all psychology's fault, as a large portion of classic science itself, including physics, remains behind the advances in theoretical and subatomic research: "In practice, science has persistently dealt with nature as if the parts and bits pressed under the microscope and accelerated in particle chambers were real" (Briggs & Peat, 1984, p. 98). Perhaps one of the most outstanding of the speculative physicists has been David Bohm. His work concerning the implicate order of the universe is highly recommended.

The chapter in this book on the brain and consciousness will focus more on the impact of quantum physics on the psychology of consciousness.

The resurrection of consciousness within the "sacred" science of physics is not only paradoxical but amusing. Psychology still tries to achieve objectivity by eliminating subjectivity, that is, consciousness, as a legitimate variable. The experimental method poses a most peculiar paradox, namely, it excludes the observer as an object of study. This paradox is of no small importance, as it leaves psychology behind the advances of contemporary physics, which has, theoretically and mathematically, accepted the observer as an essential variable in understanding the observed. As Davies (1983) states: "It is ironical that physics, which has led the way for all other sciences, is now moving towards a more accommodating view of mind, while the life sciences, following the path of last century's physics, are trying to abolish mind altogether" (p. 8).

Limiting research to the experimental method has virtually eliminated consciousness as an area of serious scientific study. Not that consciousness cannot be studied experimentally, for it can, but it cannot be studied cleanly. Over and over again, psychologists are taught to be outstanding methodologists. This trait is one of their claim-to-fame qualities. Within the infamous scientist-practitioner model, psychologists were supposed to provide objective methods of studying clinical phenomena that were valid and reliable. Methodology, objectivity, validity, reliability, statistical analyses, experimentation, and quantification of the data became their professional calling cards. The profession was struggling to establish an identity and was terribly sensitive about not being "real scientists," like the ones in Los Alamos who were splitting atoms and building devices that really measured things.

Not to be outdone, psychologists too set out to measure things, and they have been doing so ever since. Libraries everywhere are filled with an absolutely extraordinary number of methodologically sound but pragmatically useless dissertations, tomes, and analyses. The priority certainly has been design over purpose. It is unimportant that a study was done before and only pointed to the obvious; if a psychologist can add another variable, measure it, and statistically analyze it, then he does so. The clarion call of psychologists has been: "Measure, control, and analyze." At this very moment, legions of graduate students and countless professors are diligently working in academic and clinical sanctuaries on the latest variation of stimulus response theory. Schwartz (1990) provides some interesting reasons behind the continuation of empty and meaningless research, stating: "It is not good science to do the same experiment again and again—to repeat what works" (p. 13).

Certain phenomena, however, do not lend themselves to being easily measured. There might be too many random variables, and including or controlling for these variables might be too difficult. Out of the incredibly complex flux of life, the organic process of living, the experimentalist isolates single discrete variables and then treats them as if they have relevance to the whole. Pieces or parts never, however, reflect the whole. As the Gestaltists have taught, the whole is always greater than the sum of its parts. A person is more than just the sum total of his organ systems (Kohler, 1975).

Consciousness is one of those phenomena that cannot be easily or directly measured, and this problem is the main reason that psychology has ignored it. Consciousness is definitely a whole that is greater than its components, but it is still a whole that can be studied. By ignoring day-to-day consciousness as an area of investigation, psychology likewise ignores the direct study of everything that goes with it; all the daily drama of life becomes secondary. Perhaps even more tragic is the loss of serious public dialogue concerning issues of purpose, meaning, and value.

Thus, the ardent attempt to be scientific has again paradoxically had the very opposite result. The irrefutable presence of paradox and its incessant return to conclusions drawn from observations are in themselves a central aspect of this inquiry (Becker, 1973; Weisman, 1965). The problem, of course, is not science or the scientific method but its exaggerated form called scientism. Huston Smith (1976) states:

With science itself there can be no quarrel. Scientism is another matter. Whereas science is positive, contenting itself with reporting what it discovers, scientism is negative. It goes beyond the actual findings of science to deny that other approaches to knowledge are valid and other truths true. In doing so it deserts science in favor of metaphysics . . . bad metaphysics. (p. 15)

OPERATIONAL EMPIRICISM

One way to avoid the dilemma of scientism is by enlarging the scientific method through the development of an "operational empiricism." It is only by operationally defining observations and intuitions concerning reality that psychology can hope to understand consciousness. Operational definitions involve the description of phenomena or concepts in terms of the behaviors, thoughts, or feelings that are necessary for the concept or phenomenon to occur. The existential-phenomenological method, sensuous-intellectual complementarity, and the state-specific approach to science are established examples of how science can be enlarged (Blackburn, 1973; Tart, 1975, 1983; Weisman, 1965).

Another way to conceptualize this undertaking is to view science as consisting of both explanations and understanding. Explanations are more precise, measurable, and specific while understandings are more vague and global. Both processes are necessary to a science of people; neither is sufficient by itself. Unfortunately, an artificial dichotomy has developed so that science is seen as logical and realistic, while understanding is viewed in a quasi-mystical manner as the province of writers and artists. Nothing could be further from the truth. Numerous scientists have made the point that there are at least two complementary ways of conducting scientific research. Michael Polanyi's (1961) distinction between explicit and tacit ways of knowing the world is just one example of models that have developed to deal with the fact that science has been looking at the world with one eye closed.

Understanding utilizes intuition in a empathic operation and comes closer to approximating "being the object," rather than just explaining it from the outside, for example, "a large black mammal, six feet tall, weighing 180 pounds with a bite pressure of 200 pounds per square inch." While informative, this statement says very little about the nature of the creature itself. Obviously, understanding is a necessary factor for any science involved with the explanation and understanding of people. Both explanation and understanding are necessary processes included in the same operation. Understanding need not be nonscientific, as in hermeneutics or the empirical understanding of others. In these disciplines, awareness of others requires a language of understanding.

Hermeneutics is an excellent example of this suggestion. It is an ancient discipline, originally designed to interpret biblical or religious texts, and most recently modernized by the philosophers Edmund Husserl (1931) and Martin Heidegger (1962). The term itself is derived from the Greek god Hermes, who was, among other things, the god of eloquence. Hermeneutics involves the careful and meaningful study of human phenomena independent from theories or objective data. Hermeneutics complements both empirical and rationalistic or structural approaches to human experience and must be considered necessary for the scientific study of ordinary consciousness. Hermeneutic inquiry deals with day-to-day modes of engagement, that is, to borrow from Heidegger, "ready-to-hand, unready-to-hand and present-at-hand" phenomena. The "ready-to-hand" mode has the closest access to direct human experience independent of theoretical or elemental formulations. In his classic work *Being and Time*, Heidegger goes to great lengths to provide a hermeneutic interpretation of this mode of experience. According to Packer (1985), what makes hermeneutics unique is that it is concerned with the meaning of human experience as a sensibleness that can be discovered in practical action. It therefore provides well for an inquiry into the everyday nature of consciousness (Alioto, 1987). Since experience and actions (especially of the other) can be interpreted in endless ways, a scientific language of understanding becomes especially important. In this sense, a language of understanding is also a language of relationships, that is, one's relationship to the world of others and things or the interaction of one's consciousness with this outside world.

One way of constructing this language of operational empiricism is to utilize reality sense and intuition along with the usual modes of logical thinking. Reality sense and intuition are used in contrast to reality testing and logic, the analytic methods of science. Avery Weisman (1965) states:

Intuition and reality sense are composed of equivalence, equilibrium and affirmation. . . . The unique feature of intuition is the emergence of novelty. . . . The quality of novelty has little to do with inductive inference. . . . The vehicle of intuition is whatever comfortably contains a fresh version of an old problem, meaning with a new twist, or a condensation of conflicting viewpoints. (p. 66)

Reality sense is expressed as evocative affirmations often couched in metaphor, paradox or adumbrative language. (p. 33)

Weisman contrasts reality sense (one's experience of the world) with reality testing, which he describes as a logical operation that analyzes, resulting in informative propositions about the world. "Reality sense is synthetic, reality testing is analytic. . . . Reality sense experiences an event from the inside, reality testing appraises an event from the outside" (p. 33). Both reality testing and reality sense are subsumed under the general operation of the reality principle. Because reality sense is synthetic, it combines several perceptual faculties into a feeling or understanding about the world. These feelings are what Weisman refers to as "the aesthetics of mental life" and are inherently vague in comparison to the analytic statements of reality testing. Yet, they are extremely valuable: "Metaphors, analogies and emotive language, however, can arouse more comprehensive intimations about reality than can be elicited by astringent propositions despite their exactitude" (p. 115).

The present methodology, then, combines reality testing and reality sense, hopefully in both an empirical and hermeneutic creative conspiracy, to produce not just words but, as Weisman states, "a world of mutual meaning to be shared with others" (p. 34).

2   *Concepts of Consciousness*

Beasts abstract not.

—John Locke

Baby in my drink.
    —Washoe the chimpanzee observing a doll floating in her water

Before the discussion of ordinary consciousness, reality, and cultural pathology, it will be necessary to explore some of the concepts being introduced. Prior to an exploration of the relationship of consciousness to the world in new ways, earlier ideologies must also be understood. Therefore, this chapter is interested not so much in introducing concepts related to the structure of consciousness as in providing some background into the broader scientific and philosophical ideas that generate and underlie the ideas in this book.

The concepts that have been influential for the evolution of this book can be described as follows:

1. The relationship of the brain and consciousness (or mind)
2. Causal decoupling
3. Epistemic dualism (and operational empiricism)
4. Constructivism and constructionist models
5. Quantum mechanics

THE BRAIN AND CONSCIOUSNESS

Although the exploration of the relationship of consciousness to the brain is not a main focus of the book, the perennial mind-brain problem is nevertheless related and thus worthy of brief discussion. Consciousness is not the only structure that regulates interaction with the world. There is also the human nervous system, the basic neurological structure. In relation to consciousness the part of the nervous system most often considered is the brain. Like consciousness, the brain can also be understood as a regulatory structure that selectively modulates how people perceive and what they perceive. In fact, their limited consciousness is a direct result of the brain's reductive structure (Pugh, 1977). Most people maintain a rather mechanistic and naive understanding of brain functioning, as if the brain, an internal structure, helps them negotiate reality by reproducing accurate internal maps of the external world. Nothing could be further from the truth. Partially understanding how the brain's visual system operates might help clear this misconception.

When thinking about the wonders of their visual abilities, most people make the naive comparison between the eye and a camera. The eye, within this model, is viewed as a type of intricate physiological Canon Sure-shot capable of accurately reproducing an external reality. Because the visual system is so effective, this naive realism is difficult to alter. If a person looks at this book, he immediately sees a book, the perception of which can be easily verified through other senses and by other people. Consensual validation is an extremely subtle but potent way of constructing reality, and constructing rather than reproducing reality is exactly what is happening. Visual perception is not a literal representation but a highly accurate symbolic construction of a potentially chaotic reality.

First, there are language and cultural preconceptions that result in one's seeing a book rather than simply a rectangular, oblong object. This point is fairly obvious, as most people are aware that they live in socially constructed realities that are mainly dependent upon language as a common labeling device. Second, however, is the fact that very specific and specialized cells from the retina to the visual cortex are responding to and organizing the external world according to preset specifications, for example, for size, texture, horizontalness, verticalness, color, and brightness. The function of neurons within the visual system is very specific in that each neuronal optical system organizes sensory input in very predictable sequences. Verticality does not exist in the brain or in the external world but is a construction based upon the interaction of both. The final interpretation of this construction is based on numerous additional factors such as meaning, context, culture, and learning. In other words, another part of the brain interprets the constructed sensory image, and one therefore sees not just a constructed image but a beautiful sunset. People blind from birth who have had their vision surgically restored at first cannot see. They have to learn to see. In other words, they have to learn to interpret their visual constructions (Stillito, 1987).

Another interesting point about visual constructions, and fortunately so, is that in terms of constructively representing the physical world, the visual system is amazingly accurate. This accuracy seems to be true for all species, that is, people see what is necessary for people, bats for bats, fishes for fishes, and birds for birds. As a species humankind's sharp binocular vision no doubt was a contributing factor in its evolution from quadrupedal hunters and gatherers. In other words, the visual system in evolutionary terms is highly adaptable. Yet, people are capable of seeing only what is necessary. Their rough approximation of reality seems to be enough. It would be wonderful to see the world as other creatures see it, but evolution is a frugal master and leaves people with only what is essential. Within the visual spectrum humans perceive only a tiny portion of reality, yet enough to survive. They are incapable of perceiving extremely large, distant, close, or extremely small objects; for these, humans need special instruments (Ornstein & Erlich, 1989). The brain, to use vision as an example, is like evolution's spartan housekeeper, using only what is minimally necessary to survive. It is only by virtue of scientific instruments, the extensions of the senses, that people could ever be aware of other realities like the subatomic, a perspective from which this book can become nothing but vast and empty space.

Multiple Selves and Constructed Realities

Current thinking in neuropsychology indicates that the notion of linear consciousness is in error and that the brain tends to organize itself in a modular fashion. That is, instead of a group of separate organizational structures connected in series, there are independent functioning units that operate in a parallel fashion. There are clear-cut advantages for an information processing system to be arranged in parallel fashion. Research by experts in the area of artificial intelligence list these advantages as (1) a dramatic increase in processing speed, (2) a system that is fault-tolerant and massively persistent, and (3) storage of large inputs of information in a distributed fashion that can be accessed in milliseconds (Churchland & Churchland, 1990). Much of this information can be totally separate from the conscious verbal self (Beaumont, 1981). The conscious verbal self, which one tends to think of as the mind, is neurologically and anatomically located (at least for most right-handed people) in the brain's left hemisphere (Gazzaniga, 1985; Sperry, 1976).

It is interesting to note that the development of nonlinear models of brain functioning is related to the refinements of chaos theory in physics. There are several reasons for this relationship. The most obvious is that chaos theory (also described later in this chapter) takes into account the complexity of nonlinear phenomena and is therefore cognizant that the reality of experience is often more complex and unpredictable than realized. Second, chaos theory is tied in with the Platonic idea of hidden forms in that it investigates the existence of other realities underlying the reality of what is commonly perceived. Third, chaos theory examines phenomena holistically and emphasizes not the isolation but the complex unity of life. Even though the brain is composed of separate parts, it can be understood only as a unified whole. Finally, chaos theory is dynamic, especially as espoused in its concept of "flow." The study of flow explores shape plus change, motion plus form, and it is becoming an accepted method of understanding complex phenomena.

The first clue that there were two separate yet interdependent brains and hence two possible consciousnesses originated with the early split-brain studies. The conclusions drawn from these studies, once controversial, are now well accepted as fact. The two brain hemispheres, although connected through the corpus callosum, can act separately. Independent functioning of the hemispheres is, of course, most evident in "split-brain patients," that is, those who have had the corpus callosum surgically severed, or in patients undergoing the Wada test, a test that allows one brain hemisphere to be put to sleep. Although these are extreme examples, best used for experimentation, to some extent the separation of hemispheric functioning occurs universally.

In general, the right hemisphere functions in an intuitive, nonlinear fashion most suitable to temporal-spatial, mathematical, and musical operations, while the left hemisphere operates in an analytical, sequential manner most applicable to language, logical thinking, and planning. One must beware, however, of conceiving such separations as absolute, an error that is already endemic to the media and pop psychological theorists. Carrying the fact that the brain has separate functions to its extreme would lead to a simplistic view of a holistic and quite complex organ. One can envision a new form of phrenology being the next logical step.

The true picture of the brain and of its relationship to consciousness and the mind is, in fact, more complex than was originally thought. For example, the neuropsychologist Michael Gazzaniga (1985) proposes a left hemisphere-based interpreter that accommodates, corrects, and explains, in a manner consistent with the self-image, any thought, emotion, or behavior that might arise from another module. In studies once again employing the proverbial split-brain subject, it was discovered that the left hemisphere would provide explanations for phenomena that the right hemisphere had witnessed that were consistent with the subject's belief system. Even if the explanations had little relevance to the observed phenomena, they were accepted as true if they were consistent and logical. Thus, in some ways part of the brain acts as an operational constructor of reality, accepting information that conforms to one's image of the world, rejecting information that does not, and modifying information that is marginal so that it fits one's constructs. It is reasonable to state, then, that part of the brain (for most people, the left hemisphere) constructs reality. Within Karl Pribram's (1986) holographic model of the brain, the term *constructional realism* is used to describe this process. All postmodern constructivist philosophies of science likewise conceptualize the brain as being an active constructor of reality (Feffer, 1988). The constructivist philosophy is especially true of certain European philosophers (Derrida, 1981; Foucault, 1973; Pivcevic, 1986; Ricoeur, 1981).

In processing reality, one's operational constructor must exclude (deny, repress, suppress) the parts of himself that are internally contradictory to his main self-construct. In the language of cognitive dissonance theory, two incompatible belief systems cannot exist within the same system for any extended period of time without causing a severe strain to the system (Festinger, 1957). A person cannot live in a state of cognitive dissonance; something has to be modified; that is, one of the beliefs must change or be denied. In Gazzaniga's model, this denial takes place in the encoding of information within a module. Information encoded in modules may or may not have access to consciousness. Consciousness itself is generally considered to be a left-hemisphere, language-based phenomenon. Information can be encoded without the language system's awareness. Gazzaniga (1985) states: "The information becomes encoded in the brain in one of the many mental modules that records experiences. It is not, however, one that talks" (p. 84). Thus, it is quite possible to have numerous and possibly self-contradictory thoughts or feelings. The only way these alternate modules manifest themselves is through the expression of behaviors and emotions that might seem strange or "unlike ourselves." It is difficult to become aware of these alternate modules because the left hemisphere abhors cognitive dissonance and loves consistency—hence, individuals' relatively unitary and stable view of the world and themselves.

A similar concept is espoused by Robert Ornstein (1987), who views the intrinsic organization of the mind as a group of semiautonomous "talents," "modules," and "policies" coordinated by a "mental operating system." In Ornstein's model, the brain is seen as organizing the mind in a hybrid system of separate belief systems that maintain reality and the illusion of a consistent self. He speculates that the experience of reality is often illusory and that the rationale for decisions, though internally logical, is often irrational. The irrationality is due to what he calls the brain's caricatures of reality and default positions, which make the brain respond in a habitual manner. In evolutionary terms Ornstein and Erlich (1989) claim that brains are still wired to react to only short-term adaptation. In this sense, there is a mismatch between the modern world and the brain's ability to plan ahead. Unfortunately, the complex, modern environment requires some long-term planning.

What people consider their conscious selves are to a large extent verbally tagged memories associated with the interpretations they have given their emotions, thoughts, and actions. These memories, encoded in modules, can compute, remember, feel, and act. In terms of mental functioning, a module is a self-sufficient entity. Of great interest is the fact that language is not necessary for the encoding of a module. Modules may, then, always be reacting to the environment even if the person is not consciously aware of their presence. A very simple example of this phenomenon is blushing. According to Gazzaniga (1985): "Behavior elicited is the way to discover the multiple selves dwelling inside. Behavior is the way these separate information systems communicate with one another. It is probable that very little communication goes on internally. It is only after we behave in a way that is contrary to the usual principles of the verbal system that we may discover the multiple selves actually dwelling inside" (p. 356).

In summary, current thinking in cognitive neuropsychology stresses the following points:

1. that the concept of self is usually derived from the linguistically dominant left hemisphere,
2. that other "selves" exist in parallel fashion in other parts of the brain,
3. that one of the brain's functions is to construct a reality that is consistent with preexisting patterns.

Material Monism and Dualism

Two basically opposing positions are held in regard to the relationship of consciousness to the brain. The classical or conservative position claims that the brain, like a computer, is hard-wired and that consciousness is totally dependent upon the existence of the brain. No brain, no consciousness. This position is the materialistic approach. Consciousness within this model is viewed as a type of flexible software, interesting and versatile but dependent on the mainframe circuits. This position, which is basically one of material monism, adheres to the belief that states of consciousness are identical to states of the brain. Those who ascribe to this point of view are called "identity theorists" and use physicality as their scientific yardstick. The position of material monists has often deteriorated into a disguised metaphysics called scientific materialism or logical positivism that reduces all questions of consciousness and the mind-body problem to semantic and linguistic murkiness.

As Roger Sperry (1987) points out, this position results in accepting the concept of consciousness as superfluous to science. Sperry quotes the eminent neuroscientist and Nobel winner Sir John Eccles as a prime example of this type of thinking: "We can, in principle, explain all our input-output performance in terms of activity of neuronal circuits; and consequently consciousness seems to be absolutely unnecessary! . . . As neurophysiologists we simply have no use for consciousness in our attempts to explain how the nervous system works" (p. 164).

The position that consciousness can be reduced to brain activity has been taken to the point of science fiction by sociobiologists. Beginning with the seminal and still classic work of E. O. Wilson, sociobiologists have made some important comparative observations regarding the genetic basis of social behavior (Wilson, 1975). Unfortunately, they have confused the mind-brain issue by acknowledging consciousness as a higher order systems structure while at the same time reducing it to specific structural organs. The following passage is an illustration of a sociobiological position regarding consciousness:

The conscious mind (which is the rational part of the decision system) lies above the hypothalamus and includes almost all of the rest of the forebrain. It is helpful to think of the decision system as a large general purpose computation center. This conscious computation system corresponds to what has traditionally been called mind. From this point the mind is simply a particular computational subsystem of the brain. . . . Evidently the sensation of consciousness arises primarily out of the interactions between the central control system (the thalamus) and the peripheral processing components in the cerebral cortex. . . . The boundaries of consciousness seem to be limited by the scope of interactions of the control center. The control center routinely receives VALUE signals supplied by the hypothalamus. The reception of these VALUE signals (anger, fear, joy, sorrow, etc.) at the control center, combined with the "rational" interactions of the control center with the cerebral hemispheres, apparently produces (within the control system) a sensation of consciousness. (Pugh, 1977, pp. 131–32)

Within the sociobiological model not only can consciousness be reduced to thalamic activity but human values may likewise be understood simply as hypothalamic signals. At its worst, sociobiology presents itself as bad metaphysics disguised as science; at its best, it contributes a genetic and biological dimension to the complex issues of behavior and existence.

Interestingly, certain popular religious and mystical views are likewise monist in nature, only they take the opposite stance and reduce everything to mind and consciousness. Since consciousness is collapsed into a single dimension, neither position leaves much room for exploration. Monism, whether physical or mental, is an escapist solution.

In direct contrast to the material monist position are several types of mentalistic or dualist positions. Modern dualism has progressed significantly beyond the dualism established by Descartes. Dualists assert that mind and brain are two separate systems. the new dualist position, which has been championed by R. W. Sperry, is called emergent interactionism. These dualists generally take a modified systems approach and, among other things, assert that mental phenomena and consciousness are real events that operate on and in different system levels. Consciousness, then, becomes an emerging, separate yet interconnected level of the physical world.

Emergent interactionism is a modern dualism that undermines the classical dichotomy of dualistic thinking, which tends to conceptualize matter and mind as occupying two totally different universes, for example, the world of spirit (or soul) and the world of matter. Rather (and at times it almost sounds monistic), modern dualism theorizes that within the same universe, mind and matter exist on different organizational levels. These separate levels of organization can reciprocally affect one another. For example, Sperry (1987) states: "As is a rule for part-whole relations, a mutual interaction is recognized: the brain physiology determines the mental events, as is generally agreed; but also the neurophysiology, at the same time, is reciprocally governed by the higher subjective properties of the enveloping mental events" (p. 165).

This interactionist approach is in a sense both dualist and monist and leads to what is called a macro or downward control model of events (Sperry, 1988). In order words, consciousness can be understood as one of the "top" levels, and although human consciousness may be dependent upon neuronal activity, it is, nevertheless, not reducible to it. Figure 2.1 illustrates how each system level can affect the other system levels from

Figure 2.1
Hierarchical Systems Levels in Relation to Consciousness

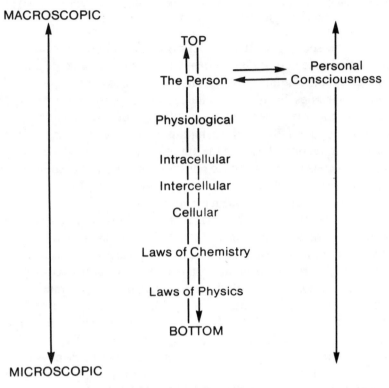

either direction, while Figure 2.2 provides a perspective on the neurological scale of organization that we are considering (Churchland & Churchland, 1990). Thus, the consciousness of a person can have a downward effect on cellular or even subatomic processes, while the bottom-level operations can have an upward effect on consciousness. For example, pancreatic cancer will have a bottom-up effect on consciousness; that is, the cancer of the organ affects the consciousness of the person, while the consciousness of having the disease will likewise have a top-down effect on the cancer system itself; that is, the consciousness of the person affects the cancer of the organ.

In a general systems approach, consciousness is viewed as an emergent, dynamic property of brain activity (Bohm, 1980; Davies, 1983; Koestler,

1967, 1978; Sperry, 1988). An important thing to remember about a systems approach is that it employs a contextual, hierarchical analysis that helps to understand and perceive the ecological embeddedness of reality, an embeddedness that is by nature intrinsically dynamic. Embeddedness refers to the fact that if one starts with what a person is thinking about at a particular time, from a downward systems perspective his consciousness is dependent on neuronal, cellular, intercellular, and intracellular processes that operate according to the laws of chemistry, which in turn are dependent upon the laws of physics, so that consciousness on this level is embedded in the atomic and subatomic processes within the brain (figure 2.1). Thus, not only are the classical laws of physics enabling the reader to read this book, but on another level so are the indeterminate quantum dynamics of subatomic particles.

According to Sperry (1988):

The principle of control from above downward, referred to as "downward causation" by Donald Campbell, Karl Popper, myself and others ... can be applied at all levels throughout nature. The outlook says that we and the universe are more than just swarms of hurrying atoms, electrons and protons, that the higher holistic properties and qualities of the world to which the brain responds, including all the macrosocial phenomena of

Figure 2.2
Levels of Organization

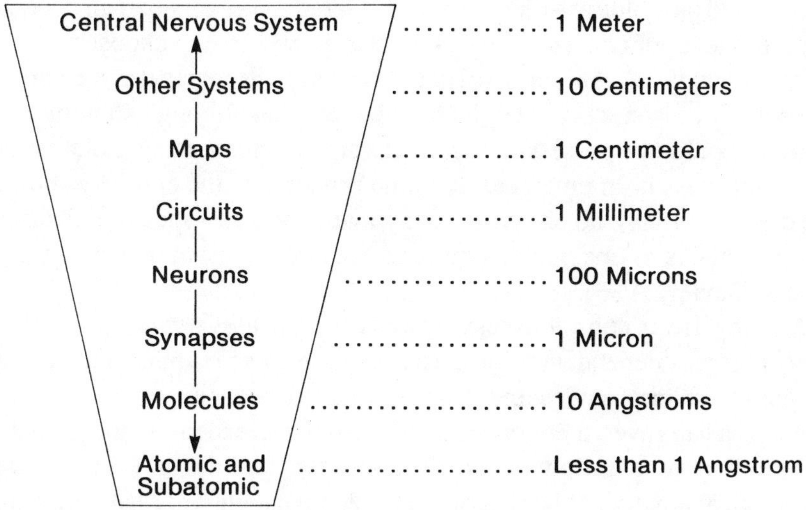

Central Nervous System .... 1 Meter
Other Systems .... 10 Centimeters
Maps .... 1 Centimeter
Circuits .... 1 Millimeter
Neurons .... 100 Microns
Synapses .... 1 Micron
Molecules .... 10 Angstroms
Atomic and Subatomic .... Less than 1 Angstrom

Adapted from Churchland & Churchland, 1990.

modern civilization, are just as real and causal for science as are the atoms and molecules on which they depend. (p. 609)

Roger Sperry's point of view, along with the new philosophical approach of emergent interactionism, is not a popular psychological position. Yet, in reading the works of psychological interactionists like Sperry and Pribram (who is also called a constructionist, a matter to be discussed later), I have discovered ideas that no only coincide with my own postulates concerning consciousness but are in accord with the philosophical speculations of physicists as well. Paul Davies has written extensively on the paradigm implications of modern physics and, along with Heinz Pagels, is a "psychological" physicist. Davies (1983) eloquently states:

The fundamental error of dualism is to treat body and soul as rather like two sides of a coin, whereas they belong to totally different categories. . . . Many of he old problems of dualism fall away once it is appreciated that abstract, high-level concepts can be equally as real as the low level structures that support them. . . . The brain consists of billions of neurons, buzzing away, oblivious of the overall plan. . . . This is the physical, mechanical, world of electrochemical hardware. . . . The two-level (or multi-level) description of mind and body is a great improvement on the old idea of dualism (mind and body as two distinct substances) or materialism (mind does not exist). (pp. 82–85)

What Davies means by two-level dualism is what Sperry implies by emergent interactionism. For example, termite colonies seem to function in a holistic and purposeful manner. Yet no one would say that an individual termite has a sense of purpose. In a sense, both the individual termite and the colony itself may be considered an organism. It all depends upon the level of contextual analysis, that is, where one chooses to look (Hofstadter, 1979). At each level of the system a different pattern emerges. Thus within a systems model, it could be said that although an individual termite would not possess consciousness, the colony as a whole would. Consciousness is an emergent dynamic property of the entire system. In the case of humans, no one would deny that they are a collection of atoms. The mistake is to imagine that humans are nothing more than a bunch of atoms (Davies, 1983).

Moving from consciousness upward within a systems model finds consciousness dependent upon certain macroscopic realities like culture, religion, ethnicity, environment, or even nutrition; for example, for someone with a hangover, the sequence and logic of these ideas would probably be extra hard to follow. Such an individual would be in the rather paradoxical position of being both at the apex of cellular organization and yet at the bottom of the larger macroscopic hierarchy. At each level of this systems hierarchy, events, although partially determined from below, are also bound by and embedded within properties of the larger enveloping structures. Within these holistic systems each level, the subatomic and the cultural, for example, has its own regulatory function and determines in part what the system is doing yet is always subservient to the general continued existence of the system itself. The principal rule of organization seems to be to maintain the function and integrity of the whole system.

Certain types of mental dualists called interactionists claim that consciousness is an emergent structure that can have a downward influence on the physical level of cell and organ. This point of view is in direct contrast to reductionistic models that basically maintain a microdeterministic, upward view of the world. Interactionism is basically a systems approach that provides understanding of how brain acts upon mind and how mind acts upon brain. Once again, according to Sperry (1987):

As is the rule for part-whole relations, a mutual interaction between the neural and mental events is recognized: the brain physiology determines the mental effects, as is generally agreed; but also, the neurophysiology, at the same time, is reciprocally governed by the higher subjective properties of the developing mental events. . . . Exerting top-level causal influence in the direction and control of behavior, the conscious mind is no longer something that can be ignored in objective neuroscience. (p. 165)

CAUSAL DECOUPLING

There are serious pitfalls involved with maintaining an exclusive top-down approach to consciousness. The main one, as Heinz Pagels (1989) so eloquently points out, is that top-down dualism leaves the door open for a proliferation of a virtually infinite number of untestable mental models. Cognitive psychologists are always, and perhaps always prematurely, developing maps of the mind, invariant mental models that seem to explain the mind but never address how the model corresponds to the brain (Hampden-Turner, 1982). (For an excellent discussion of the perils of dualism, see Heinz Pagels's book *The Dreams of Reason* as an example of good, scientific thinking about consciousness.) The fact that consciousness can be viewed as an upper-level emergent structure of the brain does not release psychologists from the obligation of discovering how this emergent order occurs. There is a connecting point between thought and matter and this connection, as a result of collaborations between various disciplines, will someday be better understood. Pagels, who postulates a "causal decoupling" mechanism between mind and brain, explains that "'Causal decoupling' between levels of the world implies that to understand the material basis of certain rules I must go to the next level down;

but the rules can be applied with confidence without any reference to the more basic level" (p. 222). At some point, the laws of genetics become causally decoupled from the laws of chemistry. It is not necessary to explain chemistry in order to understand how DNA behaves. Likewise, it is not necessary to explain synaptic connections to understand how consciousness behaves. Although there is a relationship between the two, the idea of causal decoupling between different levels renders the understanding of the brain somewhat less critical for the understanding of consciousness. In order to understand another person, one does not have to understand his neurons; his self and his neurons, although interdependent, represent different and decoupled levels of his system.

According to Davies (1983):

The essential feature in all these attempts to grope towards a better understanding of the self is the convolution of hierarchical levels. The hardware of brain cells and electro-chemical machinery supports the software level of thoughts, ideas, decisions, which in turn couple back to the neural level and so modify and sustain their own existence. The attempted separation of brain and mind, body and soul, is a confusion born of trying to sever these two convoluted levels. But it is a meaningless enterprise, for it is the very entanglement of the levels that make you. (p. 96)

Figure 2.3
Causal Decoupling

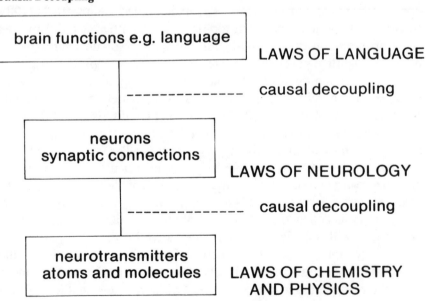

Figure 2.3 illustrates an example of causal decoupling as applied to brain functioning. Although language is partially dependent upon the laws of neurology, and the laws of neurology are partially dependent upon the laws of chemistry and physics, there are points of separation that delineate breaks where the understanding of one level (language) does not require understanding of either the basic neurology or the physics and chemistry that support it. For a clinical psychologist to provide psychotherapy, it is not always necessary to understand the underlying neurology.

EPISTEMIC DUALISM

Both the monist and dualist positions regarding consciousness and the brain can lead to untestable and fatalistic assumptions. Theoretical reason and science see the problem only from the third-person perspective, while mysticism and practical reason see the mind/body issue only from a first-person perspective. The best way out of this problem is to follow the principles of epistemic dualism, which explicitly acknowledges that people see things differently depending on whether they view them from the perspective of in practice what must be true or in principle what must be true. Epistemic dualism gives credence to both the reductionism of science and the ethical dilemmas of life. In this sense, the concept definitely embraces human values and allows for the development of maps of the mind, which have to be tested in reality.

Pagels borrows the concept of epistemic dualism from Immanuel Kant and employs it in the service of scientifically and pragmatically understanding consciousness. He describes the philosophical and practical pitfalls inherent to categorical, substance, and property dualism and puts forth the Kantian concept of epistemic dualism as a solution. Pagels's suggestion that a complexity barrier exists between the workings of the brain and consciousness is consistent with the notions of epistemic dualism. If a nonlinear complexity barrier exists for consciousness, then one may never truly understand it but can only approximate models of it. Perhaps this barrier partially explains why people can think one way yet act another. Kant's dualism is a dualism not of mind and body but rather of the reasoning processes used to examine the world. A split exists between theoretical reason, which sees in principle what must be true, and practical reason, which sees in practice what can be accomplished.

The concept of epistemic dualism is similar to the notion of operational empiricism in that it makes a distinction between in principle what must be true and in practice what a person can achieve.

Epistemic dualism gives its due to both the reductionist approach of science and the ethical dimensions of human life; it is a dualism of method or of intention, not a logical or material dualism. Furthermore, it promotes a research program because the boundary between what in principle must be true and what in practice a person can achieve is subject to scientific investigation (Pagels, 1989, p. 222).

The above statement epitomizes the intention of this book that the development of another model of the mind is quite beyond the point. C. Hampden-Turner (1982) describes in great detail at least sixty different models of the mind. Yet, these maps or models are of little use if they do not somehow translate into an improvement of everyday life, that is, a transformation of consciousness that has practical as well as academic implications. The concept of operational empiricism will become more apparent as the text proceeds.

CONSTRUCTIVIST MODELS

As part of the idea of developing constructivist proofs, real physical models must be created from ideas about the universe. The idea or theory that consciousness constructs reality is quite different from the actual construction of a physical model or experiment that demonstrates the theory. In other words, mental (including mathematical) theories require physical proof. As the mathematician Kurt Godel pointed out, not all mathematical concepts are solvable or provable (Hofstadter, 1979). This inherent uncertainty unfortunately also holds true for a major segment of human consciousness and behavior.

One of Pagels's desires is that the introduction of advanced computers will lead to the horizontal integration of separate scientific disciplines. This integration will not only enrich science but lead to the development of a true science of complexity capable of truly exploring complex nonlinear or chaotic phenomena. At present scientists are capable of developing models of either order or chaos but not the integration of both. To Pagels the blending of both order and chaos represents complexity and the true nature of the universe. The disciplines of phenomenology and connectivism in the area of artificial intelligence are contemporary examples of successful attempts in developing a science of complexity. Consciousness is also an excellent example of a nonlinear, complex phenomenon that traditionally has been explained in simple, linear, and reductionistic terms. The difference between linear and nonlinear phenomena is like the difference between simple, direct, and causally predictable events and complex, indirect, and less predictable events. For nonlinear events, the inclusion of a tiny variation in input could lead to a tremendous variation in output.

The same is clearly not true for serial or linear phenomena, which are always more predictable (Lee, 1950).

The study of nonlinear phenomena is related to the science of chaos introduced earlier in this chapter in the section of multiple selves and constructed realities. Chaos itself has no formal, set, scientific definition. Two examples of how the science of chaos is described are as follows: (1) "The irregular, unpredictable behavior of deterministic, nonlinear dynamical systems" and (2) "Dynamics freed at last from the shackles of order and predictability ... systems liberated to randomly explore their every dynamical possibility ... exciting variety, richness of choice, a cornucopia of opportunity" (Gleick, 1987, p. 306).

Perhaps most relevant to the study of consciousness is the statement that "in non-linearity and feedback lay all the necessary tools for encoding and then unfolding structures as rich as the human brain" (Gleick, 1987, p. 307).

The study of nonlinear phenomena began within the new science of chaos and originated with Edward Lorenz's study of weather. Meteorology is an excellent example of nonlinear events; in fact, the term *butterfly effect* was coined by Lorenz as an illustration of chaotic, nonlinear phenomena. For example:

The modern study of chaos began with the creeping realization in the 1960s that quite simple mathematical equations could model systems every bit as violent as a waterfall. Tiny differences in input could quickly become overwhelming differences in output—a phenomenon given the name "sensitive dependence on initial conditions." In weather, for example, this translates into what is half-jokingly referred to as the Butterfly Effect—the notion that a butterfly stirring the air today in Peking can transform storm systems next month in New York. (Gleick, 1987, p. 8)

As subsequent chapters will show, consciousness is a highly complex, nonlinear process that is highly dependent on both chaos and the initial condition effect. The initial condition effect means that the original state of any system will affect the outcome of any interaction. Initial conditions are extremely critical to nonlinear processes like consciousness.

The development of sophisticated computers has made the construction of integrated models of chaos and complexity possible. In terms of consciousness, this development has likewise made a horizontally integrated, complex model possible. No more will consciousness simply have to be reduced to epiphenomena, hypothalamic activity, or metatheoretical constructs. Constructed, integrated, computer-generated models are possible. Of course it is necessary not to make the error of substituting a computer model of consciousness for consciousness itself. Nevertheless, using a series of horizontally integrated computers as an experimental aid is a definite step in the right direction. Being what he terms a "naive realist" Pagels (1989) requires constructivist proofs and provides the following illustration, using Noam Chomsky's mental concept of transformational level as an example.

Of course Chomsky and others do not assert that these mental representations are in the brain; they assert that they are in the mind. How the mind is related to the brain is not known in sufficient detail to determine if the transformational level in the mind has a correspondence with the anatomy of the brain. This, however, does not evade the criticism I am espousing. Until the mind and its modules (if they exist) are understood on a material basis and thus pinned down, the models of the mind advanced by the cognitivists and others will proliferate, shift and slide with the tide of intellectual fashion and occasional new experimental findings and analysis. (p. 186)

Now Pagels is correct in assuming that less metaphysical speculation and more constructivist proof are needed; however, he is wrong in believing that it is necessary to lose the baby with the bath water. This is where the exception comes in. Both physical and nonphysical models are necessary for scientific progress, and to assume that physical or anatomical correlates of ideas are absolutely and always essential is, at best, a common error of physical scientists and, at worst, a bad form of metaphysics, that is, to assume that the physical universe is the ultimate proof of existence. Probably Pagels is rebelling against bad ideas, of which there is an abundance. Accurate and explanatory mental maps, in the general sense of promoting research and understanding of the world are, however, quite essential.

What Pagels fails to realize is that being a constructivist does not have to mean one is always an experimentalist. Experience is not always definable, translatable, or reproducible, yet it is always essential. The philosopher Michael Polanyi (1961), along with many other responsible scientists and philosophers who have had a tremendous influence on this book, sometimes speaks about what he calls tacit knowledge. Tacit knowledge represents a different way of understanding or knowing the world and is not always directly reproducible. Chapter 1 introduced certain concepts that suggested that there are alternate ways of understanding the world. Researchers are not, by any means, restricted to experimental techniques.

Perhaps a good way of making a comparison between experience and constructivist physical proofs is to compare Heinz Pagels with Fritjof Capra. Both men are physicists and both write about the relationship of human consciousness to physics. Capra is interested in what Pagels calls existence proofs. The following passages are examples of statements from each that are related to consciousness. The first passage is from Capra (1985), partially quoting the psychiatrist Stanley Grof:

Although the world is seen as energy patterns when the spiritual dimension enters into experience, there is still an objective, absolute space, in which everything is happening, and where there is linear time. But this changes in a very fundamental way when people begin to experience the next level, the transpersonal domain. At that level, the image of three dimensional space and of linear time is shattered completely. . . . I built a sundial to keep track of the passing hours and immersed myself completely in the cyclical rhythms that shaped my activities—the recurring passages of night and day, the ebb and flow of cool sea breezes and blazing summer sun, and in the background the endless rhythm of waves crashing against the rocks, waking me up in the morning and sending me to sleep at night. (pp. 106, 130)

From Pagels:

Yet, I would say against such views that the term consciousness and mind as we loosely use them probably do not refer to anything we can scientifically study. I believe that in the future, as the cognitive and neurosciences advance, such terms will be replaced by more precise categories of thought describing our mental experiences, categories that may also find their way into popular language. . . . Nothing destroys a poorly-thought-out idea faster than the requirement of detailed design or construction. (pp. 203, 175)

These two brilliant men's ideas, obviously quite different, very much need each other.

Existence proofs, as opposed to constructivist proofs, are dependent upon personal experience. For example, although the self may not be eternal, consciousness might. Since consciousness and the self are not identical in that one creates the other, two points of view arise. One point of view is that consciousness is a product of the brain, while the other is that consciousness is a product of all matter; that is, the universe is conscious so the brain and the self are simply two ways in which the consciousness of the universe expresses itself. There are, however, no ways of testing these two propositions. The belief in one or the other is largely a matter of faith and intuition. Pagels objects to this fact, that such speculation about existence can be endless, unproductive, and at times restrictive; however, there is still no need to eliminate experience from scientific proof.

While Capra can at times be obscure and metaphysical, he does at least include his experiences as part of his physical and psychological theories. (There were times when his experiences clearly led me not only to recollect some of my experiences, but to reflect upon new ideas as well.) Pagels, however, is clearly antiexperience. He views experience as a messy obstacle to developing an objective, physically based science. (Yet, I found that Pagels's writing also led to personal recollections and new ideas.) Both positions, existence proofs and constructivist proofs, are necessary; one really cannot exist without the other. What is definitely required for each, especially, perhaps, for personal experience, is the development of a model that correlates with an optimal reality, that is, a happy and productive reality. In a nonreductive way, it is necessary to use corroborative models of both subjective experience and the physical world. Corroboration or synthesis can only enrich the final understanding of humankind and the universe. A principal cornerstone of this book is the development of a model of consciousness that can be directly correlated to cultural productivity, cultural happiness, and the creation of a healthy and prosperous human community. It is absolutely imperative to avoid useless speculation and bad metaphysics that do not in any way improve the quality of people's lives. The next section of this chapter will provide a solid example of how new and important findings can lead to pragmatically harmful beliefs.

QUANTUM MECHANICS

> Once again, human perception of things seems out of step with reality.
> —Nick Herbert

Although there are several excellent books explaining quantum physics, two of the best are *Quantum Reality* by Nick Herbert and *Other Worlds* by Paul Davies. The following is from *Quantum Reality*:

Quantum theory was devised in the late twenties to deal with the atom, a tiny entity a thousand times smaller than the wavelength of green light. Disturbed by its philosophical implications, many physicists at that time considered quantum theory a provisional device bound to fail outside the atomic realm. Quantum theory continued however, to prosper beyond its inventors' wildest dreams resolving subtle problems of atomic structure, tackling the nucleus some ten thousand times smaller than the atom itself, and extending its reach to the realm of elementary particles (quarks, gluons, leptons) which many believe to be the world's ultimate constituent. With each success quantum theory became more audacious. Quantum physicists looking for new worlds to conquer turned their sights to the macrocosm, and now dare to model the birth of the universe itself as one gigantic quantum jump. Heaping success upon success, quantum theory boldly exposes itself to potential falsification on a thousand different fronts. Its record is impressive: quantum theory passes every test we can devise. After sixty years of play, the theory is still batting a thousand. (p. 94)

As Niels Bohr (1958) suggested, "Anyone who is not shocked by quantum theory has not understood it." Quantum theory (or mechanics, as it is often termed) among many things represents a new way of looking at the universe. It affects submicroscopic worlds, ordinary (macroscopic) reality, and cosmic orders of existence. The theory modifies the interpretation of existence itself from a realm of absolute and predictable values to an arena of probabilities and chance. Furthermore, it provides a solid basis for understanding consciousness as an integral and inevitable part of the universe. For example, Davies (1983) states that "consciousness plays an essential role in the nature of physical reality" (p. 100).

Interestingly enough, in terms of actual, observable effects, quantum theory has minimal observable impact on the macroscopic, ordinary world in which everyday life proceeds. All quantum experiments consist of ordinary events, a process Herbert dubs the Cinderella effect. The Cinderella effect refers to the fact that in the world, quantum events are ordinary in that people are fated to experience classical reality only. No one directly experiences the extraordinary implications and possibilities of a quantum existence. If a comparison may be made to a radio receiver, it is almost as if humans are mainly tuned to only the classical reality station. However, while the quantum world is ordinary, quantum reality and theory are anything but. While the experience of phenomena is almost always classical, the actual reality of the world is not; it is a series of simultaneous possibilities, a polyhistory. This point is extremely important because it implies that many of the extraordinary or mystical conclusions about the world that result from quantum theory are simply not true, especially in this world.

It is due to its philosophical impact that quantum theory has become so forbidden, especially to the humanistic and social sciences of everyday life. Fritjof Capra (1977) states:

The concepts of Quantum theory were not easy to accept even after their mathematical formulation had been completed. Their effect on the physicist's imagination was truly shattering. . . . Quantum theory has thus demolished the classical concepts of solid objects and of strictly deterministic laws of nature. At the sub-atomic level, the solid material objects of classical physics dissolve into wavelike patterns of probabilities, and these patterns, ultimately do not represent probabilities of things, but, probabilities of interconnections. (pp. 58–59)

Quantum physics implies that there are no absolute, classical realities but, rather, probabilities of connections and events between matter and perhaps even between consciousness and matter. One point of view states:

"It is not possible to formulate the laws of quantum mechanics in a fully consistent way without reference to consciousness" (Herbert, 1987).

Quantum theory reintroduces consciousness as an entity to be reckoned with. As the physicist E. P. Wigner (1972) suggests, if consciousness cannot affect matter, then it is the only scientific example where one system (matter) can affect another system (mind) without being affected itself.

In quantum theory electrons or protons possess no qualities of their own but, rather, only a relationship between themselves and their measuring device. A quantum law of motion states that matter must increase and multiply in order to fulfill all possibilities, yet in the act of measurement only one possibility can occur. In a sense, then, through some type of interaction, reality is constantly being constructed, a fact that makes quantum mechanics one of the principal verifiers of constructivism. In relation to the wave/particle duality of matter, quantum theory leads to another startling possibility. Waves, for example, do not have parts. How a person divides up a wave depends upon how and where he looks at it. "The world's wave nature makes us in a certain sense co-creators of its attributes" (Herbert, 1987, p. 132). Quantum theory teaches that people do not create reality but that they construct it and are constructed in the process of construction itself; they become correlated to the system.

Nick Herbert points out that the Hungarian-born mathematician John von Neuman wrote the quantum bible, *Die Grundlagen*, in which he proved that if quantum theory is correct, the world cannot be made of ordinary objects. This position contradicts the neorealist beliefs of scientists like Albert Einstein who believed that all objects in the world have real attributes of their own. Yet for von Neuman and other scientists, physical objects would have no attributes of their own if a conscious observer were not watching them. Another critical debate focused on whether the universe is local or nonlocal. If the universe is indeed nonlocal, its quantum nature would be verified. Locality is limited by the speed of light, faster than which nothing can supposedly go. Nonlocality implies that in some way events occurring in a far distant part of the universe can instantly affect events in another part. A nonlocal universe definitely changes the rules of the game as they are now known. It does so in ways that humankind has not even begun to understand. Years after von Neuman's postulates, the development of what is known as Bell's theorem and its subsequent experimental verification by John Clausner and later by Alaine Aspect and colleagues proved that the universe is indeed nonlocal and therefore definitely of a quantum nature (Davies, 1983).

From the position of psychology, quantum theory means a lot and a little. Quantum theory means a lot in the sense that people should not take any one theory of human behavior as absolute law; it means a little in that they must continue to develop consistent and orderly laws of human behavior. Both meanings are necessary and important. In essence, quantum mechanics as it applies to human existence in this world strongly evokes the laws of epistemic dualism. Mathematically and theoretically people can know and understand that the world is different from what it appears to be and yet, on another level, they must develop practical constructivist models as if the world is definitely what it seems to be— the reality most people are used to. For their continued personal and evolutionary success, people must do their utmost from both perspectives to make the world and their lives on it as robust as possible.

There are two critical mistakes that can be made when it comes to the practical application of quantum mechanics to everyday life. One would be to ignore totally the teachings and implications of quantum mechanics while maintaining a dogmatic and narcissistic perception of personal and cultural beliefs. The other error would be to assume absolutely that quantum mechanics is applicable to the macroscopic world and from this belief to develop a new mythology, for example, that the spirit world exists as a parallel universe, that channeling is a reality, or that one's specific religion becomes verified.

The fact, as Nick Herbert (1987) eloquently points out, is that aside from its mathematical, experimental, and applied advances, quantum mechanics still leads to at least eight possible versions of what reality may be. He describes these as:

1. *The Copenhagen interpretation* describes reality as the product of how it is measured. This version is basically the position of Niels Bohr.
2. *Copenhagen #2* states that the world is the result of some type of observation, an observation that can be nonlocal, that is, from another time or place.
3. *Phase entanglement* implies that although humans perceive it to be separate, the universe is an undivided wholeness. This position is based on a quantum formalism that indicates that once two quons (very elemental entities) interact and move apart, they are always represented by a single wave form. This position is another way of stating that matter is interconnected or that everything is represented in everything else.
4. *The many worlds interpretation* of H. Everett dictates that all possibilities simultaneously exist in separate but correlated dimensions. Measurement does not matter; only the degree of correlation between things matters. According to this point of view, an observer becomes integrally correlated with what is observed; that is, one becomes a part of it. Surprisingly, because it solves certain theoretical problems, this interpretation is a favorite of physicists.
5. *Quantum logic* is a mathematical approach to understanding reality.

6. *Neorealism* was the favorite position of Albert Einstein, a position that basically dictates that the world is composed of ordinary objects; there is no underlying quantum reality.

7. *Consciousness constructs mind and reality* suggests that consciousness is the ultimate substance. This view is the position of John von Neuman.

8. *The duplex universe* is Werner Heisenberg's understanding that somewhere in the universe all potentials and possibilities are present and their existence is independent of observation. (pp. 173–74)

Which model of reality does one choose? As Herbert states, whatever reality it is must be a nonlocal one. In this sense all eight of these possible realities could apply to how the world is structured. The acceptance of a nonlocal reality implies accepting a world that is not what it appears to be. It begs people to expand their horizons of understanding beyond their present boundaries.

The reality models of quantum theory have changed forever the traditional ways in which people understand not only themselves but the universe they inhabit as well, a crucial point to realize when extrapolating from quantum theory to their lives in the physical world. In a sense, the world becomes a more holistic place, an arena in which everything is interconnected. The quantum theorist David Bohm (1980) is a proponent of this position. Bohm's concepts of implicate order and holonomy conceptualize consciousness and matter as being inextricably linked.

Almost every idea woven into the following models of consciousness and the psychopathology of everyday life has been at least briefly mentioned. For more detailed and thorough explanations, the reference section should prove more than adequate. The following chapter will examine the actual nature of human consciousness.

3 *The Nature of Consciousness*

What will become of my whole life? . . . Is there any meaning in my life that
the inevitable death awaiting me does not destroy?

—Leo Tolstoy

Despite evasive epistemological maneuvers, one basic, undeniable fact
remains: consciousness itself. Consciousness is both the most obvious and
the most mysterious part of people's daily lives. William James was one
of the first psychologists to suggest that the understanding of consciousness should be one of the prime goals of psychology (James, 1896; Pollio,
1990). Eighty years later a Princeton psychologist, Julian Jaynes (1976),
published a book that began exploring, among other things, "ordinary
consciousness." Along with Jaynes's work came the especially innovative
and pioneering works of C. T. Tart (1983) and Robert Ornstein (1973).
Still, research within psychology and psychiatry on consciousness became
the exception rather than the rule.

Beginning in the late 1960s the study of internal phenomena such as
thought and imagery became part of what is now known as the cognitive
revolution in psychology. Cognitive psychology still operates within a
reductionistic, quasi-experimental paradigm so that for the most part
day-to-day consciousness has been neglected. Perhaps the one exception
is B. J. Baars's (1988) work on a cognitive theory of consciousness. In
addition, Howard Pollio of the University of Tennessee at Knoxville, one
of the few pioneers researching consciousness (and its relation to language), has pointed out that consciousness is by and large treated as a

minor offshoot of perception and learning. In psychology, consciousness is usually not studied as a topic in and of itself. This situation, of course, is not true in philosophy, where phenomenology and existentialism have made consciousness an enviable if often obscure object of inquiry (Merleau-Ponty, 1962). The same is true in literature, where, as Pollio has pointed out, the word *consciousness* (or *stream of consciousness*, to use the original Jamesian phrase) conjures up images of James Joyce, Marcel Proust, Virginia Woolf, William Faulkner, and Jack Kerouac (Pollio, 1990). For purposes of this chapter, however, a review of the psychological literature shows five principals who have directly written about ordinary consciousness: William James, Karl Jaspers, Julian Jaynes, Robert Ornstein, and Charles C. Tart.

The purpose of this chapter is twofold: to introduce a modified systems model of consciousness as well as to describe the preexisting and corroborative models. The descriptive approach, through its inherent empirical-phenomenological nature, avoids the thorny issues inherent in defining a process (DeBerry, 1987). Often, definitions are like last year's fashions, not fitting well but still being worn. A definition is static; a description is dynamic. Definitions can be dangerous in that they can be misconstrued as being exclusive and final. At best, definitions are suitable to static, material objects, for example, a house, a suit of clothes, or a banana. Processes such as consciousness, life, psychotherapy, or marriage, since they are fluid and dynamic, need to be described or depicted and not defined or explained. This issue is not one of right or wrong descriptions but rather one of creating a description/depiction that best approximates the reality, in other words, a good map.

SEVEN PROPOSITIONS

The following propositions about consciousness will form the basis for the remaining chapters.

1. Consciousness is a structure that can be located and measured in time and space coordinates.
2. Consciousness can be transformed as it moves along these coordinates.
3. As a correlate of consciousness, reality can likewise be transformed; that is, consciousness interacts with the world in a reciprocal fashion so that it creates and is created by external reality.
4. Language is one means by which these coordinates can be measured.
5. The externalization of consciousness refers to the evolutionary shift from an internal matrix of intrapersonal-interpersonal-impersonal consciousness to a predominantly

impersonal consciousness as manifested by a preoccupation with the external world of material phenomena.

6. A major historical transformation from the modern into the postmodern world has made the consciousness of the individual an object of manipulation, that is, a commodity.

7. The technological revolution, especially as manifested by visual media like television, movies, and video, has so accelerated and consolidated this external shift of consciousness that the illusion of the image is now the accepted and predominant reality.

- **Proposition 1:** Consciousness is a structure that can be measured in time and space.

The term *consciousness* denotes first the actual awareness of experience; second, it denotes a subject-object dichotomy; and third, it denotes the knowledge of a conscious self, that is, self-awareness. In reference to consciousness, the psychiatrist Karl Jaspers (1963) said:

But, the state of self-awareness and the objective aspects of that "other" to which the self directs itself, interlock in a mutual movement whereby the "self" is caught up by what is given externally and is at the same time driven internally to grasp at what is there. Description of what is objective leads on to the meaning of this for the self and a description of the states of the self turns into a description of the objective aspects under which these states become apparent.... Immediate experience is always in a total relational context ... founded in the way we experience space and time ... body awareness and the awareness of reality. (p. 58)

Jaspers clearly states that consciousness is not a passive receptor of the world but, rather, an integral and active processor of reality.

The psychologist Julian Jaynes claims that existing models describe consciousness as (1) a property of matter, (2) a property of protoplasm, (3) learning, (4) a metaphysical imposition, (5) a helpless spectator, that is, epiphenomenon, (6) emergent evolution, (7) behavioristic, that is, nothing, and (8) the reticular activating system. Models 1 and 2 are most relevant to this discussion. Jaynes goes on to describe consciousness as possessing the following features: (1) spatialization, (2) excerption, (3) an analog "I," (4) the metaphor "me," (5) narratization, and (6) conciliation (assimilation). Jaynes's description of consciousness is very similar to Tart's and Ornstein's in that it is basically a systems approach that comes closest to the systems model that will subsequently be described. Jaynes (1976) states that

consciousness is an operation rather than a thing, a repository or a function. It operates by way of analogy, by way of constructing an analog space with an analog "I" that can observe that space, and move metaphorically in it. It operates on any reactivity, excerpts relevant aspects, narratizes and conciliates them together in a metaphorical space where such meanings can be manipulated like things in space. Conscious mind is a spatial analog of the world. (p. 63)

For William James, consciousness was like a stream, an ever-flowing, active, and intentional process. James made the point that consciousness does not exist independently but always implies consciousness of something; that is, consciousness is always relational and potentially infinite in that there appears to be an infinite universe of which to be conscious. Human consciousness always involves a number of simultaneous possibilities that are either selected, ignored, or discarded. Consciousness, therefore, is a field event, a constant juxtaposition of figure and ground. Any definition that attempts to locate consciousness physically inside people's heads totally misses the point that consciousness is a relational and relative process or, as B. J. Baars (1988) states, a global work space. The main points to remember about consciousness are that it is an active process, that is, an operation, and that it is always relational and therefore always relative to the figure-ground configuration, that is, time and space. Because consciousness is an operation that processes an internal analog of the external world that varies through time and space, it can be measured. Therefore, it should be possible to develop coordinate reference points that trace its movements. Accomplishing this goal requires some understanding of the operation of consciousness. What exactly does consciousness do and how does it do it? Another way of posing this question is to ask: What is the structure of consciousness (White, 1982)?

GENERAL SYSTEMS THEORY

General systems theory is one of the best models in which to understand consciousness as a metaphoric operational system (Grinker, 1974; Marmor, 1983; Von Bertalanaffy, 1973, 1974). The theory itself is really a discipline of disciplines, with special emphasis on psychobiology and ecology, and is similar to Arthur Koestler's (1978) lesser-known concept of holons and holarchies, David Bohm's (1980) idea of holonomy, and Gregory Bateson's (1975) ecological model of the mind. The systems model was first applied to consciousness by Charles T. Tart (1975), who states:

As we look at consciousness closely, we see that it can be analyzed into many parts. Yet these parts function together in a pattern: *they form a system*. While the components of consciousness can be studied in isolation, they exist as parts of a complex system, consciousness, and can be fully understood only when we see this function in the overall system. Similarly, understanding the complexity of consciousness requires seeing it as a system and understanding the parts. For this reason, I refer to my approach of consciousness as a *systems approach*. (pp. 3–4)

In Tart's model the structure of consciousness can be isolated into at least ten subsystems or parts. These are identified as exteroception, input-processing, memory, sense of identity, motor output, interoception, emotions, time sense, evaluation and cognitive processing, and interaction with the environment. Although Tart seems to be the first theorist to employ a general systems approach to consciousness, he does so with a definite bias toward altered states. Tart's explorations of ordinary consciousness are used as a vehicle for developing a model of unusual and altered states of consciousness. He accomplishes this task, however, in a very scientific, scholarly, and pragmatically useful manner. Once the reader achieves a grasp on ordinary consciousness, Tart's books are a way of expanding to the areas of nonordinary consciousness. People have, however, too often made this jump to the "extraordinary" without first understanding what it is about the "ordinary" that makes them wish to leave so quickly.

GENERAL SYSTEMS AND CONSCIOUSNESS

In general systems theory, the following systems are commonly distinguished from one another: subatomic, atomic, molecular, organelles, cell tissues, organ systems, nervous system, self, self-other, family, community, subculture, culture, nation, international, biosphere, solar, galactic, and cosmic. For purposes of consciousness, this book will principally consider the self and self-other systems ("principally" because in general systems theory all systems are in some manner interdependent). The focus on system interaction is especially important to the development of an ecological approach to consciousness, and though it could be stated that consciousness operates principally on the level of self and others, it must also operate with diminishing effect on all other systems. The model is helpful in terms of reducing both egocentric and anthropomorphic thinking as well as providing perspective concerning humankind's position in the general scheme of things. Inevitably, general systems theory is a bit humbling (Laszlo, 1971).

General systems theory describes systems as complex regulatory structures of related components that maintain an open interdependence on surrounding systems. There are principles of systems in general or specified subclasses of systems that are universally applicable and can be expressed in mathematical models (Miller & Miller, 1985; Rapoport, 1974; Schwartz & Osborne, 1986). The existence of a system structure depends on its difference from its surroundings. When that difference no longer exists (as in death), the system structure, as one knows it, no longer exists. Structures act as regulatory devices, governing processes so that the system maintains its integrity from its surroundings. The ongoing identity of the system depends upon its structure, that is, it is independent of its parts. The nature of the structure in turn is always related to its purpose. Structures, therefore, are purposeful; they exist for a reason. The Italian government, a termite's nest, a family, and one's liver are all examples of structures.

However, the separate parts of a structure exhibit numerous possibilities that the structure organizes. The human nervous system has, in principle, a large number of potentials that are usually never realized. The parts, therefore, may determine the flavor or content of what the structure is regulating and expressing, but they do not alter the expression itself. For example, a structure such as language, which organizes and regulates expression will always do just that, that is, express, regardless of a change of parts, for example, grammar, words, or language employed. The Italian government will continue to govern regardless of who is in charge; the termite nest protects and promotes the development of the termite colony independent of any one individual termite; a family continues to exist after the father dies; and one's liver continues hopefully to remove toxins from an aging body regardless of what the body may look like. Parts may change, but structures do not. Structures interact with their parts to stabilize and provide boundaries:

Structures thus achieves [*sic*] a reduction of complexity. There exists, both inside the system and outside of it, a potential complexity that never becomes an actual complexity as long as the system's structures remain operative. Structures reduce the potential complexity of the parts by restraining and selecting the activity of those parts ... structures neutralize. . . . [T]hus, it is necessary for each system to possess mechanisms or strategies for selecting those processes to which it will respond and those to which it will not. (Schwartz & Osborne, 1986, p. 1215).

A MODIFIED SYSTEMS MODEL OF CONSCIOUSNESS

In general systems theory, consciousness can be described as a structure, a regulatory operation that interacts with reality in a constant reciprocity of assimilation and accommodation (Piaget, 1980). The system structure of consciousness consists of at least two basic substructures: perspective and focus. Jaspers (1963) calls perspective the level of consciousness while focus he terms attention. William James (1950) calls these substructures the center and the fringe of consciousness while Charles Tart (1975, 1983) employs an attention/awareness dichotomy. The three authors are in agreement that there are fluctuations and differences in both how and what people are conscious of. For purposes of this model, perspective can be considered the qualitative dimension of consciousness while focus is the quantitative dimension. This distinction is somewhat arbitrary and is being employed only for descriptive purposes. As this discussion continues, it will become obvious that perspective and focus are at times interchangeable (Smith, 1984).

Perspectives

The metaphor of a map illustrates perspective while the analogy to a theatrical stage illustrates focus. Maps provide perspective of unknown territory and are thus essential to the navigation of reality. Yet, the perspective provided by a map can and does vary greatly, depending upon the map. For example, a map may be local or national, topographical or surface, geological or meteorological, political or nonpolitical, secular or nonsecular, archaeological or neurological; there are many, perhaps an infinite number, of valid perspectives (Hampden-Turner, 1982). Perspectives are not simply isolated facts; they are experiential and constitute a way of looking at the world. The more useful perspectives a person has, the more direct knowledge of the world he will possess. Thus, it is helpful to have as many useful maps (perspectives) as possible.

Conversely, a diminished number of perspectives results in a loss of direct knowledge and a corresponding increase in obsolete or inferential knowledge. Simply put, the less one knows about someone or something, the more he has to either guess or rely on dogma or outdated and obsolete information. There can be an increase in the number of perspectives, as in experiences of creativity, illumination, philosophical speculation, and free association, or a decrease, as in dogmatism, reductionism, stereotyping, and ritualistic behavior. Many people are aware of only a few perspectives and unfortunately are not even conscious of the fact that their consciousness represents a perspective. That is, they take their perceptions literally and are not even aware they are using a map or that additional and possibly more comprehensive maps (perspectives) are available. In other words, most people mistake the map for the territory.

The usefulness of any given perspective may be measured scientifically by testing its applicability to the world. In a sense, it is like distinguishing and separating wheat from chaff. In an age of an ever-increasing information explosion, the identification of pragmatically useful perspectives becomes critically important (Moyers, 1989). This process, of course, depends upon numerous situational factors as well as the sophistication of one's knowledge and techniques. For centuries humanity lived within an Aristotelian perspective of the universe, which, at the time, was adequate for its purposes. The Aristotelian perspective was replaced by the Copernican perspective, which led to the Newtonian perspective of the universe, which is limited and has thus been supplanted by the perspective of quantum mechanics. The shifts from a bicameral to cameral consciousness, from an agricultural to an industrial to a technological consciousness, and from a modern to a postmodern consciousness may likewise be considered as examples of shifts of perspective (Jaynes, 1976). In general, the historical shift has been from the notion of absolute realities (Aristotelian) to a more relativistic perspective. Perspectives such as these are not exclusive or discrete categories. Rather, they represent tendencies toward constructing and interpreting experience in a certain way. Therefore, they are very much like scientific paradigms. Perspectives represent general conscious and unconscious preferences toward certain points of view. They are like epistemological assumptions that guide people's understanding of experience and their negotiation of their perceived reality.

Perspectives are like a craftsperson's bag of tools. The more tools one has, the greater the likelihood that the most appropriate tool will be used for the job. Remember Abraham Maslow's statement at the beginning of chapter 1, that if the only tool one has is a hammer, chances are that everything is going to look like a nail. The necessity of employing any one particular perspective or groups of perspectives is, of course, situationally determined; for example, in order to make love it is not necessary to understand the Marxist perspective of history, but if one's lover is a Marxist, it might certainly help the quality and perhaps frequency of his lovemaking to understand it. Arthur Koestler (1967) calls the creative connection of different perspectives the bisociative act and considers it very important to life, stating: "The bisociative act connects previously unconnected matrices of experience; it makes us 'understand what it is to be awake, to be living on several planes at once'" (p. 45).

The movie *The Gods Must Be Crazy* is an excellent illustration of the practical application of perspective and focus. In the movie, the consciousness of the Bushmen of southern Africa was complete. In terms of providing happiness, harmony, and a high degree of adaptability to their immediate world, the Bushmen had all they needed: a useful perspective and a focus on all that was essential to happiness and survival within their world. Suddenly, the twentieth century in the form of a Coca-Cola bottle drops into their lives. The changes wrought by the new object are immediate and dramatic. The Bushmen begin to fight and disagree. They do not know how to incorporate the new object into their world perspective. The movie becomes a metaphor for the plight of the postmodern world. In order to survive and be happy the pre–Coca-Cola Bushmen needed only a limited perspective and focus. To achieve the same end, happiness and survival, postmodern people need an ever-increasing number of perspectives and focuses. Yet the end result is the same.

Technology and Antitechnology

The Gods Must Be Crazy was basically antitechnological. Aside from the inherent paradox of using twentieth-century technology to produce an antitechnological product, the movie misses the basic point that it is not technology that is the enemy but, rather, people's perspective and focus, that is, their consciousness regarding technology. Technology, as O. B. Hardison (1989) points out, not only is here to stay but will probably be a pivotal force in the evolution of humanity and consciousness. One of the problems is that people do not use technology correctly; that is, they let technology operate as if it functions in a vacuum. Personal and social ramifications are usually considered secondary to practical results. Too often, people do not bother to consider the total impact that a technology, such as the automobile, for example, might have on other aspects of their experience separate from transportation or convenience. Secondary, tertiary, multiple, and usually unexpected effects will inevitably occur in any interconnected, general system. Awareness of the relationship of parts within systems is basically an ecological perspective that should be given more consideration than it is presently receiving.

The Gods Must Be Crazy makes the excellent observation that the postmodern world is increasingly complex. Most people, however, either strive to return to the simplicity of earlier times or unconsciously live as if they were Bushmen. That is, they make no attempt to expand their perspective and focus. Despite the growing awareness of how critical ecological understanding is, it still takes crises such as the greenhouse effect, acid rain, the homeless, and urban decay to spur most people into action. Even then, effective action usually occurs only when certain individuals are personally threatened. In chapters 8 through 10, some of the cultural and political reasons for this myopia are explored.

The academic label of perspective is a matter of no small importance as perspectives modulate people's construction of reality. As substructures of the overall structure of consciousness, perspectives color people's interactions with the external world by reducing what is potentially available. Each perspective is like a point of view, and each point of view is like a little internal machine that filters reality. When one is not aware of his perspectives, that is, is unconscious of them, they are usually termed preconceptions or a priori assumptions. The less conscious one is of one's perspectives, the more distorted and biased one's behavior is likely to be.

The classical Aristotelian perspective of the universe is very concerned with the philosophical notion of absolutes (Holbrock, 1981). This seemingly esoteric concern has always been a central philosophical assumption of nearly all Judeo-Christian Western theologies. Eventually Aristotle's perspective filters down to the average worshiper as a series of absolute prescriptions, laws, and metaphysical structures that are assumed to be absolute truths. By this time not only is the Aristotelian origin of this perspective gone but the fact that it is a perspective is lost as well. What was once a point of view originating in classical Greece becomes a dictum for living 2,300 years later. The following clinical vignette illustrates how earlier perspectives can affect present-day life.

The Case of Mary T.

Mary T., a thirty-two-year-old, college-educated female of Irish descent, was referred to me for depression and marital and family difficulties. Mrs. T. was a very religious person who attended church on a daily basis and considered religion to be "the cornerstone of her life in this world."

Her symptoms of depression, though mild, were very resistant to treatment. In fact, the reason she was depressed was that she could not be perfect. Her goal in life was to be perfect in everything, that is, a perfect mother, a perfect wife, a perfect secretary, a perfect homemaker and so on. The only problem, with the exception of her employer, who loved having such an obsessive perfectionist working for him, was that her efforts at achieving perfection were driving her family crazy. However, they too were already imbued with the need to be perfect so that although they wanted Mrs. T. to change (leave them alone), they did not want her to stop being perfect. The whole family loved having the perfect household and were very concerned that they be perceived as the ideal family. Several years of intensive psychotherapy were necessary before she was able to see (1) that she was living according to an impossible dictum of absolutes and (2) that her way of life was but one perspective among many alternate and healthier perspectives.

The religious perspective can easily be distorted into a fatalistic, passive way of living so that life in this world is viewed as secondary to life in some eternal hereafter. Implicit in Mrs. T.'s perspective of life was that she was in this world to suffer, work, obey the rules of God, and accept what happens to her as God's divine will. It was only because Mrs. T.'s perspective resulted in dysfunctional living in the New York City of the 1980s that she sought help and is becoming aware of her implicit assumptions and embedded perspectives.

Millions of people, however, never reach this point and would consider this example applicable only to the "mentally ill." Perspectives are very difficult to recognize and change because they provide a stable and consistent view of reality. The case of the "T" family is a good illustration of how a perspective originating over 2,000 years ago in the Middle East cannot, without much distress, be literally applied to the multiparadigmatic and rapidly changing postmodern world of the late twentieth century without a clash of perspectives.

The Focus

The focus is simply the number of factors one can identify within each perspective, that is, what one is looking at. Each perspective, then, has a potentially infinite focus, although there seems to be an upper limit as to how much information is pragmatically useful. A theater, for example, may have a stage that is only partially illuminated. The audience's understanding of the performance will be partly determined by what it is allowed to see. The more it is able to focus on the presence of monsters in the corner-stage left, for example, the more it will understand the action of the players. Being able to focus on the lighting control panel, however, will not significantly add to knowledge concerning the play. Therefore, it is important to determine which focus is essential and which is trivial; it is not necessary to focus on everything.

Like perspectives, the focus within any given perspective can also be increased, as in creative or scientific thought, or decreased, as in paranoid, constricted, autistic, or egocentric thought. One may, for example, be aware of a historical national perspective but may focus mainly on the paranoid aspects of that perspective (as in jingoism) while ignoring the other salient features. Numerous clinicians and theorists describe certain pathological states as manifesting a constriction of inner space in terms very similar to perspective and focus (Lasch, 1979; Masterson, 1985).

The focus represents objects that one is aware of within any given perspective. Traditionally, these have been termed the contents of consciousness. Once contents enter the structure of consciousness and become parts or subsystems, they can, to some extent, affect the nature of one's consciousness, although they can do nothing to alter its basic structure.

Thus, perspective/focus and structure are relatively, but not completely, independent. The purpose of consciousness as a structure is to regulate one's interaction with reality, especially within the physical world. This purpose is simply part of the structure and does not change. What is changeable, however, is how this interaction takes place. At this point, perspective and focus have their effect. The structure of consciousness is rather elastic and can be expanded or contracted accordingly. This point is crucial to understanding the world since it implies that how one thinks, as well as what one thinks about, affects one's consciousness of reality. For example, even though a person may be conscious of ultraviolet radiation as a scientific fact, he will never be able to perceive it. He may be conscious, again, in an intellectual sense, of subatomic particles and black holes, yet his perspective and focus will never alter the structure of his consciousness itself (his inability to perceive them).

However, just as one is capable of reacting to what he is not conscious of, he is likewise capable of conceptually being conscious of what is perceptually unknown. His consciousness of these imperceptible phenomena as existing in the same universe he inhabits has a profound influence on his life in that it provides him with additional perspectives, that is, maps of reality. These perspectives literally make him increasingly aware of the enormity and complexity of not only the universe, but his own life as well. Fundamentally, the same laws are true in politics, ecology, or interpersonal relations; for example, if a man is conscious of the feminist perspective, he will act differently than if he is not conscious of this perspective; if one is aware of another's feelings, he will act differently than if he is unaware.

The Case of Crystal

Crystal is a very bright, articulate sixteen-year-old girl who was referred by her parents and school for "lack of motivation and depression." Crystal lives with her parents in a very upscale area. Because Crystal is still an adolescent, I first met with her parents. Like their daughter, they were bright and articulate and were also professionally and financially successful. They were very concerned that Crystal attend an Ivy League school. Crystal's parents were likewise very concerned with their style of living, for example, clothes, house, furnishings, automobiles, friends, food, and restaurants.

Crystal's main concern with life was shopping. Her perspective was totally one of consumeristic entitlement. Her focus was exclusively centered on objects that she could purchase. There was an amazing lack of awareness concerning anything but her desire to shop for clothes. Her plan was to go to art school in the city. She had already checked into the grade requirements and knew she would be admitted. There no longer was any need to do well in school. Her plan was to become a "life-style shopper" for wealthy people. Of this she was quite confident. When she had money to buy things, she was quite happy; when the money ran out, she was depressed. Lack of money, Crystal was convinced, was the only reason that the school and her parents thought she had a problem. As long as there was money to buy things, there was no problem. Crystal was just like her parents.

Crystal's consciousness is modulated by her focus on consumption and appearance. Her interaction with the world is based on this focus. It is difficult for her to see anything beyond the world of the mall. The case of Crystal illustrates what constriction of perspective and focus can do. Operating only from the limited perspective of consumeristic entitlement blinds one to entire areas and additional issues and problems. Once locked into a specific perspective, one is capable of focusing only on objects limited to the particular perspective. Both Crystal and her family maintained a parochial perspective that not only limited their potential but severely restricted their ability to deal with serious personal, community, national, and planetary issues. The limitations of their perspective and focus precluded consciousness of their own development as well as consciousness of homelessness, poverty, exploitation, or social injustice. Crystal's friends and family, the friends of her family, and the town they live in are the same way so there is at this point very little hope for change. Crystal and her family with their uniperspective and limited focus are like cultural character disorders, that is, very difficult to change because they do not realize that their consciousness is the problem.

SUMMARY

Perspective and focus have been introduced as two suboperations within the general systems structure of consciousness. They represent ways in which consciousness limits and chooses its interaction with and construction of reality. In this sense, both perspective and focus can represent only models and metaphors of the operations of consciousness. It should be understood that perspective and focus are not fixed entities but constantly fluctuating and occasionally interchangeable abstractions. In fact, they are metaphors that exist only as a means of measuring and manipulating consciousness. In this sense perspective and focus are very much like the subatomic particles whose existence and nature depend upon the instruments of their measurement.

4 *Transformations of Consciousness*

Is what you knew yesterday still part of your mind.
　　　　　　　　　　　　—Rudy Rucker, *Infinity and the Mind*

- **Proposition 2:** Consciousness can be transformed as it moves along temporal and spatial coordinates.

Both perspective and focus may shift over temporal (past, present, and future) coordinates or spatial coordinates, namely, the intrapersonal, interpersonal, and impersonal dimensions or the standard Eigenwelt, Mitwelt, and Umwelt of the existentialists (Kaufmann, 1975; Weisman, 1965). Consciousness is capable of shifting over temporal dimensions in that one may be conscious about past events, immersed in the present, or imagining about the future. Consciousness fluctuates among awareness of self, awareness of others, awareness of things, and, of course, the infinite combinations and permutations of all three. Another dimension is the personal dimension, which is consciousness of one's presence in the world as manifested by his perspective and focus in relation to these combinations of temporal-spatial factors. The personal dimension, which is basically a synthesis of the intrapersonal, interpersonal, and impersonal dimensions, has traditionally been termed the self, ego, or identity. It is how one, at any given moment, identifies himself. For example, at a party, a person might be conscious of his thoughts (intrapersonal); of his thoughts in relation to another's thoughts as in a dialogue (interpersonal); or of what he or another person might be wearing (impersonal). His perspective across these dimensions may likewise vary in that he may be either conscious or unconscious of emotions, conscious only of his own emotions (intrapersonal) and unconscious of another's, or conscious of only certain types of emotion in both people. His focus may likewise vary as, at any given moment, he may focus on himself, on another, on everyone in the room, on the food or the music, or on any combination thereof.

Furthermore, consciousness may temporally drift, in that while talking, a person may begin to experience old feelings; he might be fantasizing about a future rendezvous with someone; he might think about a past meal or remember an old outfit similar to the one someone else is wearing. The hostess may elicit strong feelings based on a previous encounter of which he may or may not be conscious; someone may remind him of his grandmother; he might begin to think about "what you think I think you think about me," what R. D. Laing (1965) terms the meta and meta-meta dimensions of communication. One's personal consciousness is, at any given moment of time, a synthesis of this potentially infinite matrix of permutations and combinations. Usually, one is not conscious of the synthesis; that is, he is unconscious of his own consciousness and how it synthesizes the external world of the party. Obviously, this state is necessary in order for a person to function and behave in a socially acceptable manner. Schizophrenics have difficulty reducing this intensity of sensory input and are at times overly conscious of the process, an unfortunate fact that leads to self-consciousness, extreme anxiety, and an inability to act.

THE TEMPORAL DIMENSION OF CONSCIOUSNESS

What then, is time? If no one asks me, I know what it is. If I wish to explain what it is to him who asks me, I do not know.

—St. Augustine

The temporal shift of consciousness has profound effects on a person's sense of personal identity, in relation to which Victor Guidano (1987) states: "Needless to say, any transformation in one's experience of existential time produces a new space-time dimension and consequently initiates considerable changes in one's sense of self and the world. These changes have great influence on the oscillations and the course of the subsequent lifespan" (p. 119).

The time that is consciously experienced by humans is not necessarily the same type of time that is used in science (Prigogine, 1978, 1980). In physics, for example, there are several different types of time, each of which is different from experienced or subjective time. People's psychological experience of time differs so drastically from time as understood by physicists that it has prompted some scientists to question their own theories. The works of Ilya Prigogine, a Nobel Prize–winning theoretical chemist, represent, for those interested in a more thorough description of time and consciousness, the most radical and comprehensive treatment of the subject.

For most people, however, until they have an unusual or odd experience or, like St. Augustine, until they try to explain time, time itself seems remarkably consistent and objective. Perhaps the most common experience of an altered sense of time is the phenomenon of holiday or vacation time. From a personal perspective, I have noticed that when I have been fortunate enough to remove myself to another culture for a relatively extended period of time, my sense of time undergoes a profound change. Not only does it slow down but, because the familiar markings and events of my schedule are gone, I am unable to tell what time it is, and eventually I begin to lose larger temporal distinctions like the day and the week. (I have never been away long enough to lose track of years, but I would think this experience must be quite powerful.) Accompanying these pleasant temporal distortions is the growing awareness that I have been keeping time not so much by a clock, but by activity. For example, if I am sitting with Mrs. Russo, it must be 6:00 P.M. Monday and if I am teaching class, it can be either Thursday or Tuesday between 8:00 and 10:00 P.M. This shift in temporal consciousness leads in turn to a growing awareness and reflection on how I have been spending my time, which in turn lead to a shift in personal consciousness, usually resulting in a new understanding of myself and a beneficial reorganization of priorities.

Similar shifts in identity and time sense have been reported as the result of any situation that can profoundly alter the organism's sense of structural and personal integrity. The following case illustrates this point.

The Case of Gary

Gary is a thirty-two-year-old business executive who had been in psychotherapy for about one year when he suffered a near-fatal car accident. Prior to the accident most of our sessions concentrated on teaching Gary how to relax. He was an overachiever and an excessive worker who was beginning to develop stress-related somatic symptoms. Even though he was physically suffering, it was very difficult for him to modify his life. He was spurred on by a gnawing sense of time urgency that allowed him little time for himself or his family. He had been this way since childhood, when he had learned from his business-oriented parents that personal success could be measured only through achievement and acquisition. Little time was left for the personal pleasures of life or family. The accident, however, had an unexpected effect on Gary's sense of time urgency. During the sessions following the accident he was very receptive to suggestions concerning slowing down and spending more time with his family. He began to take more vacations and, even more important, Gary was enjoying them more. He could relax on the beach without having to call either his broker or the office. Gary felt that the accident had given him a second chance to live his life. He reported that he actually "experienced time differently," as if it were "a precious flower that all too soon fades away." Prior to the accident such poetic concerns were irrelevant to Gary. His near-fatal crisis made him much more accessible to my interventions.

Gary's case conveys how the sense of time can be experientially altered on a visceral level. Gary did not just rearrange his thinking about time; he actually began to feel it differently.

Even the process of aging can affect one's sense of time. Young people perceive the years as lasting forever while older people see them as flying by. Altered states of consciousness, which are basically what time sense alteration is, have long been known to cause personal changes. Intense religious or mystical states, drug-induced states, sudden scientific or philosophical illumination (the eureka experience), or even catastrophic traumas have been known to produce experiences of temporal alterations (Tart, 1975).

Most people within traditional cultures are oblivious to the temporal mosaic of existence. Time is understood as being a fixed, external variable of absolute finitude. In the bromidic reality of the everyday, macroscopic world, time indeed does seem to be a fixed and stable entity. But, the key phrase here is "seems to be," for it is only the constructive limitations of the senses and physical mortality that contribute to the notion of absolute time. Cosmology, along with discoveries spawned from the theories of relativity and quantum mechanics, has forever destroyed the notion of absolute time.

An anthropometric universe takes on certain properties only because people perceive them to be there (Harrison, 1981). Time is a relative concept dependent upon the nature of the observational measuring device, which in this case is consciousness and all the factors associated with it. The observed system is also important in that the nature of time shifts as one moves from the subatomic to the macroscopic to the cosmic arena.

The concept of cosmic time is an excellent way to put things in perspective. Scientists estimate the age of the planet to be approximately

4.5 billion years. Now, placing these 4.5 billion years within the framework of one of one of earth's calendar years creates an example where each month becomes roughly equivalent to 375 million years. Within this framework the first forms of primitive life began appearing in the primordial soup sometime in mid-September. The dinosaurs arrive on the scene about November 24, and the first small, land mammals arrive sometime during early December. Humankind's hominid ancestors begin appearing during the last week of the year, and modern Homo sapiens makes its illustrious appearance in about the last twenty-five minutes. If this time frame example is altered to include the estimated age of the known universe, approximately 17.5 billion years, then the appearance of modern people does not begin until a few seconds before midnight.

In a more prosaic scale, a generation is considered to be approximately thirty years. If a person was born as recently as 1960, then only twelve generations ago his ancestors were living in the sixteenth century and just a paltry seven generations ago his ancestors were still living in the eighteenth century (they would be his great-great-great-great-great grandparents). The world has changed dramatically in a relatively short period, yet as a species humans have not yet been around as long as the dinosaurs.

In terms of subjective consciousness, there is only the moment. Only the present seems to exist. The past is gone, and the future is yet to come. For example, as someone reads this sentence, it is impossible for him to force himself to remain in the past; the very act of reading these words moves his consciousness into the present, which is always and instantaneously becoming the future. Nothing exists except in the present. In subjective terms, the past and the future are only metaphoric abstractions employed as a way of understanding the constructivist activity of consciousness. Because consciousness of the world is constructed, it can include the past, as in old memories, or the future, as in dreams and fantasies. Thus, although existence is firmly rooted in the present moment, human consciousness is not so restricted and, like a drifting radio receiver, can move back or forward along many channels (Fraisse, 1963; Gorman & Weisman, 1977; Ornstein, 1969).

Actually, this version of temporal consciousness is not very different from the concept of time as understood within relativity theory. In objective terms, especially if one takes the theory of relativity into account, the temporal situation becomes even more confusing. Present, past, and future simultaneously exist. Time, as one experiences it, is just that, that is, something that one experiences. The theory of relativity makes perceived time a construction of consciousness. According to Davies (1983):

The abandonment of a distinct past, present and future is a profound step, for the temptation to assume that only the present really exists is great. It is usually presumed, without thinking, that the future is as yet unformed and perhaps undetermined; the past has gone, remembered but relinquished. Past and future, one wishes to believe, does not exist. Only one instant of reality seems to occur at a time. The theory of relativity makes nonsense of such notions. Past, present and future must be equally real, for one person's past is another's present and another's future. (p. 124)

THE SPATIAL DIMENSION OF CONSCIOUSNESS

Physicists have long known that space and time are inseparably woven from the same fabric. They are, in essence, inseparable. Once again, it is only sensory constructivist activity that maintains the illusion of separate things existing in separate locations and separate times. According to Harrison (1981): "The restless world is in a state of continual change; at one instant of time there is a distribution of things in space, and at a later instant, there is a different distribution. This variableness can be displayed by drawing a diagram in which things are distributed in both space and time" (p. 130).

Therefore, in addition to understanding how past and future can affect consciousness, one must also understand what the object of consciousness is. Consciousness, as William James said, is always consciousness of something. These "somethings" can be reduced to three basic dimensions: the impersonal, the interpersonal, and the intrapersonal. Because consciousness is involved with a something within one of these dimensions, the something can be objectified or given a mathematical value, and thus the something can be located on a three-dimensional graph. The spatial dimension of consciousness can be understood in terms of Figure 4.1.

If the time dimension is collapsed into the existential moment, then at any given moment a person's consciousness has to be located somewhere within these three circles. Existential philosophers, especially as reflected in the works of Martin Heidegger (1956), have lucidly described the ground of being, that is, the ontology of the individual, as having to be concerned with the impersonal, material, emotionless world of objects or the external but highly subjective and emotional world of others or the internal and likewise highly subjective world of the self. In ordinary consciousness there is really nothing else that a person may be conscious of. A person can be thinking about another person, himself, or the book he is reading. It is rare, however, for consciousness to exist for any length of time in exclusively one dimension. Consciousness is usually a synthesis of all three, the synthesis becoming one's personal dimension, that is, one's

Figure 4.1
The System of Spatial Consciousness

SPACE

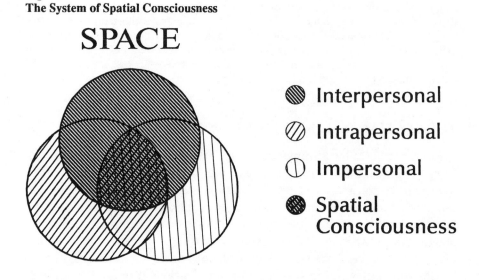

⬣ Interpersonal

⬤ Intrapersonal

① Impersonal

⬤ Spatial
Consciousness

sense of self or identity. As with time, one is unconscious of this operational synthesis; it is a product of the constructivist structure of consciousness.

Let us attempt a simple experiment with the impersonal dimension. Pick an object and focus on it. Try to be conscious only of the object itself and nothing else. Focus all your attention on it for about five minutes. Unless you are an accomplished meditator or have some very extraordinary powers of attention, you probably were at certain moments conscious of other thoughts or emotions, or perhaps even images, outside of and extraneous to the object. These extraneous intrusions were part of your synthetic operations interfering with the task at hand. The external world, although it seemingly exists independent of consciousness, is nevertheless always embedded and understood within a context of personal meaning. In the language of classical psychology, by projecting oneself on it, one fills the external world with meaning.

The above illustration exemplifies one of the differences between a classical and a constructivist psychological approach. Classical psychology subscribes to the notion that there is an objective, external world independent of a person's projections. In other words, just as there is the classical notion of absolute time, there is also the same Cartesian notion of an absolute and separate reality. Projections in classical psychology are considered either defensive or pathological. In constructivist psychology, projections are considered the rule, not the pathological exception. What constructivism dictates is that one needs to understand exactly how he puts

Figure 4.2
The System of Temporal Consciousness

TIME

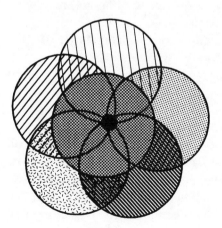

⬤ Past

◉ Present

◉ Future

● Temporal
   Consciousness

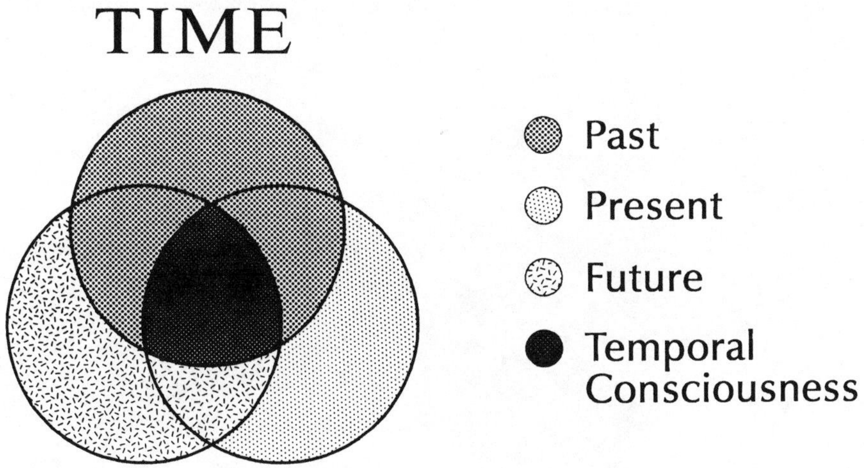

the world together, the permutations and combinations of past, present, future, impersonal, intrapersonal, and interpersonal that compose one's sense of personal consciousness. One's consciousness at a given moment may be compared to the artistic combinations of a painter blending hues, colors, and tints as a way of reproducing reality.

Figure 4.3
The System of Temporal-Spatial Consciousness

TIME

⬤ Past

◉ Present

◉ Future

SPACE

◍ Interpersonal

⊘ Intrapersonal

◍ Impersonal

● Temporal - Spatial
   Consciousness

Figure 4.4
The Synthesis of Consciousness: Personal Identity

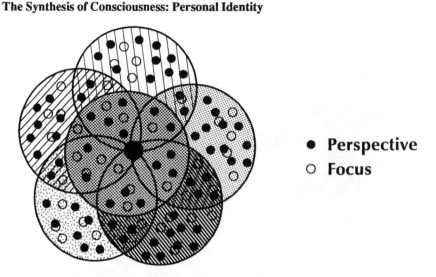

● **Perspective**
○ **Focus**

Both the spatial and temporal aspects of consciousness must be combined into a single model that includes perspective and focus. First the temporal dimensions can be placed in an illustration similar to the one used for spatial factors (figure 4.2).

The two illustrations can be combined as in figure 4.3.

Each separate circle can be imagined to be in a state of flux; in fact, it becomes more accurate to conceptualize six spheres that have one common point where they all combine. Within each sphere there are virtually an infinite number of perspectives and foci that contribute to the quality of the dimensional sphere. These can be illustrated as a potentially unlimited collection of different-colored spheres rotating and revolving within the main dimensional spheres (figure 4.4).

Out of this vibrant morass of interaction comes a singularity of consciousness. Ordinary consciousness is truly a miracle.

THE REDUCTION OF COMPLEXITY

The reason one's personal world never reaches its potential level of complexity is directly related to the regulatory function of the structure of consciousness. Structures are, by nature, regulatory and reductionistic in that they must constantly modulate input and output so that the organism maintains its integrity from the surrounding environment. Although the separate parts of a structure (in this case perspective and focus) may exhibit manifold possibilities, the structure restrains and organizes these potentials in very specific ways. A person normally considers that his senses are windows to the world, that he sees with his eyes and hears with his ears. But such a view is not entirely valid, for a primary function of sensory systems taken as a whole is to discard "irrelevant information" (Ornstein, 1977).

A systems model implies that reality, space, and time are not the fixed or absolute entities one believes them to be but rather the extrapolations of the incredibly complex structure of consciousness. A person is as unaware of this synthesis of reality as he is habituated to the blood flow in his eyes. Because the blood flow is constant, one's perceptual processes need not pay attention to it. The same is true for one's individual versions of reality. Because the synthesis of past, present, and future is a constant process, one hardly notices it. He simply takes for granted that the world is what it appears to be—"we see what we want to see."

Concerning complexity, humans find themselves in a rather unique yet paradoxical position; that is, even though they can be intellectually conscious of the complexity of the universe, they cannot be perceptually aware of it. Not only can they not see it, they rarely feel or experience it. Yet the complexity is there. The laws of quantum mechanics work, and people are capable of theoretically understanding how they work, although no one has yet reported being able either to see or to experience what the theories say must probably be happening (remember the eight basic models of reality; see chapter 2). The only exception to this rule seems to be the creative blendings of geniuses, saints, and psychotics. Yet even for geniuses and saints, such experiences are teasingly transitory, and for psychotics they are uncomfortably disruptive. (Schizophrenia is not the best way to negotiate the complex maze of reality. Madness is not, as some like the late British psychoanalyst R. D. Laing believe, the gateway to artistic and extraordinary experiences.) Even the most talented, conscious, and brilliant people must, in order to survive, reduce the potential complexity of existence. Once again psychology is indebted to Immanuel Kant's concept of epistemic dualism. Even though one may not be able to perceive the complexity of existence, he must always temper his actions with the understanding that the complexity is, nevertheless, always present.

It could be argued that in an evolutionary sense this constancy of perception and singularity of consciousness are extremely valuable. If a species were constantly conscious of its consciousness, it would fail to notice the tiger in the bush. This argument, of course, is quite true, yet beside the point. At times humans must act as if there is a consistent and absolute external reality, but on another level they must pause and ask themselves how this reality is constructed, just exactly how much past and future are mixed up in present consciousness. The famous axiom of history "those who do not remember the past are doomed to repeat it" applies to individuals as well as to nations.

The Case of Stefan

Stefan, a bright, thirty-year-old keyboard player, came into psychotherapy because of difficulty in holding a job. Despite the fact that he was a talented studio musician who was musically in great demand, he was unable to find consistent work. In our first meetings Stefan was aloof and distant. He maintained a rather stern expression that, because of his physical stature (he was also a body builder), could at times be quite imposing and often intimidating. Stefan had a long list of complaints about all of his employers: they were fools, untalented, disinterested in him, uncaring, selfish, and so on.

Whenever I made a comment, Stefan either ignored me or leaned back in the chair, muscular arms folded tensely behind his head, staring at me with a contemptuous mock smile.

Eventually I discovered, not to my great surprise, that Stefan had a very bad relationship with his father. Much to my surprise, however, I likewise discovered that he had no idea how he appeared to other people. Stefan was unaware that each meeting with an employer or authority figure, in this case myself, was a repetition of meetings with a sadistic and removed father. Stefan's construction of reality was very much influenced by the past.

Stefan's construction of the present is both temporally and spatially affected by perspectives and focuses that really have little to do with the present. For example, figure 4.5 illustrates how his perception of men in the present is influenced by other factors from the past while his perception of the past is affected by his interactions in the present. His consciousness in the future will therefore be affected by his permutation of the past and present dimensions. In this case, from the therapist's perspective, what is actually occurring in the present is, in part, the patient's construction. It cannot be literally interpreted as an experience in the present.

The idea that the past may influence the present has a long scientific and philosophical tradition that reached its zenith with the psychoanalytic movement. Psychoanalytic thought has always emphasized that the past is capable of interfering with the present. What psychoanalytic theorists fail to realize is that the extent of reconstruction, not only by the past but by the future as well, is far greater than they imagine. Freud and his subsequent analytic followers developed an intricate but often erroneous

Figure 4.5
The Construction of Stefan's Present

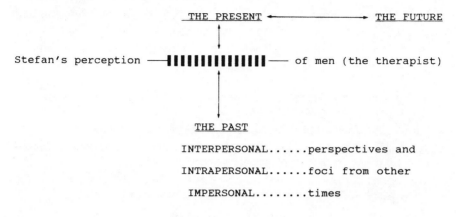

quasiscientific doctrine of internal mental dynamics. The early psychoanalysts, especially Freud, were exceptionally brilliant in that they were able to develop a comprehensive psychological model of illness. However, the classical psychoanalytic model is a paradigm that is now considered to be limited in that it bases its observations, theories, and techniques on an intrapsychic, one-person perspective (Feffer, 1988). The classical psychoanalytic perspective was, however, a necessary historical precursor to the interpersonal, the field, and now the constructivist paradigm of reality.

The psychoanalytic model is basically an extension of the Cartesian dualism that emphasizes the proverbial split between subject and object. The Cartesian dichotomy implies a continuing separation between the "knower" and the "known," that is, between the person and the external world of reality. This model is a prequantum model of cause and effect based upon the mechanistic, macroscopic, Newtonian physics of the late nineteenth and early twentieth centuries. In fact, terms like *boiler room*, *safety valve*, *steam engine*, *gear box*, and *mental apparatus* have been used by classical psychoanalysts as metaphors of explanation. Freud, as is often the case with genius, was well aware of these mechanistic and linear limitations. His followers became analytic zealots and tried to transform psychoanalysis from a science into a religion. Concerning his followers, Freud commented as early as 1921: "They are content with fragmentary pieces of knowledge and with basic hypotheses lacking in preciseness and ever open to revision. Instead of waiting for the moment when they will be able to escape from the constraint of the familiar laws of physics and chemistry, they hope for the emergence of more extensive and deeper-reaching natural laws, to which they are ready to submit" (Capra, 1982, p. 789).

Both Newtonian physics and psychoanalysis imply a strict determinism with regard to the physical and psychic realms. Fritjof Capra (1982) provides an excellent comparison between the four basic concepts of classical physics and classical psychoanalysis:

1. The concepts of absolute space and time and of separate material objects moving in this space and interacting mechanically with one another;
2. The concept of fundamental forces, essentially different from matter;
3. The concept of fundamental laws describing the motion and mutual interactions of the material objects in terms of quantitative relations; and
4. The concept of rigorous determinism and the notion of an objective description of nature based on the Cartesian division between mind and matter (pp. 180–81).

Capra goes on to compare these four tenets with the topographic, dynamic, economic, and genetic points of view and makes a compelling argument for a new, more constructivist paradigm. For those interested in a more traditional analysis of Cartesian psychoanalytic assumptions, see Melvin Feffer's work, *Radical Constructivism.*

IMPLICATIONS OF CONSTRUCTIVISM

What does constructivism mean? What are the practical implications of knowing that consciousness is an operational synthesis of numerous temporal and spatial factors? Constructivism basically implies that the concept of a Cartesian split is an illusion, that there is no superior external reality or objective knowledge or absolute truth; there are only interrelationships of constructed realities that exist between the perceiver and the perceived (Berger & Luckman, 1966; Polanyi, 1969; Pollio, 1982). Neither can be understood without reference to the other.

Constructivism revises the Platonic notion that a singular, ideal reality exists independent of a person's veiled perceptions. Separate realities may exist, but they are neither singular nor absolute. Rather, they are multiple and relational. There is no finite or absolute knowledge "out there" waiting to be discovered. Knowledge is constructed as a vehicle for understanding the relationship of consciousness to the system. Such knowledge, then, is based not on the limitations of the system (in this case the universe) but on the limitations of the observer, that is, his consciousness of the universe. If consciousness remains constricted, not only is understanding of the world one inhabits limited but his relationship to it as well becomes distorted. As with disturbed individuals whose relationship with themselves and the world becomes distorted, so too can people's relationship with the planet become troubled. In both cases, individual and cultural, constrictions in consciousness can lead to potentially self-destructive or ecologically destructive behaviors. Constructivism implies that there is no goal or end point of either absolute knowledge or environmental adaptation for which one must strive. Instead, what becomes important is the analysis and understanding of what one is now constructing. Constructivism suggests returning to and examining interactions in the here and now. In this sense, it is much more of a systems or field attempt at understanding the world. The forthcoming chapters on values, reality assumptions, and language will make clearer just what constructivism implies concerning the relationship of consciousness to knowledge. For now, as an example of one of the implications of constructivism, its relationship to psychotherapy will be explored.

Constructivism and Psychotherapy

Obviously, constructivism totally revises the notion of a psychotherapeutic "cure," a concept that still underlies the biomedical and behavioral paradigms. The biobehavioral model speaks of diseases and maladaptive behavior; the constructivist model speaks of distortions of consciousness and faulty but purposeful constructions. In the biobehavioral model there exists an expert who is outside and apart from a patient. It is the task of this expert to fix, cure, change, or in some fundamental way do something to and thus alter the patient. In the constructivist model there are at least two people trying to understand how at least one of them constructs his world. No more, no less. As a continuation of the humanist tradition, constructivism solidly and scientifically returns choice to the equation of psychotherapy and the person. It changes the role of the psychotherapist from the medical position of one who cures to the more spiritual posture of one who guides or one who helps construct conditions for change.

Furthermore, the constructivist model puts to a final rest the traditional patriarchal belief that the analyst or psychotherapist has exclusive privilege to an absolute reality concerning the patient. This belief is always a distortion of good psychotherapy, yet, unfortunately, it is a distortion that is too often the rule rather than the exception. In a competitive, acquisitive, and materialistic culture the therapist is often viewed as having something that the patient does not have, be it wisdom, happiness, or success. Health is often equated with having or possessing these qualities almost as if they were material commodities. Eric Fromm has emphasized that today's consumeristic culture tends to place almost everything within a "having" rather than a "being" mode. These factors, along with several others to be discussed later, contribute toward placing the patient in a passive, dependent role. In these cases the psychotherapist shares the same materialistic and patriarchal presuppositions as the culture, sometimes unconsciously but, more often than not, consciously. (Being patriarchal has nothing to do with gender, as women can sometimes be more patriarchal than men.)

While traditional reductionistic models are deterministic, constructivist models are teleological in that they take human meaning into account. Instead of analyzing problems as derivatives of childhood conflict or reducing the person to a series of hormonal imbalances, constructivism looks for its answers in the meanings, relationships, and purposes of world creation. Nothing exists independently; everything is a matter of relation. This view does not imply that behavioral or biological factors do not exist, only that they do not exist alone, that they are contextual and as much a result as a cause. The biological and the behavioral can be understood only within the general context of the operations of consciousness, that is, the whole person.

This model may sound like mystical monism, California pop psychology and Alan Watts. Alan Watts was an important 1960s philosopher who wrote some excellent books concerning the nature of human existence and the universe. Although Watts's philosophical speculations were quite solid, his works were too vulnerable to popular cultural simplification. His ideas had strong appeal for a generation looking for transcendent truths and mystical realities. The problem, however, is that this "I am one, and you are one, and we are one, and we are all together" philosophy unfortunately does not result in any kind of personal or societal change. Fundamental monism is not testable and therefore nothing more than escapist fantasy. Too often it is used as a justification to do nothing.

The monistic position may ultimately be true. In fact, it is totally acceptable to believe that all of reality is ultimately composed of the same interconnected substance as long as (and this is a critical qualification) it is understood within a Kantian framework of epistemic dualism. Epistemic dualism makes the important distinction between what ideally might be true and what in practice one can hope to achieve. As Heinz Pagels says, it is a duality not of substance but of method. Although theoretically people's individually constructed worlds may be arbitrary, from a practical perspective these worlds are real, consistent, and extremely durable. The macroscopic world presents itself to people as a definite cause and effect universe in which their consciousness can make a very real difference. Thus, even though at this juncture it seems as if science is showing that there are potentially an infinite number of possible realities and that, furthermore, there is no absolute reality, only arbitrary realities, one must, nevertheless, continue to proceed as if this description were not true. In other words, people have to understand exactly what it is about themselves that contributes to the way the world is. Even more puzzling is the issue of how and why most people arrive at a consensus of what everyday reality is.

Before this book explores the issue of reality consensus, it will now examine one of the less beneficial effects of constructivism. After all, because the universe is paradoxical, everything has both positive and negative effects. Humanism, especially as fired by the discoveries of quantum physics and the emergence of a constructivist paradigm, has its distortions. One of the largest and saddest humanist distortions of the late twentieth century has involved the issues of choice, control, and free will. A plethora of pop psychology literature describes how simple it is to "choose to change." The implication is that a person's problems, because they are personally constructed, can be, simply through sheer will or magic, deconstructed. Statements like "You are choosing your problems" or "Your choice is to suffer and you can change if you want to enough" are examples of popular distortions. Aside from the very few cases where such simplistic axioms do work, most of the time they make people feel guilty for not being able to change. Often, those who have received such advice wind up worse off than before.

Epistemic dualism can play a guiding hand. It is crucial for a person or psychotherapist to make the distinction between what ideally may be possible and what in actuality is possible. Reality, just like behavior, is multidetermined. Assuming a general constructivist philosophy does not exclude unconscious, biological, genetic, social, and economic forces from playing a correlative role. To the contrary, constructionism, because it has a systems orientation, attempts to identify the parts and substructures that contribute to the operation being studied.

SUMMARY

From the building blocks of general systems theory, this book has slowly constructed a model of ordinary consciousness and, within a general systems framework, has described the roles of the metaphoric substructures of perspective and focus and the dimensional substructures of space and time. This book has postulated that personal consciousness and the sense of self are the illusional, static synthesis of the dynamic interplay of these parts and substructures. At this point, however, the model is still purely hypothetical and certainly untestable.

Proposition 3 may now put some substance on the skeleton of these postulations. The text will move from an elemental to a more complex perspective. Perspective, focus, and the permutations of space and time operate within, affect, and are affected by larger, more global system levels. The system levels of values, reality assumptions, and language are larger suprastructures that affect the overall system of consciousness on the levels of community, culture, or nation and are not limited to individual consciousness alone.

5   *Values and Reality Assumptions*

There is absolutely no criterion for truth. For reason, senses, ideas, or whatever else may exist are all deceptive.

—Carneades

- **Proposition 3:** As a correlate of consciousness, reality can likewise be created and transformed; that is, consciousness interacts with the world in a reciprocal fashion so that it creates and is created by "external reality."

What does it mean to say that reality is a correlate of consciousness? The preceding chapters have developed the proposition that consciousness is a systems structure that enables people to interact with an external world of objects and people, an interpersonal world of others, and an internal world of the inner self. Because the dimensions of the operations of consciousness are potentially so complex, consciousness must be a reductive as well as a constructive processor of reality. The reality of being human is, therefore, a bit arbitrary. The only rule seems to be that there is a rough, approximate fit between one's mental constructions of the world and the physical world itself. In proposition 3, the reason the phrase *external reality* appears in quotation marks is that there are no separate external and internal realities but rather only reality. The Cartesian distinction between inner and outer is a polarity forced upon people by the operation of their sensory system. Epistemic dualism, however, rescues them from the trap of mystical monism and enables them, for the sake of pragmatic constructivism, at least to treat the external world as if it were separate. Since they have little choice in the matter, this solution becomes the only viable one.

Therefore, there is no absolute external reality; there are a potentially infinite number of constructed personal realities that are correlated with individual consciousness. Each reality presents itself as physically real and personally adaptive. The reality of the Yanomamo is as valid a reality as that of the Western urbanite. Both realities insure a smooth adaptation and promote survival.

The preceding chapters have demonstrated that there is a neurological substrate to the constructive/reductive operations of consciousness. The visual system illustrated how the world is "pieced together" by the brain. A person's nervous system reacts to only a tiny fraction of what is going on about him. Yet, this incredibly tiny bit of processed reality has been all that humankind has required as a species to survive and flourish. At this point this book must also examine the social or cultural realities that humans create. Human culture is responsible for transforming the potentially infinite number of egocentric realities into a common, shared perception of the world. In comparison to the constructed physical world of the senses, constructivism as it applies to cultural phenomena should be a bit easier to accept.

THE SUPRASTRUCTURES OF VALUES AND REALITY ASSUMPTIONS

One of the issues that constructivist theories of consciousness must explain is the matter of the potentially infinite number of perspectives and focuses that exist. Out of all the potential information that is available to construct social reality, just how does one decide what perspectives to take and on which phenomena to focus? The question is of no small importance considering that a single issue of the *New York Times* now contains more information than the average sixteenth-century individual had to learn in his entire lifetime (Moyers, 1989; Ornstein & Erlich, 1989). Unfortunately, most of the world does not have a great deal of choice in this matter and hardly gets to really decide these issues; perspectives and focuses are usually predetermined by people's cultural systems. This phenomenon is so successful, especially in the so-called Western democracies, that people are not even aware that choices have already been made for them. Most people are unaware as to either the existence or the operation of this subtle deception. Consciousness is selective, reductive, and constructive, but to say simply that this statement is an explanation does not quite meet the muster of constructive model building. There seems to be a piece missing, which may be another regulatory substructure of consciousness.

Within a systems model of consciousness, perspective and focus are determined by the subsystems of values and reality assumptions. The subsystem of values has also been termed meanings, beliefs, attitudes, opinions, or preconceptions (Watzlawick, 1984). In general systems theory, values may be considered suprabiological structures that serve a regulatory purpose (Schwartz & Osborne, 1986). Yet, despite the term, their function is the same, namely, to shape, guide, and determine one's perspective and degree of focus. Values have also been termed "axioms of certainty," which are defined as acceptances that guide behavior (Weisman, 1965). Values are, of course, shaped and determined by the numerous parts that compose the subsystems of culture, community, and family and are linguistically generated (Hampden-Turner, 1982). The fact that values must be linguistically created is a key point, for it implies that ultimately the components of language play a major role in the construction of the world.

Reality assumptions are less articulated than value systems, but their effect on behavior is just as powerful. The reason for this vagueness may lie in the fact that while values are explicitly taught, reality assumptions are not. Reality assumptions are implicitly transmitted and are, therefore, often unconsciously learned. Although hidden, reality assumptions are very evident in the everyday language and behavior of an individual, community, or nation. They might be considered values that are so intrinsically woven into a particular social fabric that they are simply taken for granted. Reality assumptions have also been termed visions of reality and are evident in personal or cultural myths, legends, customs, and enduring patterns of behavior (Andrews, 1989). In this sense, reality assumptions can be said to be a system nucleus around which values can form. The system of reality assumptions, like a special seed, generates only certain types of values. One of the functions of values, then, is to maintain the structure of reality assumptions. To continue with the seed metaphor, both the overall structure of the seed and the substructures of its environment (plants, soil, and nutrients) are interlocked in a mutual dependence. Certain seeds can grow only in certain soil, and only certain soils will do well with specific seeds. Similarly, consciousness is determined by the spatial and temporal relationship of perspective and focus, which are determined by values, which are determined by reality assumptions, all of which holistically interact to maintain the conscious integrity of the organism.*

VALUES

The section on consciousness and the brain discussed briefly the sociobiological position that regards values as intrinsic biological mechanisms, possibly of hypothalamic origin. Aside from the metaphysics, sociobiology does offer a valuable perspective in that it conceives of "value-driven decision systems" and distinguishes between intrinsic and secondary value systems (Pugh, 1977). Within the sociobiological paradigm, values become biological criteria for survival decisions that impel the organism toward purposeful survival behavior. Thus, although originating within a deterministic framework, sociobiologists are willing to admit three important points, which apply to reality assumptions as well: (1) values guide behavior, (2) values are goal seeking, and (3) values are purposeful.

These three points contain the essence of the systems structure of values. This fact is important to remember because confusion and polemics over the origin and nature of values can be as confusing as the endless debates over the nature of consciousness. One thing that both scientists and theologians have in common, fortunately, is the understanding that independent of origin, values purposefully guide goal-directed behavior. In relation to the multitude of views concerning their origin, it might also seem apparent that different theoreticians, when employing the term *values*, are talking about an entirely heterogeneous range of phenomena. Instincts, morals, ethics, attitudes, and beliefs become noticeably intertwined within the value concept. Some researchers like Milton Rokeach (1968, 1989) have produced volumes of data involving value issues and painstakingly make operational distinctions among attitudes, values, and beliefs. Others seem less obsessive about this matter. This book is interested in describing values in relation to perspective and focus only as organizing principles of consciousness.

Values are one of the keys for determining how, out of the multitude of reality data, people decide what to be conscious of. From a general systems perspective instincts, thoughts, ideas, opinions, attitudes, and beliefs could

*The word *determine* does not imply causation; the system of consciousness is a nonlinear, complex structure that cannot be understood in terms of Cartesian cause and effect. The model in this book is much closer to the models of consciousness developed by Arthur Koestler and Gregory Bateson, and it never really defines consciousness—it is a phenomenological model that simply describes what seems to be going on.

all be placed within a model of mutual interaction, with values and reality assumptions being the most inclusive. This book agrees with Milton Rokeach (1968), who defines values as follows:

I consider a value to be a type of belief, centrally located within one's total belief system, about how one ought or ought not to behave, or about some end-state of existence worth or not worth attaining. Values are thus abstract ideals, positive or negative, not tied to any specific attitude or object situation, representing a person's beliefs about ideal modes of conduct and terminal goals. . . . An adult probably has tens or hundreds of thousands of beliefs, thousands of attitudes, but only dozens of values. A value system is a hierarchical organization—a rank ordering—of ideals or values in terms of importance. (p. 124)

Thus, values, a suprabiological structure of consciousness, are a way of organizing and guiding a person through the multiple labyrinth of a constructed reality. The same process is true for larger units such as communities, cultures, and nations; there must be common values that bind the group together and, in effect, help determine its identity. In a harmonious culture there is an overall matching of individual and societal values. Throughout specific periods of history both individual and national values maintain a high degree of consistency (Rokeach, 1989).

Differentiation and Integration

In terms of consciousness this book is basically interested in the differentiation and integration of the value subsystem. *Differentiation* refers to the degree of development and articulation of the various values within the structure of consciousness while *integration* refers to the interrelation of the various articulated parts. The more complex and sophisticated an organism is, the more that differentiation and integration will play an integral part in its development.

For example, as infants grow and develop, their muscular coordination becomes finely tuned and specific, and they move from global physiological responses, for example, the startle reflex, to specific motor responses such as walking or throwing a ball. Within a Piagetian framework, such development represents both the differentiation and integration of cognitive functions through the sensorimotor, preoperational, concrete operational, and formal operational levels of functioning. Cognitive abilities become more integrated through all levels of functioning and yet increasingly differentiated so that by the time the level of formal operations is reached, abstractive understanding supersedes concrete knowledge. The same is true for values and consciousness. As one progresses through life's

stages, consciousness and values should become increasingly differentiated and integrated. For various reasons, to be discussed later, this process
does not always occur. Contradictory and often primitive value systems
often remain and operate as undifferentiated and unintegrated motivators
of behavior. As Jean Piaget has noted, a great deal of the world never
reaches the level of formal operations.

Humans are more complex than raccoons, raccoons more complex than
worms, worms more complex than paramecia, and so on. This statement
does not mean, however, that humans have a better or healthier level of
differentiation and integration than do raccoons. In fact, it is impossible
to make such a comparative statement; however, in terms of the individual
potential of each species, in comparison to humans there probably are more
successfully differentiated and integrated raccoons populating the planet.
In other words, raccoons are more successful at being raccoons than
humans are at being human, an issue that will be discussed in subsequent
chapters.

Healthy humans, however, will have a high degree of integration among
highly differentiated but interrelated subsystems. For example, the concept
of the self includes many differentiated subsystems such as work self,
social self, intimate self, professional self, and student self, which are in
part situationally dependent. The health of the person or self is determined
to some extent by how aware the person is of these separate situational
selves, that is, to what extent these differentiated "cultural selves" are
integrated and aware of each other. Often they are not, resulting in a
psychopathological or schizoid state (DeBerry, 1989b). Separate or even
contradictory values, like contradictory behaviors, emotions, or selves,
can, unfortunately exist within the same person.

Values and Constructivism

Values may change, but their function as a subsystem does not; they
still regulate and organize one's perspective and focus. Values can be
understood as the lens through which one looks at and interacts with
reality; however, this understanding is not totally accurate as the effect of
values on one's consciousness of reality is an active process, not a passive
one. Values are not static; they are dynamic in that they are always
potentially open to modification. That is, to some extent, values create
reality. To think is to react, and cultural values are a person's set of
concepts by which he interacts with reality (Pearce, 1974; Piaget, 1965).
"Since reality sense is rooted in private being, not in public contexts, reality
is as much created as it is encountered" (Weisman, 1965, p. 23). "We

interact with a mediated reality and consider the artificial result our natural condition" (Pearce, 1974, p. 46). It is the interaction of consciousness with the external world that constructs reality. A person tends to activate reality through consciousness. The constructivist implications of this position have been described as follows: "All this, of course, implies a dramatic change in our traditional viewpoint of the relationship between knowledge and reality. Knowledge can no longer be regarded as an approximation to truth—that is, as a step forward in grasping an ultimate and certain reality—since knowledge simply expresses a specific relationship between knower and known" (Guidano, 1987, p. 7). Once again reality does not seem to be something waiting out there to be discovered; rather, reality is selectively invented.

Consciousness, within this model, is the synthesis of the operations of perspective and focus and is, in this sense, interpretive and representative of the personal dimension. That is, at any given moment a person's interpretation of reality (consciousness) depends upon his perspective and focus, which in turn depend upon his values. Reality, therefore, for all practical purposes is a matter of how much he knows, where he chooses to look, and what he is capable of seeing. To repeat the analogy, if consciousness may be compared to a radio receiver, then it is for certain that people are picking up only very few channels. The value substructure of consciousness perceptually reduces their potential input of information in order that they can make sense out of the world and survive.

Values are acquired through the process of cultural learning. This process has been termed socialization, enculturation, education, or indoctrination. In a general systems sense, values represent a connecting or overlapping substructure among the larger systems of family, community, subculture, culture, and nation. The mechanisms of learning and development have been systematically worked out by theorists and clinicians of various persuasions and will not be elaborated upon here. The developmental models of Jean Piaget are an excellent way of understanding how people acquire the "tools" of adulthood. In fact, Piaget's description of development through assimilation and accommodation to reality is basically a constructivist model. Piaget possessed a dynamic view of consciousness and considered development to represent an evolution of consciousness as reflected by a person's relationship to the world. His theories of assimilation and accommodation are directly linked to the developmental concepts of differentiation and integration described in an earlier section. Piaget's cognitive theories of development are likewise related to the mechanisms of cultural learning. For present purposes, however, this book will ignore the mechanisms of enculturation and concentrate on its constructivist implications.

Values and World Construction

Each person is born into a rich tapestry of social networks that contextually determine consciousness. All learning and development occur within the framework of different levels of social control starting with the family and ending with the state. Between these end points are masses of social institutions such as religion, school, the corporation, the club, and the street gang. Each of these parts exerts a conservative, regulatory function on the development of consciousness. Thus, Catholics tend to transmit the values of Catholicism, conservative schools the values of hard work and discipline, "IBMers" the values of IBM, the Arthur Avenue Social Club the values of Arthur Avenue, and the Jamaica Warlords the values of street fighting and gang loyalty.

What a person thinks about has to be partially determined by one of these cultural parts. Furthermore, from a general systems perspective the needs or thoughts of any particular individual have to be secondary to the preservation of the structure itself. The preservation of the general culture, as expressed by the preservation of its value system, has to take precedence over the individual person. The corporation, the gang, the family, and the American culture as a system all preserve their existence at the expense of individual consciousness. Within a general systems perspective the individual exists only as a part that helps preserve the smooth functioning of the system's overall structure. Remember, parts are interchangeable; structures are not. Structures are by definition conservative and self-preserving in that one of the main goals of a system is to maintain continually its separateness and integrity from the surrounding environment. The structure must, of course, continually adapt to the environment, but its main purpose is to sustain itself as a separate and viable entity.

Since the age of five, I have personally experienced a great deal of change, yet the structure of myself, my personal dimension, and sense of identity have been remarkably consistent. As far as I can tell, I will continue to be Stephen DeBerry, and if I live another forty years, as I sincerely hope to, I assume that regardless of physical changes I will continue to be Stephen DeBerry. The values that guide my behavior are one of the ways in which this consistency is maintained. Both personal and national values are like scientific paradigms; that is, for both the individual and the nation they determine what is thinkable and do-able. Within any given cultural system individual consciousness may have a certain degree of freedom, but this freedom can never be diverse enough so that the system structure itself could be altered.

Unless a person is conscious of the fact that he is always limited by his particular value system, he will not seek out additional ones. Unless he realizes that his values are culturally determined, he will attribute them to God, fate, or the state of the world. Basically, people are all limited by values or "points of view." This limitation is not the problem. A problem arises when (1) people do not realize that they have a particular value system and (2) they act as if there are no other value systems or points of view.

The Case of Robert

Robert is a twenty-five-year-old medical student of conservative Jewish background who consulted me for anxiety and depression. Robert's parents had been concentration camp victims, and this experience (often called the children of the Holocaust survivors syndrome) left an indelible mark on Robert. Robert's entire existence revolved around a fatalistic and guilt-ridden distortion of Judaism. The inevitability of suffering was a sine qua non of Robert's life. Despite an interest and talent in classical music, Robert felt that he had no choice but to redeem himself by becoming a doctor and, in doing so, to likewise redeem his parents and compensate for their suffering. Suffering was to Robert an inevitable part of life.

Robert did not respond to any clarifications or interpretations concerning his value system. To Robert, the way in which he perceived the world was perfectly normal. Robert surrounded himself only with friends of similar orthodox Jewish persuasion who thought and felt just as he did. They were all doing something that they did not really want to do, "but hey, what are you going to do. . . . You have to do what you have to do. . . . That's what you gotta do." This aphorism, which is a favorite of many people, was Robert's anthem. Psychotherapy was supposed to help him reduce his anxiety and alleviate his depression so that he could get on with his studies and his normal level of suffering. Although it was clear to me that Robert's temporal dimension of consciousness was predominantly located in the past, there was little that I could do to change it. Robert did not want this state altered.

Robert responded quite well to a short-term, cognitive-behavioral approach, and his depressions improved, yet his values and reality assumptions remained largely unchanged.

This clinical vignette illustrates how values can determine, shape, and construct the way people interact with reality. People are born into an arbitrary cultural reality that is mediated by a consciousness that enables them to deny the mediation. In other words, individuals and groups usually maintain a realistic position concerning the world; "what you see is what there is." Robert, like most people, was unconscious of his underlying values and reality assumptions and, also like most people, did not really want to talk about them. Rarely, if ever, in this culture do people learn how values relate to day-to-day existence.

Values are usually not directly discussed and must be inferred from behavior. I have never had a patient who presented with a value problem. Like most psychotherapists, I hear complaints related to the macrocomponents of patients' lives, that is, behaviors, thoughts, and feelings that are causing distress. Sometimes, as a result of modifications in thought, feeling, and behavior, values do change. The process, however, is both inconsistent and slow. Yet, when personal changes do slowly trickle down to the subterranean caverns of values and reality assumptions, the changes become more lasting and durable. The durability stems from the fact that a personal change has been made on a deeper level of consciousness so that the person has a new and healthier relationship with the world. In psychoanalytic metajargon, it might be stated that the ego/superego of the psychotherapist has become successfully internalized by the patient. Regardless of the theoretical map, the underlying reality is identical. Lasting personal change always involves a change of values. There is no such thing as value-free psychotherapy.

It is extremely difficult to modify values. Most psychotherapies, especially the short-term, cognitive/behavioral or biological ones, rarely, if ever, get to a point where the underlying value systems can be examined. Values are very much associated with one's personal identity construct and, like precious psychological gems, are fiercely guarded. This point leads to a very special problem concerning values, consciousness, and the construction of reality. The problem is that in a general systems model of consciousness, values are a system's substructure, and a substructure's (or any structure's) primary purpose is to maintain its structural integrity as well as the overall structural integrity of the system. This point is perhaps the most important lesson of a systems approach, that structure precedes and overrides content.

The content of values is therefore secondary to the structure of values and is perhaps one of the most critical problems facing humanity: people are capable of valuing almost anything. It does not seem to matter what the value system is as long as it is present, as it inevitably is. Once established, the value system, like a self-fulfilling prophecy, must continually maintain itself. The value of racism, for example, can easily be passed on from generation to generation, yet no one bothers to explore the damage such a value may cause.

The reason for this behavior is not certain. Perhaps, as the sociobiologists espouse, values are a neurologically hard-wired part of the organism. All that the organism seems to require is that a structural value system be operative. Little attention is paid to the nature or the implications of the value system itself. Throughout history people have adopted the most inhuman of value systems as their own. Racist, Nazi, or Stalinist values exist or have existed independent of any humanistic or critical evaluation of their contents. What seems to matter is the structure, and, as Eric Fromm has repeatedly pointed out, people seem to have an overriding need for structure itself. Once values are embraced by people or groups of people, they are automatically assumed to be the only "right" ones, and little attention is paid to the overall implications of what the values actually mean. Once a value is established, the process of rationalization can keep it there. For example, the philosopher Peter Singer (1975) has eloquently pointed out how human rationalizations concerning values and reality assumptions concerning animals are related to people's refusal to stop exploiting and consuming them. This example shows how limited, short-sighted, and destructive values can override cooperative, ecological, and holistic ones.

MacIntyre's (1981) concept of practices is an excellent way of revealing how far general cultural values have deviated from a cooperative and ecological perspective. Practices can be described as complex, socially based, and cooperative forms of human behavior. Ideally, one engages in a practice for the reinforcement of engaging in the practice itself. Practices are internally motivated and self-rewarding. In this sense, they are a lot like values or at least what values should be. Practices have been described as (1) establishing their own internal standards of excellence; (2) teleological—they are cooperatively goal directed; and (3) organic, in that practices are cooperative and people can change what they are doing as a way of achieving an end (Schwartz, 1990). The idea of practices is related to notions of being a good person. Good people have good practices, which reflect their internal value structure. The development of internally motivated, cooperative, and intrinsically rewarding practices does not seem to be the basic thrust of contemporary value systems. Values do not seem to result in cooperative or healthy practices but, rather, seem to be externally focused and concerned with winning, competition, and acquisition.

How have values, reality assumptions, and practices come to be what they are today? Attempts to answer this question must examine the entire system within which people live. Although it seems as if the values have magically taken on a life of their own, the process is anything but magical and can be understood within a systems perspective. The whole is more important than the parts, but the parts as substructures also act as wholes. It all depends on the level of analysis that is used to understand the overall system. On the systems level of the person, the liver and heart, for example, are seen as parts that promote the integrity of the whole, while on the level of the organ system, the heart and liver are seen as viable wholes consisting of their own subsystems. Once the contents of the structure of consciousness are established, in this case the perspective and focus of the value system, they become entwined with the whole and are very resistant to change. People tend to value what they learn to value.

While people may have a genetic propensity to develop a value system, the content of the value system must be taught. Problems with value systems are, likewise, problems in consciousness in that perspective, focus, reality assumptions, and language and thus behavior, thoughts, and feelings are affected. The final chapters will discuss what has been called people's "crises in values."

As an illustration, the value of material acquisition has been with humankind throughout the ages. Many "things" throughout recorded history have been the substance of value systems. Different eras and cultures may have valued dissimilar materials, yet have always seemed to embrace the value of acquisition itself. An example concerns the underlying value system of a distant relative, the Duc deBerry of fourteenth-century France:

He lived for possessions, not glory. He owned two residences in Paris, the Hotel de Nesle and another near the Temple, and built or acquired seventeen castles in the duchies of Berry and Auvergne. He filled them with clocks, coins, enamels, mosaics, marquetry, illuminated books, musical instruments, tapestries, statues, triptychs painted in bright scenes on dazzling gold ground bordered with gems, gold vessels and spoons, jeweled crosses and reliquaries, relics and curios. He owned one of Charlemagne's teeth, a piece of Elijah's mantle, Christ's cup from the Last Supper, drops of the Virgin's milk, enough of her hairs and teeth to distribute as gifts, soil from various biblical sites, a narwhal's teeth, porcupine quills, the molar tooth of a giant, and enough gold fringed vestments to robe all the canons of three cathedrals at one time. . . . He kept live swans and bears representing his chosen device, a menagerie with apes and dromedaries, and rare fruits in his garden. (Tuchman, 1978, pp. 469–70)

The Duc deBerry sounds like the Donald Trumps of the twentieth century. The underlying value structure is not all that dissimilar and, unfortunately, has existed since ancient times. Although the material representations of my ancestor's values might be different from Donald Trump's, their underlying structure is identical. Acquisition or, as Thorstein

Veblen (1979) would say, "conspicuous consumption," has been a bane of humanity from time immemorial.

MACROVALUES AND REALITY ASSUMPTIONS

When values are very general and determine the subsequent development of more specific, everyday values and behaviors, they may be called macrovalues. Some examples of macrovalues are truth and freedom. Subsumed under macrovalues may be microvalues that guide everyday behavior such as cleanliness, orderliness, humility, respect, competition, greed, creativity, spontaneity, assertiveness, curiosity, cooperation, and altruism. Part of the general confusion of these times is that people often egocentrically and erroneously confuse their individual microvalues with more general macrovalues. Microvalues are more a matter of personal preference or individual style and personality. Different microvalues can express the same macrovalue. Both an orderly and an untidy person can still maintain the macrovalue of truth. Different cultures have different ways of expressing the same macrovalues. In relationships between individuals, between groups, and between nations, it is important that there be an understanding of each other's macrovalues. The macrovalue of individual dignity is drastically altered as one moves from Paris to Tehran. Ideally, there should be some correlation between individual microvalues as expressed through behavior and the guiding but more general cultural macrovalues. This issue is extremely important and will be explored in depth later in the book. A main contention of this book is that the consciousness of postmodern individualism has led to a dangerous split between values and behavior.

Sometimes, however, values and even macrovalues are so general and all-encompassing that they are best understood as reality assumptions. Although people may not express them and often do not even think about them, all people possess certain assumptions concerning the general nature of their existence. In the case of Robert, for example, it could be said that there was a certain fatalistic reality assumption underlying Robert's behavior. This fatalistic assumption, which probably included predetermination and the inevitability of suffering as being part of the human condition, was never verbalized. Nevertheless, it was there. It became clear through the passive victimization theme of helplessness that permeated all of Robert's stories. Although reality assumptions tend to be rather vague and global, they can still have a rather significant effect on the construction of one's existence. People who believe that blacks are inferior will inevitably exclude them from personal involvement in their world. The subtle yet powerful reality assumptions of racism or elitism can be applied to religion, social class, ethnicity, nationality, and even the clothes people wear and the food they eat (Farb & Armelagos, 1980).

REALITY ASSUMPTIONS

There are at least three general assumptions of reality: (1) fatalistic-tragic, (2) idealistic-romantic, and (3) existential-ironic. By no means is this list to be considered final. Likewise, the qualities associated with each assumption should be taken as only the most basic of introductions and then only as a means of illustrating the systems view of consciousness. For a more in-depth analysis of reality assumptions, see J. D. W. Andrews (1989).

These categories are not mutually exclusive; in fact, many people are capable of maintaining combinations of all three. It is necessary to be at least aware of all three and not be stuck in only one.

Assumption 1, the fatalistic-tragic orientation, is basically a negative determinism that guides the lives of many people. It usually leads to values that are a distortion of religion or the human spirit and to depression-prone, passive, helpless, and hopeless perspectives and focuses that result in behaviors that naturally continue to verify the underlying reality assumption. With the exception of cautious realism or pragmatic skepticism, there are very few positive qualities that result from this reality assumption. People with this underlying reality assumption often expect bad things to happen to them, have a way of getting stuck in situations, and have a difficult time dealing with success. If there exists, as would be considered in a biomedical paradigm, an underlying biological depression secondary to a neuroendocrinological dysfunction, then the depressive symptoms of a person with the fatalistic-tragic reality assumption would become even more serious and pervasive. However, it is not necessary to have an underlying, causative, biological problem in order to have a fatalistic-tragic reality assumption guiding one's life (as in the case of Robert). Not everyone with a positive dexamethasone suppression test reports feeling depressed (the dexamethasone suppression test is a controversial biological measure of endogenous depressions). As always, consciousness (and behavior) is a systemic, multidetermined structure with multiple parts and substructures not always possessing the same influence on the overall system.

Several psychodynamic as well as humanist clinicians and theoreticians have espoused the view that human development is affected by a multitude of factors (Adler, 1931; Fromm, 1955; Horney, 1973; Sullivan, 1953).

Long before these views became popular, Adler, for example, broke away from Freud's deterministic model of human development. Adler's personality investigations concerning individual feelings of inferiority, superiority, or sibling rivalry described how individual perceptions can affect one's course of action. If one perceives oneself as being inferior and destined for suffering, then the chances are that such suffering will occur. Karen Horney also succeeded in connecting individual development to various cultural forces and, like Adler, paved the way for a socially rooted theory of human development and psychopathology.

The idealistic-romantic assumption is a complicated but naive way of looking at the world. People with this reality assumption usually have lofty and exalted notions as to the way the world should be. Their constructions of reality tend to be a bit more positive than their fatalistic-tragic counterparts. At their best, they tend to be optimistic heroes who can make the world a better place; at their worst, they are frustrating Pollyannas, pointless martyrs, and inert dreamers.

The existential-ironic reality assumption is a favorite of intellectuals, mystics, and people who have gone through great personal upheaval. Existentialism developed in Europe and flourished as a result of the cataclysmic upheaval of World War II. This origin is one of the reasons that the existential movement, except as embraced by intellectuals, bohemians, and, to some extent, hippies, never became popular in America. It is not a popular cultural orientation but, rather, tends to be held by separate and special groups of people who have been raised in an environment conducive to the development of such an outlook. It is the reality assumption closest to embracing epistemic dualism and the paradoxical nature of the universe. At its best it can lead to values that positively correlate with an honest, inquiring openness to the world, a nondogmatic approach to experience, and a temporal orientation to the here and now. However, in its distorted form it can lead to intellectual cynicism, aloofness, emotional detachment, pervasive nihilism, and ascetic withdrawal. Actually, the irony pole of this dimension adds a humanistic touch to the potential of existential nihilism and dilutes the undervaluation of reason and the overvaluation of the individual that sometimes follow "pure" existentialism. The ironic pole admits paradox, which allows for a sense that nothing is ever quite what it seems to be. In other words, there are no absolute black and white but only shades of gray. If one focuses totally on existence, essence is ignored while if one believes there is only essence, as do some idealist-romantics, then existence is ignored. The systems constructivist approach to consciousness allows for the possibility that essence and existence are two sides of the same coin, and epistemic dualism implies that since people are incapable of distinguishing between the poles of essence and existence, they might as well forget about the issue and proceed with improving the shades of gray, that is, the actual in-between states of reality.

VALUES, CULTURAL RELATIVITY, AND SHADES OF GRAY

Asked if he had any values, an individual would probably reply, "But of course I have values." Asked to elaborate on that statement, he would probably say, "Well, I value happiness, companionship, pride, dignity, love, self-respect, ambition, and equality." Now if one asked this same person what he values in others, he might reply, "Honesty, trust, strength, wisdom, thoughtfulness, and sincerity." With further inquiry regarding cultural, national, or religious values, the list would grow, but it would also overlap considerably. There are about a dozen or so cluster values that historically, in terms of human nature, have been remarkably consistent across time and culture.

Yet, asked how he puts his values into practice, a person would be even more hard-pressed to give an answer. Within most secular societies very little emphasis is placed upon the relationship of values to behavior. This relationship is often called ethics. There is very little agreement concerning the nuts and bolts, day-to-day realities of ethics. What one person or group believes is a necessary part of self-respect might not be the same for another person or group. What is necessary for one group might be arbitrary or even antithetical for another.

However, such confusion is understandable. Except for tightly knit religious groups, the general culture does not provide prescriptions for ethical behavior. Such provision would be considered contrary to the modern and postmodern notions of individualism and the self. What modern society does offer is law. Law is a poor but necessary substitute for value-based behavior. One need not value the law but only obey it. Adherence to the law does not have to be an internalized value. In fact, for most people it is an externalized constraint. The problem with law's substituting for values, for many different reasons soon to be discussed, is that it can lead to a general disenchantment with all values, especially the so-called traditional values.

In the West, particularly in the United States during the 1960s and 1970s, this disenchantment led to the development of a new value termed value relativity. In its most distorted form, value relativity meant that since all values are arbitrary, then all values are useless. Since there were only shades of gray, behavior became situationally determined and anything was possible and permissible. Instead of values that might restrain or guide behavior, an overemphasis on immediate satisfaction became the norm (Moyers, 1989 [interviews with T. Berry Brazelton and J. Searle]). This tendency gathered momentum and became a movement that permeated all levels of society. For most people, though, this transformation did not result in an increase in happiness or fulfillment. To the contrary, it did just the opposite and for certain people and groups created a new nonvalue value structure that was even more restrictive than the original one. The main outcome of the belief in value relativity has been confusion.

Values are important. Whether one assumes the sociobiological perspective that values are a biologically determined, hard-wired constituent of the nervous system or the more spiritual position that values carry a teleological imperative of human development, they are, nevertheless, an indelible and intrinsic substructure of consciousness.

In a recent book, *The Closing of the American Mind* (1988), Allan Bloom illustrates the point that the value base of this society has eroded. Bloom places great emphasis on the deterioration of the university as the traditional cultural instrument of value transmission. However, Bloom is right for mostly the wrong reasons; furthermore, because his analysis (not his observation) is faulty, he also comes to some very erroneous conclusions and recommendations. Bloom is wrong because as a way of "fixing things" (again another reductive solution), he advocates a return to the classic dictates of a traditional education. Specifically, Bloom proposes reinstituting "teaching of the classics" as a means of correcting the present. Because humankind cannot go backward in time, Bloom's call for a return to the classics as a way of reintegrating "traditional values" is fallacious. Going back in time to an earlier era is a blatant and misguided impossibility. Unfortunately, this impossibility, along with Bloom's book, has been embraced by conservatives and fundamentalists, who have a tremendous influence in keeping things the way they have always been (Bellah, 1987; Handy, 1969; Mathes, 1981; Moyers, 1989 [interview with T. Wolfe]). Actually, the only possibility is moving ahead, and since it is becoming apparent that people are responsible for constructing their future, the details of the present and future, not the loss of past consciousness, should become the paramount issue. The call for a return to traditions of the past is only an escapist solution.

SUMMARY

These points are raised now because this book is beginning to move from the microscopic organization of individual consciousness to the macroscopic orientation of public consciousness. Through the supra-biological systems of values and reality assumptions, both public and private consciousness become intimately connected. There is one more substructure of consciousness to explore before the model becomes complete. This is the substructure of language. Linguistic abilities are one direct measure of consciousness and therefore must be understood as a part of the overall system.

6   *Language and Consciousness*

Philosophy is a battle against the bewitchment of our intelligence by means of language.
            —Ludwig Wittgenstein, *Tractus Logico-Philosophicus*

- **Proposition 4:** Language is one of the means by which consciousness can be measured.

Language has become the basic building block of human consciousness. Like a supreme artistic creation, linguistic ability is held aloft as the epitome of human separation from the "savagery" of the animal world. Opposable thumbs, outside of anthropology, have never quite attained the exalted status of Bibles and political speeches and are rarely, if ever, discussed as a point of separation of humans from nonhumans. Clearly, language is perceived as being the most human of all phenomena.

Language and rationality go hand in hand in extending humanity's boundaries beyond the jungle. Rational thought is built upon the structure of language. The consistent uniformity and lawfulness of language from phonemes to sentences have allowed for a similarly consistent and lawful way of constructing the world.

In language both underlying structure and manifest phenomena follow a remarkably stable, linear form of logic. The logic of language and, hence, of the language of thought and ideas is a causal, deductive-inductive mechanism for processing reality. In evolutionary terms it has provided an extremely powerful tool that has enabled humankind to be the only planetary species that exclusively adapts the world to its purposes. In terms of assimilation and accommodation to reality, humans, in comparison to other species, do the most assimilation and the least accommodation. They are constantly shaping reality to meet their needs. From an elemental perspective, language is responsible for the development and proliferation of human culture and technology. The word *elemental* refers to the fact that language is a very basic part of the consciousness system. Consciousness is usually expressed in language. Like it or not, humans are talking animals. As Arthur Koestler (1967) states:

Owing to the immense benefits derived from verbalizations, the verbal symbol, which at the dawn of symbol-consciousness was at first no more than a label attached to a pre-existing conceptual schema, soon became its focal member, its center of gravity, as it were. As words are the most convenient and economical means not only to communicate but also of internal discourse, they soon assume a central role, . . . whereas images and other forms of unverbalized thought are gradually pushed towards the periphery, the fringes of awareness, or sink slowly down below the surface. (p. 600)

Although it is fast on its way to being so, language is still not the exclusive contractor of consciousness. Numerous students of consciousness have pointed out that there are alternate, less linear ways of constructing the world. Since the organic source of linguistic functioning has been consistently located in the speech areas of the brain's left hemisphere, these nonlinear, intuitive, or synergistic modes of consciousness are often associated with right-hemisphere consciousness. This dichotomy, as Robert Ornstein points out, should not be taken as an example of discrete binary classification. It has become quite fashionable to speak of right-hemisphere consciousness as if it were something that exists independently. This idea, of course, is simply untrue. The brain is far too complex an organ to be so primitively reduced into localized parts. There are, however, tendencies of processing information that to some extent can be hemispherically located. These tendencies are described in the following table (Ornstein, 1977).

Left Hemisphere	Right Hemisphere
intellectual	sensuous
temporal	timelessness
explicit	tacit
analytic	synthetic
linear	nonlinear
sequential	simultaneous
propositional	appositional
focal	diffuse
causal	synchronicity
local	non-local

It is important to remember that the brain processes information in a holistic and parallel fashion. There is really no such thing as separate parts. Studies employing magnetic resonance imagery, computerized axial tomography, and positron emission tomography have conclusively demonstrated that even the simple act of speaking a syllable or moving a toe may involve numerous areas and substructures. The point here is that consciousness, like the brain, is a holistic structure. The right requires the left, and the yin needs the yang; each is part of the other. This chapter will develop the idea that human consciousness, at the expense of its holistic nature, is being restricted to a predominantly linguistically constructed reality.

IMPORTANT QUALIFICATIONS OF
A LINGUISTIC MODEL OF CONSCIOUSNESS

Faith in and focus on linguistic consciousness have led to a schizoid state of reality in which other modes of expressing consciousness are ignored. For example, when it comes to politics, Americans tend to be overwhelmingly skeptical and cynical and yet pay remarkable attention to the political language. When something happens, people immediately want to know what the president said about the event. What is said is often more important than what is actually done. The art of political rhetoric involves creating the illusion of doing something while actually doing nothing, as in the "Just say No" campaign of the war on drugs. Because words are representations and symbols of a deeper underlying reality, the Reagan administration, through the clever and deliberate manipulation of words, was actually able to construct the illusion of there being a concentrated war on drugs, while at the same time actually cutting funding. The contradiction was hardly noticed. Because the administration's rhetorical position was consistent, there was little need to look at the behavioral realities behind the linguistic ones. President Bush calls together a national summit on education during which nothing substantial occurs. Yet, the so-called summit produced so much media attention that the "appearance of substance" was provided. The language of national press coverage was enough.

Language is an abstract condensation of the underlying reality of human consciousness. It is one of the end products of the systemic spatial-temporal blendings of perspective, focus, values, and reality assumptions. But language is not the only way in which this underlying reality can be expressed. One must also take into account behaviors, emotions, images, and sensations. These prelinguistic modes of expressing consciousness are extremely important and in evolutionary terms predate linguistic consciousness. Long before a person's ancestors could talk, they had feelings about the world. They had images and sensations with which they constructed their "being in the world," that is, their consciousness. Ever so slowly, as linguistic consciousness expanded, these preverbal modes became less and less important. The preverbal modes of consciousness described in the table as right-hemisphere functions are an important tool for effectively constructing reality. In reference to the evolutionary importance of these modes of consciousness, Victor Guidano (1987) states:

Assuming that tacit, analogical processes play a crucial role in the scaffolding of the order and regularities with which we are acquainted, it follows that feelings and emotions are primary in personal knowing. When considered within an evolutionary perspective the primacy of affect becomes explicit. While cognitive abilities represent one of the final products to emerge from a long evolutionary process, feelings and emotions were probably the first organized knowing system to actively scaffold environmental regularities. (p. 25)

Language helped develop a human culture that could be generationally transmitted. Technologies could be developed, maintained, and passed on for improvement. The development of linear language and linear, goal-directed technology became increasingly intertwined. Each depended on the other. The results of linguistic consciousness have been incredible. In less than 6,000 years, just a tiny fraction of the earth's history, humans have enjoyed a material evolutionary success unparalleled by any other species. But a comprehensive analysis indicates that these evolutionary changes have been exclusively internal, that is, within the brain and thus within the mind and consciousness. Humankind's ancestors 40,000 years ago did not physically look all that different from humans today, but, in terms of consciousness, it would be like comparing neonates with mature adults. From a developmental perspective the physical self has not changed as greatly as the brain's capacity and consciousness. It was approximately 40,000 years ago in the cranium of Cro-Magnon man that the human cerebrum evolved to its present form. Yet, it took almost 30,000 years for the brain's consciousness to change enough for civilization to begin to appear (Campbell, 1988). As the British neuroscientist Steven Rose states: "Our cranial capacity or cell number may not be so different from the early Homo sapiens, but our environments—our forms of society—are very different and hence so too is our consciousness" (Hooper & Teresi, 1986, p. 60).

The development of language was responsible for the transformations that human environments have undergone. As the linear consciousness of language increased and consolidated more power, alternate modes of consciousness became less important (Chapple, 1970; Langer, 1967; Sapir, 1921; Whorf, 1941). Historically, humans are now at the paradoxical and schizoid point of paying almost exclusive attention to words often at the exclusion of conflicting and contradictory feelings and even behaviors. Over 2,000 years ago the Greek historian Thucydides said that the corruption of freedom begins with the corruption of language. The Orwellian world of Newspeak is closer than we think. A clinical vignette will provide an example.

Kathy is in love with Jack, who, she says, is in love with her. Kathy is in psychotherapy because of feelings of confusion and depression. Kathy "knows" Jacks loves her because he constantly tells her so. She wants to marry Jack. Jack, in addition to seeing Kathy, also sees several other women. Often, without any prior notice, he goes off for days at a time. Many times he has failed to show up for a date or engagement. Because he is a musician, Jack says that such abrupt trips are inevitable. Jack says that when they are married, he will support Kathy, although right now she is partially supporting him. Reluctantly and defensively, Kathy has told me that many times she has caught Jack lying to her.

Ideally, there should be a correspondence among the expressive dimensions of consciousness. In other words, there should be an approximate fit among what a person says, does, thinks, feels, imagines, and experiences. Clearly in the case of Jack and Kathy this correspondence is not so. Kathy is placing undue emphasis on Jack's words and is paying too little attention to his actions. Why doesn't it matter more to Kathy that Jack is lying, that he is saying one thing while doing another? Kathy seems to be a victim of the power of language to supersede other perceptual modes.

The same is true for what both Ronald Reagan and George Bush said and actually did about the drug problem. In both illustrations, words, despite their underlying duplicity, carried more weight than the actual behavior. Similar problems develop with cross-cultural relationships in which words and language convey entirely different dimensions of meaning. Different cultures often have dissimilar ways of linguistically transmitting social realities. Furthermore, cultures, even subcultures within a country, have diverse and often idiosyncratic ways of interpreting language. Some cultures place more emphasis on what is actually said in comparison to what is actually done. Words are valued as an expression of a person's intentions. Linguistic problems arise, for example, during Anglo-Arab, French-Chinese, or Latin–North American relations. In a sense, the case of Kathy and Jack is like an example of a linguistic clash of cultures; neither really understands the needs or behaviors of the other, and no one moves beyond words.

Although the constriction of consciousness to the linguistic mode is predominantly negative, there is at least one positive ramification relevant both to the form and to the purpose of the present model of consciousness. Because language is such a deeply rooted human structure, it can reveal aspects of oneself and others in profound but obvious ways. Furthermore, because language follows a consistent set of logical rules, its output can be assigned mathematical values and measured in a scientific way. Because language can be scientifically measured, the constructionist criteria of any model of consciousness can be maintained. It is then possible to construct and compare different models of reality and correlate the models with objective social criteria, that is, operationally defined, dependent behavioral variables such as happiness, satisfaction, meaning, and purpose, and in turn measure these concepts against objective social data like the divorce rate, the homicide rate, and the suicide rate.

In other words, for constructivist reasons language is assumed to be a direct reflection of consciousness. For purposes of initially building a testable model, language will be employed as the principal measurement of consciousness. Such an approach could be criticized as promoting a schizoid and one-dimensional notion of consciousness. This criticism is not without merit but, with the exception of one important qualification, must be ignored. The qualification is that this book's model of consciousness must be understood from the perspective of epistemic dualism. That is, although there are other modes and representations of consciousness, for the purposes of developing an experimental model they will be assumed not to exist. Theoretically and experimentally this stance parallels exactly what is happening in the world, that linguistic consciousness is being treated as if it were the only measure of reality. Tacit, affective, and intuitive modes of processing reality are not being taken seriously. These processes are being relegated to the realm os mysticism and the supernatural. By concentrating exclusively on language, the deficiencies and incompleteness of a linguistic consciousness can be highlighted and perhaps tested. Perhaps, then, a more holistically integrated version of consciousness can be allowed to develop.

In addition to eliminating alternate modes of consciousness, by taking such an approach, this book also assumes that people are speaking honestly; that is, in relation to language the book assumes a position of naive realism. In psychotherapy, what people say is at least personally true for them.

Is the world constructed of words? Obviously not. The world has its own physicality independent of words, yet it is principally through the structure of words that people express and understand this physicality in a manner that allows for its manipulation and control. As Kahil Gibran (1926) says, "We shall never understand one another until we reduce the language to seven words."

For some linguistic theoreticians, consciousness is always expressed in terms of language, and people can be conscious only of what they can put into words (Brown, 1988; Chomsky, 1968; Lieberman, 1981; Ronat, 1979). Benjamin Whorf is one of the main proponents of the perspective that reality is linguistically created. The famous Sapir-Whorf (or Whorfian) hypothesis states:

Human beings do not live in the objective world alone, nor alone in the world of social activity as ordinarily understood, but are very much at the mercy of the particular language which has become the medium of expression for their society. . . . The fact of the matter is that the "real world" is to a large extent unconsciously built up on the language habits of the group. No two languages are ever sufficiently similar to be considered as representing the same social reality. The worlds in which different societies live are distinct worlds, not merely the same world with different labels attached. (Sapir, 1921, p. 209)

Notice that Whorf makes the distinction between social and physical reality. This is because although language is successful for approximating physical reality regardless of culture (for example, the sentence "Look out, the bull is charging!"), it is not as successful for conveying a social reality. It is generally accepted that avoiding a charging bull is an act of physical wisdom. The social reality of the bull is quite another matter. The word *bull*, a symbol for the actual bull, has an entirely different range of meaning depending on whether one is an American farmer, a Hindu, or a Spanish matador. Another classic example is the Eskimo, who, in comparison to Americans, has at least twenty different words for snow.

LANGUAGE AND THE SYSTEMS MODEL OF CONSCIOUSNESS

To summarize, within systems theory consciousness is a structure that maintains the integrity of the system of the person. Since it is a structure, it is by nature conservative, reductive, and selective. That is, out of the vast array of possibilities consciousness must selectively attend to only a narrow range of stimuli and from that narrow range construct a viable reality. Both the brain and the mind act together in such a reductive fashion. In terms of the mind, that is, consciousness, the substructures of perspective and focus construct reality in interaction with temporal and spatial substructures (past, present, and future; intrapersonal, interpersonal, and impersonal), which in turn interact with the substructures of values and reality assumptions, all of which combine to generate a language that represents reality, an arbitrary reality but a reality nonetheless.

On physical levels the arbitrariness of reality has many reductive system correlates. For example, there is nothing sacred about the wave nature of perceived reality being between 400 and 700 billionths of a meter, and yet this wave nature is the visible spectrum and is thus the slice of reality that humans are neurologically able to process. Robert Ornstein repeatedly makes the point that the primary function of the senses is to discard irrelevant information and reduce the potentiality of the universe into stable and consistent images. For modern Homo sapiens this reductive process seems to have reached its zenith with language.

The proposition that language constructs reality is by no means a new perspective. Aldous Huxley's ideas regarding language and consciousness are quite similar. For example, Huxley (1954) states:

To formulate and express the contents of this reduced awareness man has invented and endlessly elaborated those system-systems and implicit philosophies we call languages. Every individual is at once the beneficiary and the victim of the linguistic tradition into which he has been born—the beneficiary inasmuch as language gives access to the accumulated records of other people's experience, the victim insofar as it confirms him in the belief that reduced awareness is the only awareness, and as it bedevils his sense of reality, so that he is all too apt to take his concepts for data, his words for the actual things. That which, in the language of religion, is called "this world" is the universe of reduced awareness expressed and as it were, petrified by language. (pp. 23–24)

Employing language as a measure operationalizes consciousness while maintaining the importance of the contents of consciousness, that is, people's interior world. This approach results in a "scientific mentalism," capable of embracing the paradoxical duality of existence. In keeping with epistemic dualism it allows construction of models of linguistically generated realities.

Through careful analysis of a person's words, one can locate consciousness as sets of measurable temporal-spatial coordinates for each perspective and inclusive of every focus (Rucker, 1982). In order to measure the temporal dimension, one would simply maintain a frequency count of grammar, words, sentences, and ideas as they refer to the past, present, and future. To measure the spatial dimension, one would again maintain a frequency count of grammar, words, sentences, and ideas as they refer to the self, to the self and another person, and to things. In order to evaluate the perspective, one would again count the number of words, sentences, and, especially, ideas that refer to the perspective being studied, and the procedure for evaluating the focus would be identical.

Crude Experiment Number 1

Thirty graduate students from a masters level psychology class were divided into six groups of five subjects. For the next thirty minutes they were then asked to discuss anything they wished to. Each conversation was taped. Preliminary results are as follows:

A. Percentage of linguistic structures related to time
  1. Past: 69%
  2. Present: 11%
  3. Future: 20%

B. Percentage of linguistic structures related to spatial factors
  1. Intrapersonal: 1%
  2. Interpersonal: 8%
  3. Impersonal: 91%

Because the impersonal nature of school along with the fact that these people did not know each other very well might have distorted the results, the experiment was repeated, using people who personally claimed to be "good friends." The first group consisted of four women and three men who had known each other for at least sixteen years. The subjects volunteered their time at a barbecue get-together. The second group consisted of ten psychotherapists (psychologists, social workers, and psychiatrists), six men and four women who worked together at a clinic and had all known each other a minimum of two years.

Group 1

A. Percentage of linguistic structures related to time
  1. Past: 65%
  2. Present: 18%
  3. Future: 17%

B. Percentage of linguistic structures related to spatial factors
  1. Intrapersonal: 3%
  2. Interpersonal: 17%
  3. Impersonal: 80%

Group 2

A. Percentage of linguistic factors related to time
  1. Past: 67%
  2. Present: 21%
  3. Future: 12%

B. Percentage of linguistic structures related to spatial factors
1. Intrapersonal: 2%
2. Interpersonal: 25%
3. Impersonal: 73%

These pilot results suggest that the consciousness of three rather different groups of people, at least under the experimental conditions, exists in a predominantly past and impersonal dimension.

The notion that language is a quantifiable as well as qualifiable measure of consciousness is an accepted premise of postmodernist thinkers (Engels, 1984; Feldstein, 1978; Foucault, 1973; Lutz, 1989), who stress its importance in defining reality. The act of creating language is not a passive or neutral event but, rather, the end result of the operations of the structure of consciousness. Words enable people to highlight one focus at the expense of others; that is, they are a necessary factor in the regulation of consciousness in that they illuminate people, situations, and values. Language is one way in which values are expressed, and it is through the interaction of one's values with consciousness and the external world that one's image of reality is created. Language, then, is a key substructure within the structure of consciousness (Bloom, 1988).

If a person relates to another only by talking about himself, his language will reflect this perspective, for example, "I, my, me." If one relates to another through talking about their relationship, his language will reflect this perspective, for example, "we, us, you and I, John and I." If one relates to another through discussing impersonal things external to both, his language will likewise reflect this dimension of consciousness, for example, "the car, the house, the baby, the body, the wife." In addition to simple word and grammar analyses, thematic analysis is also possible. Such analyses have been performed on metaphor, the thematic content of patient vignettes, and the thematic analysis of language-expressed time (Dapkus, 1985; Pollio, 1982). Likewise, various clinicians have stressed that language is directly related to psychopathology and diagnostic categories (Guidano, 1987). The following passage is a direct transcript of a patient discussing his relationship with his wife. The consultation was due to marital difficulties.

I know it's not me . . . I mean the old lady is such a pain in the ass. Women always nag, don't they. I am so sick of this. Nobody knows how I feel. I deserve more than this. [long pause] I'm always thinking about other women, especially this one chick I knew in high school. Man, it was so easy then. I think about those days all the time. Sometimes I think I should look her up . . . look up my old friends

. . . maybe go back to the old neighborhood. I know she'd see me. I think that's what I'm gonna do.

The remainder of the session was fairly similar in its narcissistic litany of complaints. Out of approximately 100 words the first person "I" is utilized thirteen times. There are no personal references to the person who is his wife; she is impersonally classified in the "old lady" category. The general theme of the vignette concerns the past. This patient's consciousness can be spatially located predominantly in the impersonal dimension and temporally in the past. Such locations of consciousness are common to narcissistic disorders.

The fact that language is capable of shifting consciousness along the intrapersonal, interpersonal, and impersonal dimensions is indeed a double-edged sword. The good part about this phenomenon is people's ability to personify the impersonal world. People are capable of projecting their inner world of thoughts, ideas, fantasies, internalized objects, and emotions onto the outer world. Such projections, when performed within certain limits, make the world a more exciting place as, for example, when people become personally involved in their material possessions, home teams, works of art, and literature.

LANGUAGE AND THE LOSS OF INTIMACY

Unfortunately, language also enables people to communicate about the most personal of dimensions in the most impersonal of ways. Through language, anything can be objectified to the impersonal dimension where intrapersonal and interpersonal variables are no longer of any importance. Martin Buber considered relationships of categorized others as *It—It* or *I—It* encounters. Jean Paul Sartre (1957), Richard Chessick (1985), and R. D. Laing (1965a, 1965b) called these types of relationships inauthentic or manifestations of *mauvaise foi* (bad faith). Most of the time, consciousness is a fluctuating synthesis of all three dimensions, that is, one's personal world. Problems arise only when there is a constriction of consciousness as manifested by a predominance of time spent in impersonal space. Such a constriction of consciousness can be measured through linguistic analysis.

A person can relate to another as a thing or as a person. If he relates to another as a thing, that is, a category such as wife, boss, or Chicano, his relationship to the other becomes simplified in that it becomes prescribed by the cultural rules and values associated with that particular category. People, in short, are capable of being categorized and thus related to as things, for example, slaves, the underclass, or the enemy. Christopher Lasch, for example, points out that for centuries women and children have been treated as either slaves or classes of things (Lasch, 1984).

Relationships do become a bit more ambiguous if one relates to another in a more personal sense as Linda, Brian, or Eduardo. In other words, the other is being related to not as a static "thing" but as a fluid and dynamic person. All the person's potentials and possibilities can then be taken into account. These latter categories can be far more inclusive of the intrapersonal and interpersonal dimensions that contain the innumerable potentialities of a person's existence. In a general systems sense, the personal names are more inclusive of all the potential modes of existence of Linda, John, and Eduardo. However, what is gained in terms of inclusiveness and authenticity is lost in terms of clarity and specificity.

A name is a personal symbol. Because it is a personal symbol, it has a rich potential of possibilities that represent the reality of the symbolized person. The reality of the person is always more complicated than the symbol. There are words, like Chicano, Jew, Arab, or schizophrenic, that become symbols for a more general class of phenomena. These words do not have a wide range of possibilities but instead denote very specific characteristics peculiar to the general class. Thus, there are degrees of abstraction through which language may represent reality. The more abstract and general a language becomes, the more it removes itself from the reality it is trying to symbolize. As language becomes increasingly abstract and general, the less personal it becomes.

There are degrees of abstraction by which language can distance itself from reality. For some scientific and mathematical processes this degree of abstraction has proven to be quite helpful in terms of advancing science and technology. For the world of human relations and the applied uses of technology, this distancing phenomenon has proven itself to be a dangerous process because the rarefied atmosphere of abstraction, metaphor, and euphemism allows very important personal decisions to be made without full access to consciousness.

As a species humans talk and think excessively in abstractions. Using abstract armor, they employ language as a means of defense. As they endlessly dance around their true inner feelings, they continue to avoid closeness and personal connections with others. What they reveal to the world is not what they are but, rather, what they either pretend to be or, out of fear, try to be. The often irrational, fluid, and dynamic possibilities of the intrapersonal and interpersonal worlds frighten people into a semiconscious, impersonal retreat. Humans are increasingly existing in a make-believe, impersonal dimension of fantasized intimacy. Communication is desperately avoided. Fantasized intimacy, like pretend-closeness or make-believe love, is an abstract dimension, negotiated by language and empty values that only increase alienation while avoiding entirely what might truly be happening.

There is a very strong correlation between people's reliance on the realities of linguistic abstractions and their predominantly abstract sense of vision. Out of all the senses, the visual system provides the most removed and abstract image of the reality with which people are interacting. In a cool and detached sense, very much separate from the external object of its appraisal, vision constructs the world. Human existence and interaction are becoming a primarily image-related, visual world concerned with appearance. It is not how one smells or feels that counts (unless, of course, one does not smell or feel in a culturally acceptable manner) but rather, unfortunately, how one appears. To expand this example, humans are increasingly becoming a global culture that worships the image while spending millions of dollars to hide and eliminate the wonderful and idiosyncratic realities of the human body. Chapter 9 will further explore this phenomenon as well as humans' transition into a neutral but controlled, visual image of impersonality.

Human consciousness is partially a systems blend of intrapersonal, interpersonal, and impersonal factors. In the final construct of personal consciousness, all of these factors must be involved. Furthermore, there must be an optimal but fluid blending of the three factors so that, depending upon the situational interaction, an optimal reality is constructed (see figures 4.1–4.4 in chapter 4). There is no need to be conscious of inner feelings regarding oneself or others when fixing a carburetor, performing a mathematical equation, or living in an impersonal dimension. These are basically operations of an impersonal mode of consciousness. However, not all human interactions are impersonal.

I—It, I—Thou, and *It—It*

In terms of linguistic consciousness Martin Buber's ideas are worth exploring. Buber believes that the full, potential humanness of people can be expressed only in a fully open and accepting relationship of the total *I* meeting with a total *Thou*. Buber contrasts the *I—Thou* relationship with the *I—It* relationship in which "it" represents a static, predetermined, objectified form of relating. The term "it" refers to a person frozen in space and time—a person incapable of being himself. The "its" in *I—It* relationships refer to a singularity of identity and purpose, independent and separate from the individual.

This means that the most complete type of encounter that people can have is when they openly and totally communicate everything about themselves with each other. Buberian *I—Thou* dialogue could be summarized as follows:

1. *I—Thou* exists in the lived present.
2. *I—Thou* is not an idea.
3. *I—Thou* involves feeling but does not originate with feeling.
4. *I—Thou* is love as responsibility; its goal is the love of all people.
5. *I—Thou* is undulating, cyclic, dynamic, dialectic.
6. *I—Thou* involves relationship with the whole world (Heaney & Heaney, 1973).

Effective psychotherapy is a healing and complete relationship that is based upon a Buberian paradigm. In an earlier paper I wrote:

In an *I—Thou* relationship the other is met as a complete yet separate individual. By complete I mean that all aspects of the person's being are allowed to be available within the relationship; that is, one does not have to pretend, act, or be deceptive about aspects of one's self. . . . An *I—It* relation is described as a subject-object relationship whereby one person becomes a thing i.e., a property or object of desire and manipulation. *I—It* relationships are characteristic of three basic pathological forms of relating. These forms can be described as: 1. relating to others as self-objects, 2. relating to others as transitional objects and, 3. relating to others as part objects. (DeBerry, 1987, p. 240)

The case of Tony represents an example of deviation from the desired *I—Thou*, interpersonal, intimate relationship. Tony was a thirty-six-year-old married male who consulted me because he was unhappy in his marriage. Tony was married for the second time to a successful and practical woman from an affluent, middle-class family. Tony's presenting problem was that he had a hard time not flirting with other women to whom he was sexually attracted. Other women, especially if they were available, elicited an intense feeling of lust in Tony. However, he had never cheated on his wife because she was "a source of valuable stability." Tony felt that his wife's affluent background made it easier for him to make a lot of money and be successful. He felt that because his wife had come from a fairly affluent background, she knew how to appear and act wealthy and self-assured. Without her, Tony was not certain that he could be as successful as he presently was. The only problem was that he did not feel a strong sexual attraction for her.

This clinical vignette is an excellent example of a relationship based on self, transitional, and part-object needs. Tony was not interested in a complete, *I—Thou* relationship with his wife. He was more concerned with what parts of his wife could do for certain parts of himself. Tony used his wife as a part object to satisfy certain transitional needs. In this sense, his wife became a part object herself who had only a partial *I—It* or *It—It* transitional relationship with her husband. On some level, apparently this was all that Tony thought he wanted or needed. Psychotherapy revealed that neither Tony nor his wife was conscious of these developmental deficits.

Numerous philosophers, including Buber, feel that one of the major shortcomings of contemporary life is that relationships are too easily reduced to the *I—It* or *It—It* variety. Although Buber's emphasis of the *I—Thou* encounter originated from a predominantly religious perspective, he nevertheless stressed its importance to human relations. In the frenetic, everyday, marketplace exchange of goods and services, sometimes the loss of an *I—Thou* encounter is inevitable. But what about intimacy and love? What about the case of Tony? In these cases there seems to be both a conscious and an unconscious withdrawal from *I—Thou* dialogue and thus the type of intimacy that can originate only within *I—Thou* encounters. People seem to be increasingly settling for a watered-down *I—It* form of intimacy. As discussed in the next chapter, when consciousness becomes reduced or becomes predominantly externalized, true Buberian intimacy becomes terrifying. To paraphrase both Eric Fromm and Rollo May, *I—Thou* intimacy becomes a process to be avoided or escaped from. In its absence people begin to use each other. They settle for a piecemeal gratification of different parts of themselves from assorted parts of another. People reconcile themselves to a partial complementarity and avoid the potential of a more total *I—Thou* consciousness. Tony was using parts of his wife as a source of identity. She was filling certain voids in Tony. This process was probably reciprocal; Maria (his wife) partially might have wanted or thought she wanted a verification of her "wealthy person background" status. Undoubtedly she would receive this from Tony. But what about her other needs, as, for example, her need to be loved, understood, and verified as a person? Where did they go? Would not Maria begin either consciously or unconsciously to resent the situation and pull back? Was Maria, somewhere else, complaining about unhappiness to another psychotherapist or lover? Whether she was or was not is perhaps secondary to the *I—It* dilemma itself. After all, neither option is the most desirable. The preferable option is that Maria and Tony realize what they are doing and begin to engage in a real *I—Thou* encounter, that is, mutually begin to recognize, acknowledge, and discuss the problem.

But this intimacy would be painful, and too often it is the pain of intimacy that people ignore. In this case, a painful *I—Thou* relationship would at least be more real than the constricted *I—It* or part-object relationship they were both enduring. As painful as such intimacy would be, at least it would be a step toward acknowledging the reality of the situation and thus creating conditions for it to change. Sadly, however, a bad relationship is often considered better than no relationship at all.

Joseph Campbell (1988) has pointed out that the American Indians addressed all life as a *Thou*. He believed that one can address anything as a *Thou* and claimed that the self that sees a *Thou* is quite different from the self that sees an *It*. Unfortunately, in modern cultures people are increasingly seeing *Its*. The loss of *I—Thou* relatedness represents the loss of personal involvement.

Personal Involvement

Just what is personal involvement and what does it have to do with the externalization of consciousness? In chapters 2 and 3, the personal dimension was described as a synthesis of the substructures of consciousness: perspective and focus; the spatial factors, that is, the intrapersonal, interpersonal, and impersonal dimensions; the temporal factors, that is, past, present, and future dimensions; the value and reality assumption factors; and language. Therefore, at any given moment, one's personal identity is determined by the blendings and permutations of all these subsystems. Personal involvement, then, is simply an *I—Thou* encounter of all the substructures of one person with all those of another. It is important to remember that people do not have to be actually conscious but only potentially conscious of the different contributions to their personal identity. To be persistently conscious of the operations of consciousness would, of course, be chaotic and virtually impossible. In other words, the more aware people are of their different selves or elements of consciousness, the less schizoid and the more conscious they become. It is also important to realize that being conscious of different feelings, other selves, or hidden desires does not mean that one has to act upon them. Increased awareness does not require the abandonment of either impulse control or an ethical framework of action. People do not always have to act on or express their feelings; they just have to be aware of them.

But if most of the synthesis of consciousness is subconscious or unconscious, how, then, can one become aware of not only his other selves but the elemental components of his personal consciousness? The answer has to do with feelings, behaviors, and thoughts. Chapter 2 discussed the theories relevant to the decrease in the brain's awareness and expression of emotion. Likewise, the chapter on language explored the ideas central to the ascendance of left-hemisphere, linguistically generated consciousness as being one's principal measure of reality. As the abstractive and logical realm of language predominates consciousness, one's awareness of the alternate but less logical and affective components of consciousness becomes diminished.

In evolutionary terms, these alternate ways of processing reality have mainly to do with emotions, behaviors, and, to some extent, nonrational thoughts that do not mesh with people's linguistically generated identity. In neurological terms, the consciousness of the right hemisphere and the limbic system is becoming less available to people. In relation to the mind or the systems operations of consciousness, human consciousness is becoming restricted to a reduced *I—It* or *It—It*, impersonal dimension of personal involvement, which paradoxically is really impersonal involvement masquerading as *I—Thou*. Language clearly takes precedence over behavior in that what a person or agency says is becoming more important than what they actually do. Words now have priority over inner thoughts and feelings. Prelanguage emotional consciousness is becoming less and less available. This occurrence is what externalized consciousness implies.

The externalization of consciousness refers to the fact that intimacy, closeness, relationships, communication, and, in a sense, human love have increasingly less to do with an *I—Thou* sense of personal involvement. Human relationships have now more to do with the external, impersonal dimension of consciousness. Things and appearances now take precedence over emotions and substance. Most people are aware of themselves and others only in a very nonemotional and superficial manner.

SUMMARY

Within a systems model of consciousness, this chapter has described the role of language. In evolutionary terms, language was depicted as a more recent acquisition of consciousness. Imagery, sensation, and affective consciousness were discussed as parts of the general system that predate language. It was emphasized, however, that language has now come to dominate the generation and construction of conscious phenomena.

The proposed model is relatively complete. Within a systems perspective, the structures and operations of perspective, focus, values, and language have been developed. The ability of these substructures and parts to fluctuate temporally and spatially has been explained. The second half of the book consists of applying these components and individual consciousness to social or cultural consciousness and demonstrating that what goes on in one's head is directly related to the problems of everyday life. Chapter 7 will describe externalized consciousness.

7 The Externalization of Consciousness

Man is nothing else but what he makes of himself. . . . Man is at the start a plan which is aware of itself.
> —Jean-Paul Sartre, *Existentialism and Human Existence*

- **Proposition 5:** The externalization of consciousness refers to the evolutionary shift from an internal matrix of intrapersonal-interpersonal-impersonal consciousness to a predominantly impersonal consciousness as manifested by a preoccupation with the external world of material phenomena.

The external shift of the analog "I," in its metaphorical space, means that people are becoming more conscious of the impersonal world and less conscious of their intrapersonal and interpersonal dimensions. Consequently, they are losing the ability to articulate their experience of these dimensions and, hence, their real experience of themselves and others as active, dynamic, relational "beings in the world." In short, they are losing the language of relating and, with it, the ability to be truly intimate.

Since perception depends upon both external and internal factors, one could say that people are paying more attention to external cues. The situation, however, extends beyond the limits set by theories of perception. Externalized consciousness does not imply that an external locus of control is superseding an internal one. Rather, in terms of what one is conscious of, it implies that external factors are becoming internalized. People will say that their perceptions originate freely from an internal locus, yet what they fail to realize is that the contents of their internalized locus are increasingly derived from the impersonal dimension. Intrapersonal and interpersonal factors, within people and as experienced with others, are becoming less important. Focus, perspective, values, reality assumptions, and language are becoming increasingly reflective of the impersonal dimension. This development is what externalized consciousness implies. The psychological laws of perception are not changing; rather, the nature of what is perceived is changing.

The more that consciousness is externalized, the less aware people become of themselves and others. Paradoxically, the more they become conscious of and dependent upon external events as a source of personal identity, the less conscious they become of internal events. This notion is contrary to the belief that this age is one of increased personal and interpersonal consciousness. Actually, in comparison to expanded intrapersonal or interpersonal consciousness, the postmodern age is much more characterized by a preoccupation and involvement with external images, things, and appearances. External shifts in consciousness are exemplified by the case of Tony, presented in the previous chapter. Both Tony and his wife seems to be interested in external aspects of each other. Other examples of externalized consciousness are the following:

- placing emphasis on physical appearance over inner values
- judging people by where they live and not how they live
- the idolization of celebrities, sports heroes, and millionaires
- the prevalence of greed and the desire to acquire possessions
- appraising people by what school they have attended, how much they own, or what social class they belong to
- confusing the reality of television with reality

As consciousness becomes externalized, people's personal sense of self becomes more internalized. In retreating from the vagaries of intrapersonal awareness and interpersonal dialogue, they become increasingly isolated, more preoccupied with themselves, and increasingly narcissistic. As a species, people are less able to be intimate, more protective of their inner self, more likely to act or pretend, and less aware of emotions and their reactive need for dialogue and communion with others. Pertaining to isolation, Rollo May (1953) states:

We remain spiritually isolated and at sea, and so we cover up our loneliness by chattering with other people about the things we do have language for—the world series, business affairs, and the latest news reports. Our deeper emotional experiences are pushed further away, and we tend, thus, to become emptier and lonelier (p. 68). . . . The capacity for consciousness of ourselves gives us the ability to see ourselves as others see us and to have empathy with others. . . . In the achieving of consciousness of one's self, most people must start back at the beginning and rediscover their feelings (p. 86). . . . Their connection with their feelings is as remote as if over a long distance telephone. (p. 105)

It is frightening to realize that the above passages were written forty years ago. A new generation has already grown up, and yet nothing that Rollo May has pointed out has changed. If anything, most people have accepted that alienation from interpersonal and intrapersonal consciousness is basically now a fact of life. Values and reality assumptions have also been altered so that the problem with the constriction of consciousness is no problem at all; it is simply the new reality, the way things are, the way the world is. It is amazing that in the United States no one really pays notice to the fact that within the last few years many consumer products have become safety sealed. No one is really conscious that this situation came about because, as a way of making money, someone poisoned a bottle of Tylenol capsules. People are cautious and slightly paranoid simply because that is the way the world is. The fact that there was a time when people did not have to protect themselves from each other in this manner no longer seems to matter. The way things were is too soon forgotten.

Rollo May is certainly not the first person to espouse this position, yet most people still do not realize that a problem exists. This strange and very problematic resistance to change that human consciousness possesses will be explored in a future chapter. For now, this chapter will attempt to understand why the rather astute observations of many great people have had a minimal impact on the general evolutionary progression of consciousness.

The paradoxical quality of diminished consciousness is reflected in the finding that being less conscious does not imply being less concerned. Examination of the state of the world, the average intimate relationship, the writings of the popular press, and the average psychotherapist's caseload reveals that people are more concerned than ever about intimacy and relationships. The problem is that concern, unlike consciousness, has a different origin and, likewise, different consequences. The origins of concern have more to do with anxiety, fear, and an assortment of negative thoughts and emotions. If the concern is healthy, it can lead to positive consequences, that is, an improvement of the situation. In terms of relationships, however, people are predominantly dealing with negative concerns in that communications and relationships between most people are not improving; in fact, they are deteriorating. The dramatic, almost exponential increase in the amount of help and information available is hardly improving the situation.

Perhaps two of the most dramatic examples of the external shift of human consciousness are (1) the frightening inability of most people to be aware of their own feelings and the feelings of others and (2) the near elimination of meaningful private and public dialogue.

PUBLIC DIALOGUE

Martin Buber's (1970) concept of *I—Thou* communication has repeatedly emphasized that dialogue is essential for human life. In the following passage, Thomas Merton (1972) best summarizes the problem: "To live in communion, in genuine dialogue with others is absolutely necessary if man is to remain human. But to live in the midst of others, sharing nothing but the common noise and general distraction, isolates a man in the worst way, separates him from reality in a way that is almost painless. It divides him off and separates him from other men and his true self" (p. 63).

Anthropologists report that different cultures manifest a wide variation in how much meaningful public dialogue is accepted. (From the rather parochial perspective of a westerner living in the northeast section of the United States, I would have to say that meaningful public communication is virtually nonexistent here.) As a society people have become incredibly efficient at ignoring each other. If, perchance, a stranger or neighbor is encountered, the interaction and the conversation tend to be quite superficial. As a way of meeting new people a person may buy a dog only to find that people stop to relate to the dog and continue to ignore him. When shopping, people tend to ignore each other. Although in stores parents act as if a person were invisible, one can have conversations with their children. Students were assigned to go into local shops and measure the frequency and duration of eye contact, smiles, and conversation. With the exception of a few developmentally delayed people, who in this culture "do not know any better," the frequency of smiles, eye contact, and conversation was slightly greater than zero. Apparently, children and developmentally delayed people aren't smart enough to be as inhibited as others.

Meaningful dialogue has become virtually extinct. Conversations become monologues in which each person waits his turn to talk. For example, someone who was recently in a serious car accident said that never in his life had he heard so many serious accident stories. Following a cursory inquiry concerning his condition, most people were bursting to tell their own stories. No one really listens anymore. Everyone seems aching to talk.

The need to talk to someone and to have an empathic listener is certainly a contributing factor to the contemporary increase in psychotherapy patients. Empathic listening and mutual dialogue are essential elements of any good psychotherapeutic endeavor. Alienation and estrangement are both a cause and a result of the fact that people do not really listen to each other. Although the problem often manifests itself individually, it definitely has a cultural and community context. The following case study begins to explore the idea that community and individual consciousness are intertwined.

The Case of Joseph

Joseph is a thirty-seven-year-old married male of Irish descent who came into psychotherapy because of depression-related problems. About four years ago, Joseph had moved to the suburbs of Westchester County, New York, only to discover that on three occasions he had to relocate houses. Joseph's depression was related to the fact that he blamed himself for his family's inability to remain in one home.

Shortly after living in his first house, a group of neighbors with whom he had never had contact came over to meet him. The purpose of the meeting was to tell Joseph that he had to mow his lawn more frequently, cut down some large weeping willow trees that were causing a messy leaf problem, and cut his hedges more frequently. Joseph was told that this behavior was required if his family was to be accepted into the "community." For months no one talked to him. His wife and children were also ignored. At times garbage or feces were thrown onto his lawn or front window. He felt forced into moving to a new neighborhood, where for other reasons he felt ostracized and ignored. Finally he moved into a condominium complex because he felt that interactions with his neighbors would be so structured and controlled that there could be little reason for a problem. Unfortunately, Joseph was right.

In treatment, Joseph felt depressed over his failure to be friendly and have strong community ties for himself and his family. He felt guilty and blamed himself for his inability to get along with his neighbors. Part of the problem was that Joseph, who was by nature very warm and friendly, failed to realize that he had moved into what might be called "pseudo-communities." Because they superficially resemble true communities, Joseph assumed that the inhabitants would have the same needs to be close and friendly and the same open value system that he had. Most of Joseph's therapy concentrated on getting him to realize that the problem was not his own but, rather, a reflection of the alienated and estranged community of the 1980s.

The above clinical vignette may seem like an unusual or extreme example, but, regrettably, it is not. There are extensive clinical and personal examples of similar phenomena. Part of the problem in the preceding case study has to do with changes inherent not only to the individual but to the values of community. From a systems perspective, the subsystem of the individual is always intertwined with the subsystems of larger structures such as the community. It is important to note that the people who so callously rejected Joseph's family were not "bad" people. In fact, except for the episodes described in the vignette, they seemed to be quite decent people. With certain exceptions most cases of racism or discrimination involve decent people. What happened to Joseph's family has always been a common occurrence in black-white or majority-minority affairs. The thought that it was not the criminal elements but, rather, the "ordinary" components of society that are responsible for such behavior should be terribly frightening. Most people, however, accept the behaviors presented in Joseph's story as part of their culture's general value system. Certainly few people in Joseph's community perceived their behaviors as either problematic or contradictory to morally acceptable actions. Clearly, with the exception of some very structured or unusual situations, humans are losing the ability to relate, be intimate, and act naturally with one another.

The community's discrimination against Joseph for not "being like they are" is very much related to the problem of racism. Racism and discrimination are related to the absence of meaningful dialogue. People are physically and emotionally separated from each other not only by neighborhood but by skin color as well. The chapter on values mentioned how racism always involves the reality assumption that other groups of people are inferior. Because they are perceived as actually being inferior, people do not include such individuals or groups in their personal lives or talk to them. Joseph was discriminated against for not being what his neighbors thought he should be. As is often the case in situations of racial discrimination, no one bothered to discuss what was going on.

The Western emphasis of agency over community, an emphasis especially powerful in the United States, is a major contributory factor in the deterioration of personal relationships (Moyers, 1989 [interview with W. Gaylin]; Hampden-Turner, 1982). Agencies by definition are impersonal organizations responsible for the implementation of certain tasks, for example, social service agencies, religious agencies, and health care agencies.* Communities by description are personal and informal collections of individuals or family units cooperating for the implementation of certain similar tasks. Communities have always been somewhat informal, very personal, and, likewise, dependent upon cooperation. In contrast, agencies are especially impersonal, much more formal and bureaucratic, and definitely more inclined to competition. Having structured agencies mandated to handle certain aspects of existence precludes the need for personal involvement.

PRIVATE DIALOGUE

There is a rather weak but prevalent illusion that the problems with intimacy and communication that affect public life do not apply to private relationships. Most people, however, are unhappy with their personal experience of relationships. To use marriage as an example, in the United States, surveys indicate that the divorce rate is exceeding the 50 percent point and that a significant number of spouses will eventually have an affair. Clearly, people seem to be searching for that elusive "something" that seems missing. Many signs indicate that Thoreau's description of "lives of quiet desperation" has become even more of a reality than Thoreau imagined.

It is hard to believe that, despite difficulties, many people perceive their relationships as stable. Part of the reason for the need to see individual relationships as the cornerstone of stability has to do with the lofty and ideal values Americans place on this type of relationship. Relationships are important to people, especially for the American notion of family, an ideal that is still the magnetic clarion call of politicians everywhere.

In truth, relationships of intimacy are in trouble. Things are not quite working out, and everyone is concerned, yet no one really knows just how to make things better. Since behavior is essentially multidetermined, there are several rather important reasons for this decline; subsequent chapters will explore some of these reasons. In terms of consciousness, however, the externalization process plays a major role. In most cases, when someone is seeking or engaged in a relationship he looks for and values external, impersonal factors. Consciousness of impersonal factors takes precedence over the intrapersonal and interpersonal dimensions. Some-

---

*Utilizing the term *Western world* does not in any quasi-mystical manner, as some popular books suggest, imply a superiority of Eastern cultures. Eastern cultures, for a variety of different reasons, have their own set of similar problems.

times this precedence is rather blatant and obvious; at other times it is subtle and often unconscious. The following clinical vignettes illustrate these two types of consciousness.

The Case of Mary

Mary is a very likeable, attractive, forty-two-year-old female whose grandparents were born in Italy. Mary has been married for twenty years, has two teenage children, an Italian-American husband who is a middle-level business executive, and a rather nice house in the suburbs. Mary is a college graduate who works part time as a real estate broker. Mary's life appears to be perfect. According to Mary, everyone thinks that she has the perfect life, the perfect family, and an ideal husband and that she is, in fact, a perfect wife. Mary likewise feels that this picture is basically true, so she can't understand why she feels unhappy. Her reason for coming into psychotherapy had to do with feelings of depression.

Quite early in therapy Mary and I realized that she was very passive and had a real problem being honest and assertive. After about six months of twice-weekly sessions we both came to realize that Mary was leading a very false-self, as-if type of existence. In order to maintain this false image, Mary had to cut herself off from her emotions. Mary's perfect existence was created by her in order to satisfy the needs of other people. Crucial to her life were the external images, objects, and appearances (especially as reflected by behaviors, emotions, and expressed thoughts) that would make other people happy.

Mary began to remember that, as a child, making her parents happy was of paramount importance. She always had to have the right appearance, correct and acceptable behaviors, and perfect friends from perfect families. She married a man from a socially prestigious family whom she did not really love but, nevertheless, felt that she had to marry as a way of proving herself. Her expensive wedding became the ultimate social affair and was totally orchestrated by her mother. Mary eventually became the perfect wife and mother. She was an asset to her husband at business and social gatherings. Her children went to the right schools and always maintained the proper appearances. In reality, Mary was terrified because she felt that she was living with a stranger. She felt that she was a stranger as well, "empty, shallow, and unreal." In fact, her depression was partially due to the fact that she was both intrapersonally and interpersonally impoverished. Mary was living an as-if, false-self existence. Her connection to other people was based on external images, appearances, and approval.

The Case of Vivian

The case of Vivian is very much like the case of Crystal described in chapter 3. Vivian was part of an upwardly mobile, nouveau riche family. She had the same materialistic, status symbol perspectives, focuses, values, and reality assumptions as her family. The entire family was consciously and deliberately preoccupied with status and appearance. Vivian was in marital therapy because she did not like the way her husband, Dan, acted. Apparently, despite initial appearances, he was not classy or sophisticated enough for her. The motivation to be in treatment was totally due to Dan, who was terrified that Vivian would leave him for someone wealthier and classier. Eventually, Vivian did in fact leave.

Both these clinical vignettes illustrate the increased effect that the external world has on people's lives. In the first case, the influence of external factors was mainly unconscious. In the second example, the values of the external dimension were blatantly flaunted and embraced in a reality assumption that stated, "Look at me; I am rich, valuable, important, and powerful." Much of the world, especially the United States, has been through a decade in which materialism, acquisition, power, and wealth have reached not only social acceptability but desirability as well. Society, especially as conveyed through different forms of media, has come to prize these values highly. Like the case of Crystal's family presented in chapter 3, Vivian and her family represent cultural character disorders. One of the criteria for diagnosing character disorders is that the patient does not consider the identified symptom as a problem. The symptom is termed ego-syntonic or self-syntonic, a phrase that refers to the fact that what the therapist or some significant others might view as a problem has become an integral part of the patient's personality. This process is exactly what is happening to consciousness, especially as reflected in cultural character disorders or "value psychopathology." Because both Vivian's values and her behaviors are culturally conditioned, sanctioned, and encouraged, they become very resistant to change. Part of Vivian's problem, perhaps her main problem, is that she does not realize that she has a problem.

The case of Mary is a bit different. Although Mary likewise reveals a blind adherence to external symbols of status, she remains somewhat unaware of them and manifests symptoms. Because of these symptoms, Mary was at least open to acknowledging that she had a problem. Mary's awareness that she was unhappy and did have problems meant that her symptoms were ego-alien or self-alien. In an analytic model, Mary could be said to have a cultural neurosis. Mary was unaware of the origin of her difficulties; she just thought she was doing what was right, that is, what she was supposed to do and what she thought everyone expected of her. Although explanations into the reasons for this statement are beyond the scope of this book, Mary's cultural neurosis is easier to change than Vivian's cultural character disorder.

There are numerous people like Mary and Vivian. In both cases, the impersonal interactions of the external world took precedence over the intrapersonal and interpersonal dimensions of consciousness. Furthermore, the problems inherent to both their disorders are representative of values taught and encouraged by the general culture. The following case exemplifies how consciousness of external images or appearances takes precedence over consciousness of more fundamental and certainly more crucial factors of intimacy and relating.

The Case of Susan

A bright, thirty-six-year-old attorney, Susan came into psychotherapy for difficulties in relationships. She was married for the third time and was very much afraid that her present marriage, like the first two, would end up as a failure. In treatment, I found Susan to be very narcissistic and self-preoccupied. She had a tendency to want things to appear a certain way. She was, for example, unhappy with my haircut, my manner of dress (especially my shoes), and my office decor. A great amount of time was expended discussing her feelings about what annoyed her about me. Although Susan refused to admit it, she was quite pleased that I was able to engage her in a meaningful dialogue. Her present husband, like her earlier two, refused to deal with her unhappiness and either "sulked or ignored" her. Concerning her present husband, Susan was unhappy about his looks, his profession, his earnings, and, especially, that he did not enjoy the gourmet club to which they belonged. Susan very much wanted her life to resemble that of her wealthy acquaintances. She wanted her husband and herself to look and act exactly like them.

The case of Susan, like Joseph's case, is an example of typical, contemporary situations in which an external image or appearance takes exclusive precedence. In Joseph's case the image was his maintenance of the appearance of his house. Susan's case depicts unhappiness over the impact of one's personal image. The image of "how things should be" precluded seeing or accepting "how things really are." The world of external things and appearances is only minimally connected to the rich inner world of human experience. The impersonal dimension is basically what it sounds like, a neutral, emotionless dimension of symbolic objects. It is only through their abstract and symbolic tie to human experience that the impersonal dimension maintains its value. Yet, by itself, the impersonal dimension is not enough. The lack of true relationships partially explains why Susan was so pleased to see me. At least I was willing to engage her in a meaningful dialogue. I reacted and responded to her in an alive and real manner that was based not on my image but, rather, on my real feelings and thoughts.

DOGS, BABIES, AND GOLDFISH

The chapter on the transformations of consciousness mentioned that humans have an almost endless capacity for projecting often highly charged emotions onto external objects. Projection is an essential component of human consciousness and in and of itself is certainly not the problem. The process of emotional projection onto impersonal, external objects such as cars, houses, money, art, and other material possessions can, in fact, make the world a very interesting place.

Paradoxically, the opposite seems to be occurring. The projection of emotion nearly exclusively onto external objects and images is partially responsible for the construction of a rather boring, materialistic life-style in which external, impersonal objects are given primary value. Human emotions, dialogue, and intimacy are given plenty of lip service but in reality rank second to material acquisition and external appearance. As stated, it is mainly through emotions and, to some extent, behavior and thoughts that the full depth of human consciousness can be expressed. Of these three phenomena, emotions, because they are nonlinguistic and often irrational, play the dominant role. Irrational occurrences are just as real as rational phenomena; they are simply constructed differently in that irrational events are nonlinear and do not always conform to linear forms of logic. Therefore, irrational feelings are very unpredictable. Language and emotional consciousness are not mutually exclusive; in fact, they are complementary. Language and emotions originate from different areas of the brain as well as from different operations of the mind, but both are necessary for the experience of consciousness. Because irrational phenomena, especially emotions, are erratic, they are often assigned second-class status. In this culture, the linear logic of rational thought reigns supreme. As a species, humans are definitely losing their affective communication with each other.

Perhaps the example of human communication with nonlinguistic organisms is the best way to illustrate the loss of *I—Thou* affective communication. Experience has clearly demonstrated that human interaction with infants and animals, especially pets, is for many people the epitome of communication. Because complete emotional projection is possible, this type of exchange becomes very desirable. The unique desirability of these types of communications is so strong because the preverbal infant or the animal is naturally unable to respond verbally. This inability allows a person to be totally self-referential about what the cute little infant or the adorable animal is really feeling. Almost total emotional projection is possible. Through the operation of projection, whatever the person may be feeling, the animal or infant must also be feeling. Thus a very narcissistic yet self-satisfying bond develops.

I have known patients, relatives, and friends who became totally self-absorbed in an animal, especially a household pet. The relationship with the pet then becomes the most significant one in the person's life, and the pet becomes the repository for the person's feelings as well. One of my patients maintains a most "significant relationship" with a pet dog and with a goldfish. The patient is brought incredible satisfaction by the dog's understanding of emotions and the goldfish's sensitivity to nuances of moods. Such projection of emotions as well as the creation of fantasized companions is common and certainly not limited just to patients. Although this type of relationship can be satisfying and in this day and age is often helpful and necessary, it must nevertheless be recognized as a weak substitute for human relationships.

Human babies, because they do eventually develop linguistic abilities, provide the best yet most problematic example of affective projection. Very young infants are capable of evoking very intense emotions. A healthy mother-child interaction is undoubtedly one of the most comforting and rewarding varieties of relationship. At certain stages, the healthier the interaction, the more the mother and child are able to merge into a positive and reassuring symbiosis (Winnicott, 1988). Despite the intense bonding, the healthy mother can recognize the child's own emotional needs and as a way of responding can separate herself from the child in order to make the child feel responded to. The virtually universal need of a person to feel that he responds and is responded to as a unique, valuable, and interdependent person is incredibly important and very much connected to the *I—Thou* concept of a complete relationship.

Unfortunately, this version of optimal mother-child interaction remains an ever-diminishing ideal. Increasingly, emotionally damaged parents, especially those who have an externalized consciousness and those who are narcissistic/borderline, are having babies. As Eric Fromm states, generations of disturbed people are giving birth to generations of disturbed children (Fromm, 1976). I have known and have worked with numerous families and single-parent families in which the child becomes the receptacle for the parent's or parents' emotional needs. I have likewise known and worked with numerous children who, upon developing the capacity for language, find themselves living in either highly stressful or at times psychopathological conditions. These children have great difficulty in developing an identity, maintaining an *I—Thou* intimacy, being affectively aware, and feeling like an autonomous, responding, responded-to person.

THE FALSE-SELF CONSCIOUSNESS

The feeling of being an ecologically interdependent person who honestly responds and is responded to is being seriously hampered by the development of a predominantly externalized consciousness. Just as consciousness has historically changed, so have the criteria for being a person.

Because humans are a self-conscious, reflective, language-using species, their existence becomes inherently dynamic and, at times, paradoxical and contradictory. These dynamics are manifest only when they are conscious of their intrapersonal and interpersonal worlds and are not evident in the impersonal dimension of things, which reflects what Søren Kierkegaard (1954) describes as "shut-upness." Several theorists have postulated that humans are quite capable of unconsciously leading an "as-if" life, predicated upon a "false self" that is quite capable of appearing alive (DeBerry, 1989b; Laing, 1965b; Masterson, 1985). In reality, however, the false self is an artifact, a categorical imperative of the impersonal world. The false self does not react, but rather "acts," as if it were reading a script based upon the impersonal values of the culture. Consciousness that is based on the predominance of a false-self system has to be a constricted consciousness that contributes to the construction of a constricted world. In order to maintain the illusion of the false self, it is necessary to constrict consciousness of the intrapersonal and interpersonal aspects of one's world. It is especially crucial to constrict consciousness of any kind of emotions, especially empathy, which tends to interfere with the script the false self has created as an ontological safety net (see case of Mary in this chapter).

From an evolutionary perspective, the elimination of affective awareness from consciousness produces devastating effects in that people lose a phylogenetically established way of knowing and processing reality (Guidano, 1987). Prior to the ascendance of language, affective awareness and communication were the main methods of communicating. Because they were able to complement each other, language originally was able to enhance affective (emotional) communication. Classical, romantic, or premodern literature, poetry, mythology, and drama clearly reflect the presence of both intense and tumultuous emotions as well as rational and logical language-based ideas. Modern and especially postmodern writing tends to distance itself from the first person, emotional perspective. Emotion becomes much more of an abstract and metaphoric process, often beyond the immediate reach of the principal characters. If one subscribes to the theory that art reflects life, then postmodern literature is simply expressing the values of the culture.

DOUBLESPEAK AND EXTERNALIZATION

The loss of affective awareness unfortunately enables people to remove themselves and, in the most dispassionate of manners, ponder what should be the most personally meaningful subjects, for example, love, death, or nuclear war. People are capable of and should be more affectively conscious of a rather long list of potential, critical catastrophes. Along with the threat of global nuclear destruction, there are the dangers of ecological pollution, the greenhouse effect, the budget deficit, the homeless, the underclass, and the rising national homicide rate. People need to feel much more when it comes to these topics, especially the subject of nuclear war. Nuclear war is an issue of not only life and death but intense personal suffering and the potential destruction of life on this planet. What is perhaps the most meaningful personal issue is usually dealt with as if it were a removed, dry, and abstract impersonal issue. The persistent, euphemistic use of cool, logical language, a language that contains phrases like deterrence, mutually assured destruction, and star wars defenses, contributes to the problem. The real dangers of nuclear war are concealed by the use of impersonal euphemisms and the veneer of political jargon. This jargon has been termed newspeak or doublespeak and is representative of language that pretends to communicate but really doesn't. Doublespeak can make the bad seem good, shift responsibility, mislead, deceive, and obfuscate the truth. Military invasions become "peacekeeping operations," and weapons become part of "defensive strategies." According to the Pentagon, the island of Grenada was not invaded but, rather, experienced a "pre-dawn vertical insertion" (Engels, 1984; Lutz, 1989). Placing extra emphasis on rational, linguistic consciousness eliminates the need for affective consciousness. When it comes to nuclear war, people are told not to get too emotional or irrational, as if being emotional and affectively aware of the danger could be dangerous. The real danger is that people are emotionally removed from a very real threat of destruction and tend to deal with it only as an abstract, distant possibility.

The real question is, Why aren't people more concerned and afraid deep down in the gut? Numerous patients, diagnosed as psychotic, have been terribly afraid of nuclear war. Why is being afraid of nuclear war part of psychosis? When did this happen? How is it that fear of nuclear war is labelled as a psychotic syndrome? Why are only patients afraid? Could the answer partially be that the consciousness of patients, in some ways, is more complete in comparison to the consciousness of others? In certain ways the answer to this question is yes. This answer in part requires a reexamination of some of the criteria for psychopathology. People who are sensitive to affective awareness and the intrapersonal and interpersonal dimensions of consciousness are often considered deviant or pathological. Again, although lip service is paid to inner consciousness and affective awareness, the reality seems to be that a constricted, impersonal consciousness is becoming one norm by which one measures psychopathology and classifies normalcy. In a twisted manner of speaking, then, according to these criteria, for a person's own good, he should not be too sensitive.

The constriction of intrapersonal and interpersonal affective awareness reduces intuitive knowledge of reality while placing undue emphasis on the evolutionary younger, language-dominated, logically functioning left hemisphere. Victor Guidano (1988) calls intuitive knowledge, tacit knowledge, and, in reference to the importance of affective awareness to cognition, he states:

Assuming that tacit, analogical processes play a crucial role in the scaffolding of the order and regularities with which we are acquainted, it follows that feelings and emotions are primary in personal knowing. When considered within an evolutionary perspective the primacy of affect becomes explicit. While cognitive abilities represent one of the final products to emerge from a long evolutionary process, feelings and emotions were probably the first organized knowing system to actively scaffold environmental regularities. (p. 25)

The constriction of the intrapersonal and interpersonal dimensions and, hence, the reduction of empathic, affective awareness and tacit, intuitive processes are partially responsible for one of the great paradoxes of twentieth-century existence, that as people become more "aware," they also become more self-centered. This paradox has become most obvious in the "therapized, me" decades of the 1970s and 1980s, in which legions of people in search of increased "awareness" and "expanded consciousness" instead find themselves stuck in the quicksand of narcissism and estrangement (Lasch, 1979, 1984; Montagu & Matson, 1983).

Part of the problem is that people cannot simply sit down and commence an organized discussion about their emotions the way they would discuss a car or a game of golf. As Rollo May (1986) states, in diminishing their consciousness of reality, they have lost the "language of emotions," as well as the ability to express and describe their inner world and understand the inner world of others. In the absence of a language of empathic observation, people are forced to make inferences about others and resort to a "jargon of pseudo-intimacy" (Bellah, 1987). Increasingly, these inferences concern impersonal aspects of existence. A patient once said, "I can tell more about someone by looking at the car they drive and the clothes they wear, than I can by spending time with them." Affective consciousness of the intrapersonal and interpersonal dimension of reality can only be resurrected experientially; it is not a process open to didactic manipulation and logical processing.

To compound matters, a contemporary by-product of the loss of the ability to be conscious of and express feelings has been the creation of a professional army of empathizers, such as psychotherapists, channelers, gurus, and healers, who, in being allowed to claim exclusive privilege to the language of relationships, sometimes create a "flabby language," a "psychobabble" of pseudo-intimacy (Bloom, 1988). In addition to cults of intimacy, the Western world likewise has the entertainment industry and its armada of actors, who, along with psychotherapists, are taught to maximize their empathic abilities. The rapid technological evolution of the media industry has made the combination of a robotized mass culture and a professional group of empathizers and entertainers a very dangerous combination. The next chapter on postmodern existence will explore these ideas further.

COSMETIC SURGERY, NUTRITION, AND
THE TRANSPERSONAL DIMENSION

Two contemporary cultural obsessions that clearly reflect the shift to an externalized consciousness are cosmetic surgery and nutritional therapy. Liposuction, face-lifts, and breast augmentation are three of the most popular surgical procedures in this country today. In an attempt to create a certain look or image, more people, especially women, are having their bodies remade. For models or people in the entertainment industry, cosmetic surgery has become a norm that is increasingly moving to the general public, which over the past ten years has witnessed a 30 percent increase in such operations. The external image of an ideally constructed person is becoming an increasing technological reality. What one looks like is now more important than what one is. In fact, increasingly, what one is is becoming what one looks like.

Proper nutrition, health, and fitness are important matters. Yet increasingly they have become a national obsession that has helped shift emphasis from inner to outer change. External modification is both more apparent and certainly more valued than internal change. Some people have become totally convinced that whatever upsets them can be traced to what they are eating. Others have become preoccupied with weight training, body sculpting, and jogging. A depressed patient recent left psychotherapy because his cholesterol level was under control.

In these cases people often project their conflicts onto an external dimension that is much easier to control. If one cannot control what he feels or thinks, he can at least control what he eats or what his body looks like. It is not that physical activity and nutrition are nonessential, but that by themselves, without their internal counterpart, they are incomplete and misleading.

Perhaps one of the most misleading aspects of this externalized culture is the contemporary preoccupation with the transpersonal dimension. The transpersonal dimension is the home of mystical and occult phenomena that supposedly transcend "normal" human experience. Spiritual channelers who can connect people with 30,000-year-old entities have become the current rage (Lasch, 1987). People's need for UFOs, channelers, cults, and the occult world might be considered a new repository for the parts of their consciousness that they are losing. If people cannot relate to each other, then at least they can relate to a mythical entity in another dimension. Although it is certainly possible that numerous transpersonal phenomena have validity, it is the preoccupation with them at the expense of interpersonal and intrapersonal consciousness that is becoming the problem. The transpersonal dimension can become an outlet for emotions and behaviors that are becoming difficult to express. As relationships in the here and now become estranged, the mystical aura of the transpersonal unknown becomes more appealing and, unfortunately, much safer.

SUMMARY

The crux of the problem is more than solely the externalization of consciousness; it lies within the individual and cultural processes that are causing this externalization. People are becoming more connected to impersonal things, images, and abstractions than they are to each other. They are losing each other, and in this loss some of the criteria for what it is like to be human are changing. Unfortunately, many people manifest problems in consciousness similar to the cases described. The externalization of consciousness is directly correlated to individual, community, national, and planetary psychopathology. The remaining chapters will focus on understanding this correlation.

The ideas introduced in this chapter definitely represent particular perspectives, focuses, values, and reality assumptions. The experimental development of impersonal and personal models of human interaction is the best and most advantageous method of testing these concepts.

Another important, perhaps statistical qualification is that the observations in this book concerning consciousness are from a nomothetic perspective. Statements concerning the externalization of consciousness do not apply to everyone in the same way. A normal curve distribution can be constructed for any measurement, including operational measurements of consciousness. In this sense, most people, but not all people, will be clustered next to the general mean of external or constricted consciousness. Some people or families will be quite distant from the mean, a phenomenon indicating that although they still represent a minority, there are a substantial number of very conscious, highly intimate, and personally involved *I—Thou* people. Even if 1 percent of the American population falls into this category it still represents approximately 2.6 million people.

In actuality, the number, or at least the potential number, of borderline conscious people is probably much greater. The fact that people with *I—Thou* consciousness do not know each other very well may seem strange. Yet, this seemingly strange phenomenon of alienation is not odd at all and has to do with numerous factors indigenous to the impersonal, restrictive, yet seductive culture that people live in and by which they are manipulated.

8 *Postmodern Consciousness*

We're so engaged in doing things to achieve purposes of outer value that we forget that the inner value, the rapture that is associated with being alive, is what it's all about.

—Joseph Campbell

- **Proposition 6:** A major historical transformation from a modern into a postmodern world has made the consciousness of the individual an object of manipulation, that is, a commodity.

Why should there be concern that consciousness is becoming externalized? After all, since humans first developed reliance on the abstractive nature of vision and language, interest and concern with external phenomena have been an integral part of life. The development of culture, religion, social classes, and bureaucratic hierarchies, the Renaissance, and the industrial and technological revolution make it apparent that consciousness of external phenomena has been evolving as a "normal" part of civilization. However, these statements, while true, lack a basic systems approach in understanding the dilemma of externalized consciousness. One of the problems is the fact that such criticisms are basically reductionistic. They examine isolated segments of the externalization process while somewhat ignoring the larger contextual effects, that is, the relationship of the externalization process to other parts of the system.

In that it examines all levels of consciousness, a systems approach is ecological and thus includes the interrelationship of all levels of the parts and subsystems that have been part of the postulates of this book, namely, perspective, focus, values, reality assumptions, and language. The opposite of a systems approach might be labeled a singular method, in which each part is studied in isolation. Within such an approach, emphasis is placed on understanding and explaining isolated parts. It becomes impossible to extrapolate from a single structure, part, or subsystem to the overall system itself. Information about a part may be valuable, as in the understanding of a synapse, yet the information may not be completely relevant to the understanding of larger structures such as mind, brain, and person.

Both quantum and systems approaches maintain a contextual or holistic perspective and teach that the understanding of a system cannot be performed in isolation. All parts are in some way connected to the overall purpose and structure of a system. In an of themselves, parts may be understood as parts, but in terms of the entire system, parts need to be understood in terms of how they relate to each other. For example, in order to understand how water molecules operate to produce the phenomenon of surface tension on a lake, one does not have to understand the subatomic process that binds the elementary quarks and leptons together. The molecular and the atomic represent two different levels of the general system of water. Within a systems model the relationship between these two levels and not the levels themselves is what becomes important. In a systems model complexity becomes more important than simplicity. According to Davies (1983):

There is a growing appreciation among scientists of the importance of the structural (systems) hierarchy in nature: that holistic concepts like life, organization and mind are indeed meaningful, and they cannot be explained away as "nothing but" atoms or quarks or unified forces or whatever. However important it may be to understand the fundamental simplicity at the heart of all natural phenomena, it cannot be the whole story. The complexity is just as important. (p. 225)

The overall system of consciousness depends on the interplay of the intrapersonal, interpersonal, and impersonal structures, as well as the perspectives, focuses, values, reality assumptions, and languages, all of which interact with the world. A problem this book is considering is related to the complex interrelationships among these parts. The focus, therefore, is on the relationship among the substructures of consciousness. The concern in this book is not that the external dimension of the impersonal structure of consciousness exists but, rather, that it predominates and so has a negative and constrictive effect on the intrapersonal and interpersonal structures. Perspective, focus, values, and reality assumptions originate, unfortunately, not from the operation of a total consciousness system but from the operation of the impersonal dimension's construction of and interaction with "reality."

THE PACE OF LIFE: THE ACCELERATION PROCESS

Another issue (perhaps the most serious part of the problem of operating with a predominantly impersonal consciousness) is that what was once a slow development of the impersonal dimension has now exponentially accelerated. This acceleration process has caused people's consciousness and thus their construction and involvement with the world to be changed in ways that are virtually impossible to understand. The acceleration process is not limited to consciousness alone; everything is affected by it. The accelerated pace of life is perhaps one of the most prominent features of postmodern existence. Everything is happening so fast. Even friendships have become fast, brief, and transitory. People have learned the language of friendship and can say, "Let's do lunch," but they certainly have not remembered to learn the experience of friendship itself.

Many people, instead of trying to understand the frenetic nature of modern life, opt for either stagnant survival or a fundamentalist return to the mythical "good old days." The rapid growth of the impersonal structure of consciousness is responsible for the predominance of an externalized human consciousness and can be compared to the human birthrate. It took millions of years for the human population of the planet to reach the 1 billion mark. This occurred approximately around 1800. Because of a vast number of external changes in people's interaction with the planet, by 1930, only an additional 130 years later, another billion humans were added. From this point the situation exploded so that only thirty years were necessary for the addition of another billion people, then just fifteen years so that by 1975 the world's population was approximately 4 billion. By 1987 the earth's population became 5 billion and in about ten years is anticipated to reach the 6 billion mark.

This startling example is provided to illustrate that under the right conditions, not only are events capable of occurring extremely fast but what happens now is very dependent upon what happened before. Once the population starts increasing, its future expansion depends upon earlier increases. The same holds true for consciousness. As impersonal consciousness thrives, its future growth is going to depend upon what has already happened to human consciousness. Furthermore, since the foundations have already been laid, the transformation of human consciousness into a predominantly external and impersonal nature is going to occur almost instantaneously and, unfortunately, with very little awareness that it is happening at all. There are two recent historical developments that significantly contribute to this acceleration process and that make it so difficult to compare the consciousness of the average sixteenth- or even nineteenth-century person to the consciousness of the 1990s. These developments are the emergence of a postmodern era and the expansion of visually based technology.

POSTMODERNISM

The term *postmodern* has literally become a buzzword; unfortunately, there is no generally accepted working definition of it.

As a way of describing the style and orientation of certain new structures, the term originated in the field of architecture. Rather soon, in typical fashion it passed on to other art forms so that by the 1980s society had postmodern dance, literature, poetry, drama, and so on. Following a natural cultural evolution, postmodernism soon seeped into academe via philosophy, and by the 1990s it became a standard, avant-garde academic subject. Yet despite the lack of clarity inherent in what postmodernism suggests, it is still a general concept that conveys certain truths and is therefore worth exploring. As the sociologist Todd Gitlin (1989) suggests: "To argue about postmodernism, therefore, is to argue about more than postmodernism. Postmodernism is more than a buzzword or even an esthetics; it is a way of seeing, a view of the human spirit, and an attitude toward politics as well as culture" (p. 52).

The best way to view the concept is to consider postmodern occurrences as a very heterogeneous evolutionary phenomenon. Not everyone or every place is postmodern. Depending upon where one is located, some places, fortunately in some ways, are not yet even modern. However, most large, urbanized nations and states that have already gone through an intensive and extensive industrial and postindustrial period have likewise been exposed to a modern period. Postmodern culture suggests what is becoming of the modern culture as it matures and evolves beyond the industrial seeds of its birth. In this sense, postmodernism is reflective of a very dynamic and transitory state to which a large portion of the world is undeniably being exposed.

Todd Gitlin (1989) identifies at least six applicable theories that have surfaced as an explanation of postmodern trends. Briefly, these are:

1. The "global shopping center" theory explains postmodernism as an outgrowth of the consumerism spawned by an increasing global capitalism. The global market crosses all customs and cultural boundaries and becomes the major source of individual styles and interests.
2. The "advance of science" theory explains postmodernism as an outgrowth of the implications of scientific theories, especially quantum mechanics.
3. The "television generation" theory explains the postmodern style as a result of the anesthetizing and unidimensional effects of television.
4. The "American grab bag" theory explains postmodernism as an extension of the polyethnic, consumer-oriented American culture.
5. The "post-60s syndrome" theory explains postmodern tendencies as a reaction to the loss of the idealism prevalent twenty years ago (at least in the United States).
6. The "yuppie factor" theory explains postmodernism as the natural outgrowth of a generation raised to have everything.

As Gitlin points out, none of these explanations is sufficient on its own, nor are they mutually exclusive or complete. Yet each contributes a valuable perspective that will be further explored in chapter 10.

From a psychological perspective postmodernism represents a desperate attempt to contend with conformity. At its worst, postmodernism represents a frantic attempt to halt the death of people's inner consciousness and, hence, their true aliveness. As Joseph Campbell explains, the myths and rituals that for centuries have connected humanity to the full richness of being alive are dying. The slow atrophy of myths and rituals began with the modern era but seems to be climaxing in the postmodern phase (Campbell, 1988). There is a growing yet unspoken awareness developing, especially among young people, that people are increasingly living in an age of recycled debris. Accompanying this subtle awareness is the rather terrifying and also unspoken idea that everything has been done before; nothing really original can happen, and the old simply has to be repackaged and remarketed as the new.

These frightening yet unacknowledged thoughts and emotions contribute to the growing tendency to try to establish oneself as successful. The emphasis shifts from an expressive and spontaneous internal creativity to an external and commercial emphasis on selling oneself. Doing and having takes precedence over being alive. As one high school student put it, "There's not much space left by you guys [grown-ups], and making money is the only way I'm going to get anywhere." Among adolescent patients, the healthier ones are the ones that realize that they are in a sense being programmed to make money and be successful. Unfortunately these are the students that are increasingly labeled as disturbed or rebellious and benefit little from the existing educational system.

Every era has had its postera period, a stretch of time during which the old era begins to die and the new era hesitantly begins its emergence. There have, for example, been postclassical, postmedieval, post-Reformation, and post-Renaissance periods. All the phrase really refers to is a transition period. Since the structure of the basic cultural system forces that shape human consciousness is transforming, no one really quite knows how to act or what to believe in. Everyone is searching for a new way to be. Nothing is happening, yet everything is occurring. Consistency becomes boring, but the unique is frightening and anxiety-provoking. The "post-anything" label attempts to decrease anxiety by recycling the old disguised as the new. This pretense, however, does absolutely nothing to arrest the actual transformation of consciousness. This cycle of era transition has been constant throughout human history. The historian Barbara Tuchman (1978) has written an intelligent and articulate book comparing the transitional cultural changes of the fourteenth century with those of the late twentieth century. As usual the history of established systems tends to repeat itself.

POSTMODERN COMMUNITY: THE INDIVIDUAL

Certain languages, especially English, are languages that emphasize having over being. Possession of a thing is usually valued more than the experience of the thing or even the thing itself. If fact, the need to possess what should be dynamic and experiential is partially responsible for their becoming things in the first place. People, especially women, children, and minority groups, are precociously vulnerable to becoming depersonalized into things or properties of ownership. In agreement with other dynamic social critics, Eric Fromm clearly states that most cultures are increasingly becoming vehicles of having as opposed to vehicles of being. A consciousness of having is highly correlated with external things and is increasingly becoming the sensibility of postmodern existence.

In terms of consciousness, postmodernism refers to the transition from an individually oriented, often isolated, and industrially based world into an information-based and globally linked system. These transformations are, of course, dependent upon technology, especially the technology of television and the computer. For purposes of the present chapter, however, what postmodern consciousness does to the phenomenon of the person will be explored. Historically, the nature of a person's identity, consciousness, and world construction has been very dependent upon the macrovalues of his particular society.

Prior to approximately the sixteenth century, most of humanity lived in different epochs of the premodern world. In terms of approximating a date for the emergence of the modern individual, most scholars would agree upon the late fifteenth and early sixteenth centuries as the turning point for the emergence of modern consciousness (Sampson, 1988). Although it could undoubtedly be argued that there was a host of negative consequences related to a premodern and early modern existence, there was, nevertheless, one factor that had some positive value. This factor was the absence of the self-contained, autonomous individual and the almost universal presence of the community-based individual.

Recent conceptual schemas of the self have partially been a reaction against the repressive nature of earlier self-concepts. Until the emergence of the modern period, the average individual lived a restricted existence, during which the expression of numerous thoughts, feelings, behaviors, and desires were forbidden. Freud's studies of Victorian repression of sexual feelings are a classic example of what premodern humanity had to contend with. Thus, the emergence of the modern, expressive individual could be considered an improvement. This position implies that in comparison to premodern periods, intrapersonal and interpersonal consciousness has also evolved. In brief, a partial description of this evolution could be described as follows:

- a decrease in the repression of sexual consciousness
- a decrease in the expression of socially unacceptable feelings, thoughts, or behaviors
- an increase in the autonomous individual
- an increase in egocentric and narcissistic relationships
- a decrease of community or communal values and communal bonding

Thus, the evolution of consciousness has been anything but a homogeneous process and, at best, has been a deceptive improvement. The remaining chapters will further discover why modern consciousness did not evolve as history might lead one to believe. Lost in this shift was the individual's contextual connection to an active and dynamic community. This loss eventually contributed toward the present situation, in which impersonal consciousness exponentially exceeds its two counterparts. While spontaneous individual expression has positive value, such expression attains value only within a communal framework. In the absence of sharing, the expression of one's inner impulses eventually becomes a narcissistic trap, an empty vessel of hollow, reverberating noise. The loss of a communal bond is a matter of immense consequences. Essentially, it has led to a growing distortion of both the individual and the community. Edward Sampson (1988) calls this distortion self-contained individualism, which he contrasts against ensembled individualism. Self-contained individualism is the classic blemish of the modern and postmodern individual. It is characterized by a narcissistic, image-oriented concern with self-satisfaction. Alexis de Tocqueville thought this type of individualism would be extremely dangerous to the culture of the United States (Moyers, 1989 [interview with H. S. Commager]). Self-contained individualism places extraordinary value on an independent self, operating according to its own impulses, apart and separate from any societal influences, and requires the separation of the individual from any teleological context of community. Its ethos is total self-absorption. As the ethicist Michael Josephson says: "The cumulative impact of individual selfishness is a terribly selfish society, where we don't know what to expect from people any more. If we translate the Golden Rule—'Do unto others as you would have them do unto you'—into 'Do unto others as you think they will do unto you' or 'Do unto others as they have done unto you,' you have an awful society in which I don't want to raise my child" (Moyers, 1989, p. 25). The self-contained individual is especially prominent in the United States.

In contrast, the ensembled individual represents the best of both worlds in that individual consciousness, whatever it may be, is expressed within the fluid and healthy boundaries of self and community. The separateness of the individual blossoms within the ecological conditions that connect him to others. Ensembled individualism represents a holistic conception of an interconnected yet independent self. As the biologist Lynn Margulis (1989) states, "Of all the organisms on earth, only bacteria are individuals" (p. 25).

The premodern self was always defined in relation to and in the context of a larger organization, such as the state, a religion, or an extended family. This is not to say that selfishness or narcissistic behavior did not exist; rather, consciousness was tied to a larger community context or telos, that is, purposeful behavior. According to Edward Sampson (1989):

Premodern Western society understood persons as defined by their particular social contexts. . . . Unlike our current understanding, which distinguishes between real persons and the roles they must play, in premodern society, roles were the elements which constituted the person as such. Roles were not appended to the "real" person who somehow continued to dwell authentically somewhere behind them. There was no stepping outside one's community and one's roles within it in order to act differently; one always acted within the community and in its behalf. To be outside was in effect to be nonexistent, a stranger, or dead. (pp. 914–15)

Edward Sampson and others stress that economic, political, and technological changes forced the emergence of the individual and shifted the focus of consciousness, values, and behaviors from the larger context of a particular community to the egocentric universe of the supreme self. These larger communal contexts became increasingly arbitrary and functioned as instruments for self-satisfaction. One clearly sees this transition in the differences in the concept of the individual when comparing early literature, as in Homer's *Iliad* or *Odyssey*, with the works of later periods. Odysseus, the hero of Homer's epic tale, was clearly identified, along with his comrades and enemies, as part of a greater community context (Jaynes, 1976). By the time of the Renaissance and the birth of early modern literature, especially after the printing process took hold, the person was already moving to center stage. The solidification of the individual's central position continued both in literature and the arts and in society itself and is, in effect, still continuing today. Nowhere is this process more apparent than in the repetitive individual themes of popular literature and arts (Hardison, 1989).

Although the emphasis remains on the individual rather than on the community, the themes that reflect the individual have always been historically tied to the general community culture. The problem, as in the preceding chapter's example of Joseph's predicament, is that there is no community culture. The term itself is a classic oxymoron. In reality what exists is a terrible crisis of community. The bioethicist Willard Gaylin states that

the most important thing we face is a rediscovery of community. We're a very individually oriented country. . . . But somewhere along the line we've gotten a peculiar idea of what an individual is, what individual pleasure is, what individual purpose is. We see everything in terms of personal autonomy—in terms of not only my rights under the law, but also in terms of pleasure, in terms of privilege. I think we have trained a whole generation of people to think in terms of an isolated "I." But anyone like myself, trained in biology, knows that the human being is not like an amoeba, it's not a thing. We're much more like coral, we're interconnected. We cannot survive without each other. But now, communities have broken down. (Moyers, 1989, p. 119)

With certain minor exceptions, the macrovalues of the general culture have replaced the original premodern, teleological context of what community once was. In the United States and most developed nations, a collection of individuals exists, living an independent "liberalist" tradition, each and everyone doing his own thing. According to Christopher Lasch (1984): "The liberal tradition sides with the rational, reality testing faculty, the ego, against both impulse and inherited morality. . . . In its crudest form, liberalism identified itself with the utilitarian morality of enlightened self-interest, according to which the individual seeks to max-imize pleasure and to avoid pain not, of course by giving in to impulse but by putting off immediate gratification in the anticipation of future rewards" (pp. 205–6).

ENSEMBLED AND ALLOCENTRIC VERSUS
IDIOCENTRIC AND SELF-CONTAINED INDIVIDUALISM

The loss of community and the growth of self-interest were already manifest when the so-called modern self and especially the emancipated, post-sixties individual began to emerge. Although during the transition to modern times a liberalization of the individual was experienced, it was unfortunately an unequal evolution (there is a partial summary of this evolution in chapter 7). The impersonal dimension was increasing while the intrapersonal and interpersonal realms were shrinking. Because the full depth of consciousness was already constricted, the modern and postmodern self evolved as a type of self-contained, selfish, and independent individualism.

What happened in the sixties in the United States, for example, is that people, although seeming to become freer and increasingly aware, were actually becoming more self-centered and narcissistic. As discussed ear-lier, this type of self-structure could be termed self-contained individual-ism. According to Edward Sampson (1988), this type of self-structure is inferior to what he calls ensembled individualism. Ensembled individual-ism represents a separate, yet connected, community self in which all people can reach their full potential only in connection with each other's well-being.

Other researchers, using different terminology, have come to the same conclusions. The problems of modern individualism have been intensively researched by Harry C. Triandis (1988) and his colleagues. As a way of distinguishing cultural styles of living, Triandis employs the terms *allocentrism* and *idiocentrism.* Allocentrism refers to a collectivist/coop-erative mode of being while idiocentrism refers to an individualistic, self-oriented mode, very similar to self-contained individualism. Allocent-ric cultures were found to be positively correlated with social support and low levels of alienation while idiocentric cultures were found to be associated with emphasis on achievement and a high degree of perceived loneliness.

Within Triandis's model, postmodern culture is described as neo-individualistic, a style reflective of a high degree of emotional detachment from people and groups. Although in comparison to an allocentric person, a neoindividualistic person may have a greater number of friends or acquaintances, the relationships are more transient and superficial. For example, Triandis (1988) states that

idiocentric persons in individualistic cultures find it completely natural to "do their own thing" and to disregard the needs of communities, family, or work group. But allocentric persons feel concerned about their communities and in-groups. The former will show consistency of the behavioral, affective, and cognitive elements of their social behavior, which is governed by hedonistic and social exchange concerns; the latter may also be consistent, but their behaviors may be governed by in-group norms. (p. 325)

Research within the allocentric/idiocentric dimension indicates that people in highly industrialized or technologized cultures tend to be less cooperative, more competitive, more alienated, and less capable of meaningful intimacy and social dialogue. Furthermore, people in allocentric cultures experience less stress, feel they have a better quality of social support, and manifest fewer stress-related symptoms, such as cardiovascular diseases (Triandis et al., 1988). Most social research suggests that a cooperative, community-oriented style of living creates conditions for the optimal development of both individual and group consciousness. This category of consciousness represents an *I—Thou* commitment to the development of both the individual and the community. Ensembled individualism or allocentrism is a contextual and ecological systems model of what consciousness can be. This type of individualism allows for the expression of a full range of human consciousness, an expression that by nature includes the nearly extinct experiences of ethos, telos, agape, and pathos. These emotional experiences are necessary for the feeling of being alive and will be discussed more in depth in the next chapter. Ensembled individualism is, however, secondary to the self-contained individualism so common to the world today.

Thus, the macrovalues of the general culture, with certain notable exceptions, tend to override and infiltrate the values or microvalues of any community. As in the chapter concerning community in America, the contention in this book is that real community is a constructed illusion that in reality does not exist. The values and especially the telos of these pseudo-communities are either ineffectual relics of the past or designed artifacts of the media and the prevailing technologies. As Christopher Lasch states, the general macrovalue is connected to "enlightened self-interest," a defense against impulse or spontaneous expression and the deification of an ego-based rationality. Today, these values distill to money, acquisition, and power. There is no telos in these pseudo-value entities, only pleasure and self-interest.

The word *telos* implies a meaningful and purposeful concern for the future. For example, the value of telos represents exactly the opposite of what the United States is doing by continuously raising the national debt to astronomical levels. The national debt is a vivid illustration of how government and consciousness interact on the levels of the individual and community. The debt, after all, is going to affect not only all contemporary people, but future generations as well.

Within a postmodern framework the accepted role and purpose of government and social order change. The domination of modern, liberal individualism, as well as the high-tech, information-saturated, and mobility-emphasizing values of the postmodern self, establishes government as an organization that promotes the pleasurable pursuit of a plurality of interests. Without interference and without interfering with each other, people are allowed to be separate, self-contained individuals pursuing their own paths of satisfaction. In reality, of course, this description remains just an abstract ideal. In terms of personal fulfillment, the United States remains one of the most unequal, biased, and traditionally conservative of all nations. Yet, the ideal and myth of unparalleled opportunity to make money continue to attract millions of people to these shores.

GOVERNMENT, LAW, AND CONSCIOUSNESS

Clearly, the book's focus is shifting from an individual to a community or cultural perspective. This book is concerned not with community per se, but with the complex relationship between elements of culture and community and individual consciousness, especially in the United States. One of the elements of culture that plays a predominant role in the development of community and individual consciousness is government. The role that government has assumed, especially in the postmodern era, represents a significant transformation in its relationship to the development of consciousness.

Within the modern, evolving system the purpose of government becomes the maximization of individual rights as a way of maximizing individual profit. Since there is a plurality of both individuals and interests, the goal of government becomes the insurance of fairness. In order to accomplish this, the government must be value-free: "The state was to remain indifferent and neutral, neither taking sides nor espousing any one purpose over any other beyond ensuring that no single purpose would dominate" (Sampson, 1989, p. 915). The method that a government must utilize to ensure at least the minimal application of this goal is law. As agency and government replace the individual responsibility of a value-based, community-oriented culture, law must take precedence.

For the premodern or even the exceptional modern individual, consciousness, as expressed through perspective, focus, values, reality assumptions, and language, is derived as a product of cultural custom. The daily practices and telos of the community would determine how the individual constructs the world. Under these conditions, the expression of human consciousness can be total and yet focused toward a mutually cooperative and satisfying common goal. A certain reciprocity of consciousness develops in that what makes the community happy makes the individual happy, thus making the community happy, and so on. In the absence of a community-based system, as where impersonal agencies or liberal individualism predominates, the dictates of behavior cannot come from a contextually based relationship with a larger teleological structure but must be derived from the external authority of law. Law becomes the sacred ways and means, and although most people no longer accept its divine origin, they nevertheless acknowledge its absolute authority.

Within a governmental and legal system that is required to balance fairly an extraordinarily skewed plurality of interests, certain skills are required. As Max Weber noted, it will be necessary to have not only a vast and complex bureaucracy but also a bureaucracy that values efficient management and administration. Management and administration are the postmodern hallmarks of American government. The Bush administration, for example, in its responses to the radical and important changes occurring in the Soviet Union and China, responded in a "cautious and restrained manner," reflective of a very contemporary, postmodern organization waiting for all the necessary information to arrive. This response of caution was really a means of insuring that the political-economic balance remain fairly intact. This achievement would mean that efficient administration and effective management had been successful. Such responses are only marginally connected to purposeful human values and have much more to do with the government's agency role of managing and administrating a profitable and efficient plurality of interests. Management, administration, and the efficiency of the system must take priority. It is almost as if modern and postmodern tools of management are a historical extension of the general tendency for any system to prioritize its survival.

Within an agency-oriented government of administration and management, the legal branch, in a somewhat different manner, must serve the same function. The original purpose of law shifts from maintaining a just or "right" community to maintaining an efficient one. This purpose was not always the case. Originally, even as compartmentalized, hierarchical societies grew, the law attempted to balance individual power with community consciousness. Law then evolved as the formalized and ritualized expression of the inner dynamics of consciousness, that is, perspective, focus, and so on. As such, law was dependent upon the successful correlation with these inner dynamics and the success of the individual and the community. As communities and nations grew larger, the ritualized expression and propagation of the community consciousness became increasingly necessary. In this sense, issues of right versus wrong remained germane. Either an act was right for the individual and/or the community in that it helped, or an act was wrong in that it caused harm to the community and/or the individual (Moyers, 1989 [interviews with R. Bellah and J. Lukacs]).

The laws of a government or efficient agency are, however, dependent not upon issues of right or wrong but rather upon a very abstract and impersonal notion of efficient justice. In this sense justice and law have become externalized from the full range of human consciousness to the impersonal dimension of linguistic abstractions, metaphors, and euphemisms. In a culture of efficient administration the image of the law becomes more important than the letter of the law. Law Professor Mary Ann Glendon states:

We've put a lot of weight on the law. There is a question of whether law can bear all the weight we've put on it, and whether it's really desirable for the law to be such an important value carrier in society. Montesquieu and Tocqueville, among others, though that what was really important was what undergirded the law—*manners, customs and mores. If a law wasn't grounded in the mores, the philosophers didn't think there was much hope for it* [emphasis added]. (Moyers, 1989, p. 471)

Glendon makes several astute observations concerning the absence of a contemporary connection between law and values while likewise acknowledging the role of the law in constructing and shaping reality. Specializing in the areas of family law, child care, and abortion, she suggests that law does not always serve the best interests of the individual or the community. Just as human consciousness should reflect the totality of its potential, law should be grounded in the totality of a community's "manners, customs and mores." A key aspect of modern and postmodern existence is that such grounding does not occur. Under the present conditions, laws change not because of issues of right and wrong or the improvement of the individual and community but because of a muddled potpourri of interests, management styles, and administration. Separated from its community value base, the law tends to become not only impersonal but schizoid as well. This schizoid quality can be seen in the recent Supreme Court's decision to reverse some of the critical doctrines of affirmative action and abortion while affirming the legality of flag burning.

Along with a masters in business administration degree, the law degree is the most popular graduate degree in the country. This popularity is not surprising since becoming a lawyer is highly correlated with the cultural macrovalues of money, power, success, and acquisition. Only a few lawyers continue to practice from a value-based perspective, although the popular image of television (as in the show "L.A. Law") and movies would have one believe otherwise. In terms of the relationship of the external-ization of consciousness and law, it must be pointed out that modern and postmodern law, like consciousness, is becoming increasingly external. Few people believe that the law reflects their internal consciousness. Law reflects an external constraint on people that may have little correlation with their true needs or desires.

LAW AND MORAL DEVELOPMENT

Numerous studies on the stages of moral development indicate that a great many people obey the law out of fear of exposure or punishment (Kohlberg, 1971, 1973, 1976; Piaget, 1932; Turiel, 1972, 1979). This behavior is a more primitive form of morality or ethics very much comparable to the developmental difference between shame and guilt. As the child's conscience or superego develops, the first internal restraint on his behavior is fear of being shamed through either exposure or punish-ment. Therefore, the restraint is essentially external and can be regarded as a primitive precursor of a more developed superego. For example, a child operating on the moral level of shame may not take food or money if other people are present but in their absence may engage in the forbidden behavior. Once the inner structure of guilt develops, the child refrains from unfair actions because of empathic identification with the intended victim. That is, the child or person has a fully developed, internalized image of not only the other person but what it would be like to be the other person (e.g., "I will not steal Richard's lunch money because its loss would make him feel bad, and I too would feel bad if someone stole my lunch money"). What is so wonderful about the human capacity to reach this developmen-tal level is that guidelines for behavior are internalized. How one acts depends not upon his feeling that he may be caught or punished but rather upon an internalized and empathic set of values. The shift from an internal to an external set of constraints and legal behavior is very similar to the above developmental comparison. Furthermore, external legal constraints, like shame, do not hinge on an empathic relationship with other people. Empathy, like guilt, represents a higher level of human development. The maturation of both guilt and empathy is highly associated with successful relationships with other people in which, as in the growing child, for example, the other person is internalized or reciprocally identified with in a very total way. Given a proper and healthy relationship, children can easily become autonomous, unique, ensembled versions of the parents. Successful human development, however, can occur only in a total *I—Thou* context. The necessity of the *I—Thou* context makes a healthy relationship very dependent upon a complete and uninhibited affiliation of consciousness. Likewise, ensembled individualism is very contingent upon the consciousness of an *I—Thou* relationship. In an *I—Thou* parent-child relationship, nothing in the best interest of the child is held back. The relationship occurs as an optimal blending of the intrapersonal, interpersonal, and impersonal levels of consciousness. It is interesting to note that the best models of good psychotherapy always compare the treatment process with a healthy parent-child relationship.

This excursion into the developmental ontogenesis of guilt and empathy is by no means meant to imply that these emotional experiences are always positive. In a multidetermined, paradoxical universe, events have multiple effects and are often not what they appear to be. There can be a range of potential pathological distortions of empathy and especially of guilt. The above example concerns the healthy development of these emotions, primarily as they relate to law.

But modern and postmodern law is not the product of a healthy relationship. There is no empathy, nor is there an optimal blending of consciousness. The entire intention of law is impersonal, an external manifestation of self-interests, management, and administration. In law there is no need to empathize with the accused or to explore related, relevant factors such as race, class, religion, or social status. Since postmodern law is intrinsically impersonal and a cultural example of externalized consciousness, it can ignore affective or nonlinear factors and operate consummately in the abstractive dimension of language. In the linguistic dimension, any person or process is capable of becoming objectified. People can become reduced to nonentities such as slaves, minorities, Jews, Arabs, or Chicanos, abstractive realms in which the richness of personal factors has no bearing. Things or nonentities do not have the same rights as people. At its worst, postmodern law can manifest itself this way.

To observe a sample of law disconnected from an internal sense of right and wrong, one need not look much further than most major governments. In the United States, for example, all branches and all levels of government have experienced a general change in ethics. Out of abundant examples, perhaps the recent Contragate-Oliver North affair provides a rather typical illustration. It is now quite clear—perhaps as a post-Watergate as well as a growing postmodern phenomenon—that in matters of national ethics, guilt does not play a major role. This nation is experiencing a developmental regression to the emotion of shame. Certainly, for either Oliver North or any of the other principal protagonists, guilt was not present. What was present was an irrefutable sense of: "Unfortunately I got caught, but I was only doing my just and patriotic duty. I was only following orders." Nearly all the responses to the Contragate affair are representative of a shame-oriented, primitive form of morality. This self-centered, non-empathic morality is not limited to government but tends to pervade all strata of society. Like art, government is a reflection of, as well as a cause of, what occurs in society. In the cultural system everything is in some way connected.

Thus, postmodernism represents the surreptitious development of new sets of rules. In a connected, globally linked, instant information, and service-delivery world, almost anything can happen. Boundaries are not as encompassing or firm as they once were. They might appear to be, but they are not. The surreptitious part becomes manifest because often a change of rules is not recognized. People pretend that nothing new has happened, and a growing tendency to resort to older, more traditional beliefs becomes evident. For example, the Soviet Union is still the enemy, missiles and nuclear weapons defend world freedom, and multinational corporations (like Exxon) are ecologically minded. In a psychologically postmodern existence, it becomes increasingly difficult to distinguish truth from lies and reality from image.

POSTMODERN RULES

The phenomenon of change in rules is not restricted to law but pervades all strata of society. Guidelines for how things are accomplished are changing. Postmodern rules mean that there really are no rules. Under these conditions, pretense becomes more valuable than substance. The goal, which in most cases is winning, becomes more important than guidelines of behavior. That the end justifies the means has become a postmodern reality.

An area in which this change is quite evident is personal achievement. Achieving fame or being recognized has become the new prerequisite for professional and personal advancement. A patient once remarked that all that people were interested in about her was whom she knew; knowing famous people or celebrities was definitely a plus in that it allowed her access to quasi-celebrity areas to which she would not otherwise have passage. Being a sports hero can lead to an acting career, a modeling future, doing lucrative commercials, or becoming a music or entertainment star. The boundaries and rules between what one might do for a living and what one has access to have been altered (Moyers, 1989 [interview with J. Lukacs]). Mobility and success come from being recognized as a celebrity. Politicians and professors write revealing or best-selling books and gain access to talk shows and lucrative lecture circuits. People commit crimes and find themselves in movies or novels. Jesse Jackson, who started out as a radical black leader, evolved into a presidential candidate and eventually a television talk show host. In a strange and often unrecognized way, the postmodern world amplifies the connections among things. Movie stars become mayors and presidents while the leader of this country's traditional adversary nation becomes a hero.

As in its unique architectural origins, what is unusual about postmodernism is that in a novel way it combines elements of past, present, and future. A traditional phenomenon unknowingly undergoes a metamorphosis only to appear as something new yet old. In this sense, the present, though constantly evolving, tends to contain elements of a recycled past. Style, entertainment, fashion, or the return of Woodstock and the sixties era are common examples of this occurrence. In architecture, postmodernism tended to blend classical, traditional, and modern modes to produce a new style that could be a little of all three, yet unique. In a sense, then, postmodernism represents a nostalgic method of moving forward. The legal system has changed, yet in the impersonal dimension of externalized rhetoric it can be defined as it existed 200, 50, or even 10 years ago. Law is only one example of this process. Postmodernism and externalized consciousness work together to produce an orchestrated, "twilight zone" version of reality. In the external dimension of language, experience can be created or arranged not as it is but as it should be.

If language is not simply the instrument of thought but the mirror of the soul and if its structures are so deeply rooted, then it must be capable of betraying even those persons who are ordinarily quite adept at handling it (Engels, 1984, p. 19).

THE POSTMODERN FAMILY

An example of a recycled, postmodern phenomenon is the postmodern family. The contemporary family has definitely changed in its structure and dynamics. Psychotherapists have been seeing families for years and have long recognized that a group of people who are blood-related and living under the same roof by no means always constitute a family. Yet in the media, advertisement, religious, and political arenas, these collections of people are still treated as if they represent a family. Americans are very nostalgic concerning the sanctity of the "traditional" family. The image of the traditional family now takes precedence over the understanding of the various alternative arrangements that people have willingly or unwillingly created. It is very difficult for alternative families to be recognized and understood for what they are.

The fundamental tendency is to perceive and treat all families as if they represent the traditional image of a white, middle-class family. The perception of the Wasp, although partially mythical, is nevertheless indelibly imprinted upon the collective psyche. But just who are the Wasps and how do they behave? How do they live? How the traditional, white, middle-class American family actually behaves is an illusion that exists only as a media image, not as a homogeneous reality. Wasp consciousness is just as heterogeneous as black consciousness, feminist consciousness, or whatever consciousness one wishes to consider. The point is that people have accepted the media image of Wasp over the myriad reality of whatever a Wasp might really be. This image bias has affected how people understand and treat non-Wasp groups. In real life, problems of single-mother families, working mothers, day care, and medical and legal rights still remain an issue. When a politician calls for a return to the value of the American family, does he mean the traditional image of the Wasp family or the postmodern family, or are his words just another example of the enormous capability of language to manipulate and betray?

It is perplexing that for years people have been writing about the equivocal nature of language. The basis for most of the ideas introduced here is certainly not new, and yet the problems of impersonal language and external consciousness seem to be spiraling. The question arises, then, that if the postmodern era is a heterogeneous extension of the modern era, what forces are responsible for the acceleration of postmodern impersonalness? The answer can be discovered in the extraordinary effects of modern high technology. To answer the question thoroughly, one must understand how current technology, especially the visual technologies of television, movies, videos, and postmodern advertising, affects and is affected by consciousness.

SUMMARY

Postmodern consciousness is described as a self-contained type of individualism, functioning in a rapidly changing, globally linked, and information-based environment. Postmodern events are both surreptitious and yet obvious in their impact.

Nearly all events are ambiguous in that they have more than a singular effect. Positive and negative ramifications are standard features of existence. There are some very positive features to the flourishing postmodern existence; however, because what is happening to human consciousness has a globally negative and perhaps deterministic influence on life, it becomes incumbent to deal with the deleterious aspects first.

It is impossible to move backwards, and a return to a mythical, pristine past is not advocated. The fact that community-bound individuals were the norm 400 years ago does not mean that their quality of life was better. Likewise, it does not imply that people were more intimate and had better personal relationships or a more complete form of consciousness. It would be very difficult to make a precise statement concerning the intrapersonal and interpersonal consciousness of premodern times. The consciousness of premodern people was restricted in a different fashion. The church, the state, the quality of education, the lack of public hygiene, and the reduced lifespan are but a few of the enormous number of additional variables that must be considered. Comparisons must always be tempered by the reality of time.

Consciousness is constantly evolving. The model in this book is a model for the present. The conditions of human consciousness never have and never will be what they are now. Things can never be the way they once seemed to be. Like the present, the past is constructed and can never be recreated in the present. The multiple conditions of modernity have caused the interpersonal, intrapersonal, and impersonal dimensions of consciousness to evolve to a point that did not exist in premodern times. Now, additional factors are causing the impersonal dimension to expand faster than the rest of consciousness. For human happiness and progress to continue, certain qualities, such as community, morality, telos, dialogue, and intimacy, need to be further developed. These qualities are closely related to human consciousness, which has to change in order for any type of everlasting transformation to occur. Making comparisons can develop ideas and models for future directions.

9 Visual Technology and Consciousness

Face reality
                              —advertisement for a giant NEC television screen

- **Proposition 7:** The technological revolution, especially as manifested by visual media, for example, television, movies, and video, has so accelerated and consolidated the external shift of consciousness that the illusion of the image is now the accepted and predominant reality.

In the preceding chapter the nature of modern and postmodern self-contained individualism was described. Yet, postmodernism alone is not enough to explain what might be described as the rapid proliferation of a predominantly external human consciousness. There have to be other variables contributing to this mushrooming phenomenon. This chapter will examine technology, in particular the sophisticated, visually directed mass technologies of the twentieth and approaching twenty-first centuries. Technology, like external consciousness, may be considered as an extension of oneself. In this sense, a very solid relationship already exists between modern technology and external consciousness. As Professor O. B. Hardison (1989) states, "Technological culture is constantly introducing useful materials and objects into the world. Because they are useful, they are accepted without thought. Sometimes they are so retiring that they are hardly noticed unless they are being used. Their relative invisibility has little relation, however, to their influence on the shape of consciousness" (p. 83).

This chapter will discuss the role that technology assumes in shaping consciousness. This role has to do in part with the nature and quality of the technology itself. The nature and quality of any technology are related to the extent to which it affects human life. Just what manner of technology is it and how will it affect people's lives? Sometimes effects are minimal, and life goes on very much as before, while in other cases the effects are total and pervasive, and human existence becomes permanently and inexorably altered. Quite a gap existed between the development of the technologies of fire or the wheel as compared to the invention of Formica and AstroTurf. In addition to the technology itself, a temporal factor must also be considered which has to do with the fact that historically the development of technologies has not been a consistent process. Certain discoveries have led to inventions or technologies that have had a tremendous impact on the way people construct their lives. These changes have likewise tended to cluster within particular time periods that tend to define eras of unique transformation.

The development of fire, agriculture, the wheel, the printing press, electricity, and television, to name a limited few, have all been technologies of transformation. Since the world is understood as a system, it must be realized that the effects of any technology will not be homogeneous. Different parts and substructures will be affected at different times and in different ways. Sometimes there is a long time lag between personal or cultural change and the more immediate, applied effects of a technology. As a rule, philosophical and paradigmatic changes tend to come more slowly.

Although a synchronicity exists between new ways of thinking and the unfolding of novel technologies, it is, nevertheless, a delayed and complicated one. As pointed out in the section on values and reality assumptions, the world in many ways is still dealing with numerous premodern and even prehistoric issues. Change is rarely, if ever, a uniform process.

In terms of human impact, the modern and developing postmodern era reflect the most extensive and intensive period of technological modification. Slightly over 100 years ago the world was not a connected place. No one thought of the possibility of a global village concept. It was not until 1868 that the first transatlantic telegraph cable was implemented, and at the turn of the century radio and flying machines were just being developed. The technological changes of the past 100 years have been barely short of incredible. Technological change always affects consciousness.

Out of this vast progress, perhaps the invention of televised images is the technology that has had the most pervasive and immediate impact on what it is like to be human. To quote O. B. Hardison (1989) again: "There is another fact about cultural innovations. If an innovation is basic, simply because it is so, a generation after it has been introduced, it becomes part of the world as given—part of the shape of consciousness. Television seemed to the generation of the 1940's to be an amazing triumph of human ingenuity and pregnant with social implications" (p. xii).

Over twenty years ago Marshall McLuhan (1964) coined the phrase "the media is the message." McLuhan's ideas concerning the effect of media, as well as their tendency to create a global village, were amazingly accurate. This chapter will explain how technology began affecting consciousness in a manner that was capable of eliciting accelerated change. The chapter will start with the approximate birth of the modern era and ask, How might changes in consciousness have started?

TECHNOLOGY AND CONSCIOUSNESS

Americans have preferred not to think about the social and political realities that link technology to our individual lives. But that's what we have to work on.
—Robert Bellah

The answer to the above question might originate in fifteenth-century Germany when the first public clock was introduced to community life (Lasch, 1984). This technological innovation marked the beginning of a highly effective, culturally accepted means of coordinating human affairs and, thus, human consciousness. Events no longer needed to be structured around internal and variable individual needs such as hunger or fatigue but could be controlled by an external priority, that is, dinner time, bedtime, or leisure time. Describing this technological transition point, Montagu and Matson (1983) comment: "We can only guess how this must have felt to those caught up in this wrenching phase of transition; but a peculiar and profound form of dehumanization was taking place, involving the loss of a sense of self-control, even participation in the conduct of daily life. . . . The new imperatives . . . were external, imposed from without" (p. xxii).

During the Renaissance, the historical period that gave birth to the modern notion of the individual self, human consciousness was especially vulnerable to the effects of new technologies. The introduction of increasingly powerful technological devices made the potentially negative facets of humanity's linguistic consciousness more apparent. For the first time, consciousness could be controlled not only on a mass basis, but in such a subtle, indirect, and fine-tuned manner that few people would notice. Furthermore, and perhaps most important, is that, in a general systems sense, a new and incredibly powerful substructure was added to the system, a substructure (in this case, public time) capable of changing the entire system of consciousness from a system predominantly based on internal regulation to a system of external regulation capable of maintaining the illusion of internal control, so that for most, nothing important at all had happened. Unfortunately, when a part, substructure, or subsystem is no longer integrally needed as part of the osmotic dynamics of system equilibrium, it becomes eliminated (Von Bertalanaffy, 1973, 1974). In an evolutionary sense, this process is exactly what has been happening to human consciousness; from the moment that first clock was triumphantly placed in the town square to the ubiquitous placement of televisions in every home,* people have been steadily losing portions of their internal worlds. This loss manifests itself as a quantitative and qualitative constriction of the perspective and focus of intrapersonal and interpersonal consciousness.

THE EVOLUTION OF THE IMAGE

Following the clock, it was probably the development of the printing press and publicly available printed literature that contributed to the next major alteration of consciousness. Information concerning public and private modes and styles of accepted and expected behavior no longer had to be personally or verbally conveyed through the spoken word. Most people became either capable of reading or, through someone who could read like a missionary, of having the written word available to them. Through print, the concept of style or public fashion became more general and available, not only to a limited and exclusive aristocracy but to the growing public consciousness as well. By 1500, following the establishment of Gutenberg's movable type printing press, 20 million books were already in existence (Thomas, 1979). Their effect was undoubtedly profound.

When it came to the proliferation of the printed word and the evolution of literacy, innumerable beneficial effects have occurred. Literacy had a tremendously positive impact on humanity. But in that it created the opportunity for consciousness to be altered on a large scale, the availability of mass printing changed things. The reason printing is especially relevant

*Television sets, along with stoves, refrigerators, and beds, are now considered by public welfare law to be indispensable family items.

to a discussion on technology and consciousness is that the printing press was the first technology to introduce visual images on mass scales. Words, after all, are visual symbols. In this sense, the printing press was one of the first inventions capable of having both an intensive and extensive impact on consciousness.

Following books, photography was the next major technology to cause an alteration of consciousness. Stuart Ewen (1989), a professor of the media, claims that in 1839 the world changed with the invention of photography so that the image became predominant and the object itself, dispensable. After photography, the technology of television extended the impact of the image, as introduced by the mechanical camera, a quantum leap forward. In comparison to the effect of the printed word, the revolution of the electronic image has resulted in an accelerated ascendance of the image and has had even more of a drastic effect on consciousness (Boorstein, 1964). Historically, in comparison to our Renaissance ancestors, the proliferation of video technology has rendered twentieth-century humanity far more vulnerable to external influences. As Marshall McLuhan (1964) states:

After three thousand years of explosion, by means of fragmentary and mechanical technologies, the Western world is imploding. Today, after more than a century of electronic technology, we have extended our central nervous system itself in a global embrace ... the technological stimulation of consciousness (p. 3). ... The new media and technologies by which we amplify and extend ourselves constitute huge collective surgery carried out on the social body with complete disregard for antiseptics. (p. 64)

The potential for a new technology to alter life and have unexpected or unintended effects is well accepted. It is, however, crucial that people always be aware of the dangers of potentially negative effects. In terms of television, the technology itself is not negative; its effects depend upon the purposes for which it is used (Schallow & McIlwraith, 1986–87). Video feedback has been employed as a therapeutic tool capable of expanding consciousness, improving self-awareness, body image, movement, or expression, and putting people more in touch with their feelings. In this sense television can be a wonderfully creative process. The way television is currently utilized on a mass basis in this culture does not represent a positive use of the medium. Television is used mainly for entertainment and commercial purposes, both of which tend to manipulate and restrict consciousness. The medium is decidedly not living up to its potential beneficial effects.

EXPERIMENTALISM AND TELEVISION

The beginning of the book discussed how the experimental method can sometimes lead to skewed conclusions. The experimental method tends to explain isolated parts of a given whole. With this idea there is no problem. The mistake that experimentalists make is that they generalize explanations of parts to an understanding of the whole. This problem becomes especially apparent when reviewing the experimental literature on television. In general the experimental data on the effects of television are at best equivocal. The most recent and perhaps the best book on the psychology of television is John Condry's (1989) aptly named book, *The Psychology of Television*. Professor Condry brilliantly summarizes and comments upon television-related research from its inception in the early 1950s to its present-day status. Most of the research supports the contention that the purpose for which television is used and its interaction with the personality and cultural environment of the viewer cause negative effects. According to the historian Barbara Tuchman: "We're being fed on—well, all I can say is trash, through, I regret to say, the organ of television. Television is moved by the desire to make profits, by appealing not to the audience of quality, but to the largest number—I suppose what used to be called the lowest common denominator. This is not the way to increase the thinking of the public on truth or serious matters, or to help it recognize the values in life that are creative" (Moyers, 1989, p. 6). Condry recommends an ecological approach to television studies, an approach that would understand television not as just as another appliance, but as a total environment.

Some studies suggest that television's structure and content can have negative effects while other studies state that it is the behavioral interaction of the viewer that determines whether positive or negative effects will occur. Most experimental studies tend out of necessity to examine only a limited number of personality, behavioral, and content values. Required is a large-scale, contextual analysis of how, in general, television affects viewers in this culture.

Examples of contextually based experiments are the studies that compare television viewing and imaginal style. It is believed that in comparison to visually scanning a televised image, reading involves different subsystems of the mind and brain. These different operations should reflect themselves in mental processes such as imagination. Yet when comparing the effects of reading and television viewing on imagination, the experimental results have been equivocal. Under certain conditions television can actually have an enhancing effect upon fantasy and imagination. What matters are the conditions of interaction between the viewer and the image.

When something is read, an image must be constructed by the brain and mind. Because the image is not provided a priori, a great deal of creative freedom accompanies this constructive process. In a sense, because less information is provided by reading, there is more room for active individual contribution. In comparison to words, images affect consciousness in a very different manner. It would seem that information continuously presented in a visual manner would preclude the need for the active, personal involvement of consciousness. Along these lines, it would further seem that if an image is provided, there is no need to construct one. Yet, research does not validate these contentions (Condry, 1989). If the nature of the program, the history of the viewer, and the context of the program's interaction with the viewer are taken into account, results indicate that television does not necessarily decrease imagination. If used within the proper context, television can be an incredibly creative and consciousness-expanding tool. This effect partially depends on the viewing habits of the person watching television. Large differences in effect exist, for example, between heavy viewers (four hours or more a day) and light viewers (four hours or more a week). The effect of a technology such as television depends upon how it is used. Empty entertainment and crass commercialism, not television, are eroding consciousness. Unfortunately, television always has a temporal effect in that it has to take time away from other activities. These other activities include socializing with friends, time spent talking, hobbies, romance, sports, and other arenas of human interaction.

Televised Images

While countless studies are available on how the content of television influences people, there is very little research that explores how the structure of television affects consciousness and behavior. The structure of television has to do with the continuous, electronic presentation of an image. The image is the key to the structural effects of television. Ashley Montagu and Floyd Matson (1983) consider the externalization of consciousness to be a form of dehumanization and a direct consequence of the predominance of the visual image, stating: "The tyranny of the image has begun to undermine our sense of reality and delete our conception of ourselves (p. xxxii). . . . the triumph of the image and the exile of the self in sociology may seem to be an arcane matter of interest only to academicians; but in fact it finds a remarkable parallel in the general drift of public consciousness towards the embrace of illusion and the retreat from reality" (p. xxxvi).

Empirical research has documented that television itself is not responsible for "the embrace of illusion and the retreat from reality." The effects of television depend upon the intent of its utilization. If television is employed to manipulate and distort reality, then it will manipulate and distort reality to such an extent that illusion will be embraced and reality will be retreated from. The manipulation and distortion of consciousness and reality are the way television is generally used in this country. With the exception of Bill Moyers and some public broadcast stations, television is not used to educate but, rather, to entertain.

Within the three dimensions of consciousness and their consequent synthesis, namely, the personal self, it is the impersonal world that is most accessible to external manipulation. External control of the impersonal dimension is most readily accomplished through manipulation of visual input. The semantic reality of the impersonal world is free from the affective processes and irrationalities of the intrapersonal and interpersonal dimensions. Like the televised image, the impersonal dimension is a "cool" medium of information transfer. As noted, one's intrapersonal and interpersonal worlds, though closer to a more inclusive reality, are also more chaotic in that they include domains of autistic reference as well as richly complicated empathic, affective experiences of tacit and intuitive knowledge.

Because the intrapersonal and interpersonal dimensions are by nature nonlinear and chaotic, information concerning reality that is derived from them is not easily manipulated. Therefore, information of this sort tends to be ignored or considered inconsequential. It just cannot compete with an image. Increasingly, then, consciousness of reality comes from highly distorted but easily manipulated visual media. Christopher Lasch (1984) states that "more and more our impressions of the world derive not from the observations we make both as individuals and as members of a wider community but, from elaborate systems of communication that spew out information, much of it unbelievable, about events of which we seldom have any direct knowledge" (p. 133).

Christopher Lasch would consider externalized consciousness as a product of the growing industry of technological self-improvement, which paradoxically (understandably, though, within the present model because it operates predominantly in the impersonal dimension) has resulted in a society of selfish people who appear to be intimate but are really narcissistically engaged and emotionally detached. Montagu and Matson (1983) perceive this process as "postwar technocratization . . . carrying a transvaluation of values in which democratic purposes, human needs and public interest would become mere dependent variables of the overriding technical ethos of efficiency, organization and social equilibrium" (p. 76).

THE ILLUSION OF THE IMAGE

Nowhere is the illusion of intimacy more easily generated and sustained than through the visual media. Television can provide the illusion of intimacy just as religion can provide the illusion of understanding (Goldsen, 1975; Landers, 1989). According to O. B. Hardison (1989):

The blurring of the distinction between computers and animate beings is complemented by a weakening of the human sense of what reality is. This weakening is the direct result of technology. Movies and television create an illusion of presence at the unfolding events. Interactive environments like arcade games, training simulations and artificial realities create illusions that are even more vivid. At their best, they come close to obliterating the difference between reality and illusion. They are related to image manipulation in advertising and politics and to the curious but well-documented fact that for many people today an event is not authenticated—is not real—unless it has been seen on television or in a photograph. (p. 321)

The illusion of the visual image has now become predominant. What is so dangerous about this fact is that it has created a climate in which reality can be orchestrated by technology. The orchestration is, of course, an illusion, but people are increasingly mistaking the illusion for reality. They begin to want reality to resemble the illusion. When it does not, they consider it to be an inferior version of what the image makes them believe reality is capable of. For example, many men tend to prefer women who have a cosmetically altered, model, or photographic appearance. Unfortunately, many women prefer this type of image and become dissatisfied with themselves when they do not achieve it. Numerous women become depressed because they find themselves unable to conform to the culturally prescribed image of beauty. Although the desire to fit an image affects men as well, more pressure is exerted upon women, both by themselves and by society in general (see section in chapter 7 on cosmetic surgery).

Herbert Marcuse (1955, 1964) would have conceptualized television as another cultural repressor capable of generating false needs, manipulating consciousness, reconciling contradictions, and creating a mindless unidimensionality of thought. According to Marcuse, the effect of technology on consciousness is to unburden it of autonomy, in reference to which he states:

The manipulation of consciousness which has occurred throughout the orbit of contemporary industrial civilization has been described in the various interpretations of totalitarian and "popular cultures"; [it is a] coordination of the private and public existence of spontaneous and required reactions. . . . This coordination is effective to such a degree that the general unhappiness has decreased rather than increased. We have suggested that the individual's awareness of the prevailing repression is blunted by the manipulated restriction of his consciousness (pp. 85–86). . . . With the decline in consciousness, with the control of information, with the absorption of the individual into mass communication, knowledge is administered and confined. If anxiety is more than a general malaise, if it is an existential condition, then the so-called "age of anxiety" is distinguished by the extent to which anxiety has disappeared from expression. (1964, p. 94)

Perhaps more than any other contemporary philosopher, Marcuse elucidates quite clearly the vicissitudes of the manipulation of impersonal consciousness and the concomitant constriction of interpersonal and intrapersonal realities. Likewise, his theory of unidimensional existence provides a cogent explanation for the predominance of paradox in everyday affairs. In agreement with the present model, Marcuse perceives the impersonal dimension of consciousness, for reasons of political-economic importance, as being the most easily manipulated, dominated, and controlled. In his philosophical inquiry, Marcuse focuses on the contemporary loss of the immediate, that is, the linguistically unprocessed, erotic, and intuitive pleasurable sensations of daily life. "Such immediacy is incompatible with the effectiveness of organized domination, with a society which tends to isolate people, to put distance between them, and to prevent spontaneous relationships and the 'natural' animal-like expressions of such relations" (Marcuse, 1955, p. 195).

The diminution of intrapersonal and interpersonal awareness allows for the large-scale control of people and events through the electronic, video manipulation of the now predominant impersonal consciousness. Quite simply, feelings no longer get in the way, and responsibility is transformed into a vague, bureaucratic anonymity that seems to guarantee the survival of the general culture, but at the expense of the self.

Christopher Lasch (1984) calls this process "a strategic retreat into paranoia," away from the self and the interior world, and claims it is a general trend in art, literature, and most science. This process has likewise been described by others as dehumanization, inauthenticity, ontological insecurity, and alienation (Boorstein, 1964; Schor, 1977; Sennet, 1978; Sontag, 1977). In agreement with Herbert Marcuse, most social critics would agree that the change in consciousness is a direct result of two factors: (1) deliberate psychological behavioral manipulation and (2) the replacement of reality by the video image. Ashley Montagu and Floyd Matson (1983) state: "The combination of the new technology and the new psychology has produced an unprecedented and potentially lethal threat to the essential faculties of the human mind: the ability to reason, the capacity to choose, and the will to act upon that choice" (pp. 110–11).

Several theorists perceive the restriction of consciousness as a means of political repression, while others view it as a historical outgrowth of Western emphasis on agency over community (Brown, 1959; Marcuse, 1955, 1964). Eric Fromm believes that the television-exacerbated, externalized consciousness represents a shift from a "being" to a "having" mode of existence, while Christopher Lasch (1984) postulates it to be the economic manipulation of capitalistic consumerism and interestingly disagrees with Herbert Marcuse that anxiety has disappeared, stating: "The state of mind promoted by consumerism is better described as a state of anxiety and chronic anxiety. The promotion of commodities depends, like modern mass production, on discouraging the individual from relying on his resources and judgement: in this case his judgement of what he needs in order to be healthy and happy" (p. 28).

Contemporary consciousness has evolved to the point where life's trivial concerns promote anxiety and really consequential matters are forgotten. Anxiety concerning really important ecological, political, or personal matters is too often considered either irrelevant or a fringe issue of malcontents, rebellious adolescents, and neurotics. Disturbed patients seem more aware and concerned about the really important matters while better-adjusted individuals are preoccupied with issues of self-importance. As measured by the yardstick of cultural achievement, so-called successful people clearly manifest the manipulated consciousness and pseudo-happiness that Herbert Marcuse described. What these people are anxious about is "making it." Issues involving achievement, power, money, status, and image achieve anxiety status while truly notable problems of consciousness and the world are missing. For the cultural celebrities of today, the consumeristic anxiety of buying, having, and making it has become a reality.

THE MANIPULATION OF CONSCIOUSNESS
AND THE VISUAL IMAGE

The predominance of the visual medium for providing processed information provides an unprecedented opportunity not just for controlling consciousness but for homogenizing it. Humans are now at a time when existing conditions for control go far beyond simple consumerism and product choice. At times, psychotherapy meets the criteria for such conditions. Referring to the proliferation of psychotherapies and psychological self-help techniques, Christopher Lasch (1984) states: "These techniques of emotional self-management, necessarily carried to extremes under extreme conditions, in more moderate form have come to shape the lives of ordinary people under the conditions of a bureaucratic society widely perceived as a far-flung system of total control" (p. 58).

General statistics from a 1988 National Institute of Mental Health survey indicate that the percentage of people either seeking or in some form of psychotherapy has been steadily increasing. These people do not have major psychoses or other serious psychiatric illnesses. In fact, throughout modern times the percentage of any given population that could be legitimately diagnosed as schizophrenic has remained remarkably consistent at approximately 1 percent of the general population. There is no doubt that for people with serious and genetically influenced psychological disturbances, some form of psychotherapy is required. These people do not, however, comprise the subgroup causing the increase in the patient population. The statistical increase in psychotherapy utilization is due to a greater utilization by either the marginally adjusted or well-adjusted people of this society. This tendency is somewhat alarming. Why is this new category of adjusted to well-adjusted "consumers" swelling so rapidly? Although there is a multitude of causative factors, this chapter will discuss those associated with television and illustrate them with a case study.

Sharon has been hospital-diagnosed as a young "borderline personality disorder," which is a postmodern, "wastebasket" diagnostic category especially popular in the 1980s. Two diagnostic categories, borderline and narcissistic personality disorder, are to postmodern times what hysteria and obsessive neurosis were to Freud's Victorian era. Some of the hallmark criteria of the borderline status are anxiety intolerance, lack of sublimatory (diversified) channels of expression, poor impulse control, and transitory and usually temporary and spontaneously reversible psychotic states that typically include intense mood fluctuations, emotional sensitivity, and identity confusion.

The Case of Sharon

Sharon was an eighteen-year-old attractive and intelligent white female who, upon the recommendation of a former patient, came to see me. Prior to her consultation with me, Sharon had been hospitalized three times; two of the hospitalizations had included potentially suicidal behavior. Sharon's parents were divorced, and she had two siblings, a younger brother and sister, who were described as being model children. When I asked Sharon what a model child was, she replied, "A child that always does what she is told. . . . You know you can't have any feelings of your own."

Because there is a mild correlation between the borderline syndrome and depression, when she first started psychotherapy, Sharon was on an antidepressant called Pamelor. Pamelor did nothing to change Sharon's inner problems, but it did provide her with the energy not to become depressed or tired over how she was living her life. As she was growing up and prior to her parents' divorce, watching television was the principal family activity. Her parents quarreled about many things, including which television shows to watch. Sharon felt that her mother preferred shows that portrayed the woman as dominant and in charge, with the man or husband representing some kind of a good-natured buffoon. Her father, however, preferred the opposite type of program with the male portrayed as strong, effectual, and positive while the female was characterized as empty-headed and foolish. Sharon claimed she had no idea who her parents really were. When I first started seeing her, she watched about eight hours of television each day (the United States average is about four to five hours). She likewise had little idea who she was. Sometimes Sharon would come to the sessions dressed like a man, sometimes like a woman, on other occasions like a child, and often like a combination of all three. Her speech, manners, and emotions also reflected these changes.

I explained to Sharon that I tended to think of her problem as being, among other things, a disturbance of her sense of self. That is, her personal identity was confused; her consciousness kept radically shifting, and she did not, in a very existential sense, know who she really was. Sharon was one of my longest-term and most frequent patients. For more than six years she was in treatment four to six times a week. Eventually she began to develop a consistent but somewhat shaky sense of a stable self (relationships with men were still very difficult for her) and watched television only a few hours each month. Sharon is currently living with a friend and attending a university.

Sharon's case is an excellent contemporary example of identity confusion. Her confusion has a great deal to do with the externalization of consciousness and the ascendance of the image. In the absence of healthy parenting, Sharon's sense of identity had to come from external sources. Because external images are so valued by our culture, Sharon could not perceive that she was hurting herself. In the absence of stable parental relationships, her reliance on television, video, and movie images seemed a feasible solution. Such external dependence on images neglected the internal development of intrapersonal and interpersonal consciousness.

When adolescents first start socializing, as a way of reducing their anxiety and directing themselves, they adopt roles. Often these roles are taken from popular cultural heroes. For example, when I first started going out with girls, I tried to act like the television rock star, Ricky Nelson. Fortunately, I eventually learned that in order to be liked, I did not have to be someone else. Sharon never was able to evolve out of this phase. It was not until years later and as a result of psychotherapy that she was able to develop a somewhat stable internal image. Sharon no longer had to act like someone else.

Years before the invention of television, the great German poet Rainer Maria Rilke wrote the following passage: "We discover that we do not know our role; we look for a mirror; we want to remove our make-up and take off what is false and be real. But somewhere a piece of disguise that we forgot still sticks to us. A trace of exaggeration remains in our eyebrows; we do not notice that the corners of our mouth are bent. And so we walk around, a mockery and a mere half; neither having achieved being nor actors" (1975, p. 141).

IMAGE AND PERSONAL IDENTITY

What is it like to be a man? Does one pretend to be Roseanne's husband, or is Bill Cosby's version closer to the real thing? Is one's behavior an extension of a "Dynasty" script or a soap opera, or is a Tony Danza or Ted Dansen situation comedy more appropriate? Perhaps if one is into music, an MTV rock and roll star would be better. Then again, should one be macho and tough like Arnold Schwarzenegger, Clint Eastwood, and Sylvester Stallone or is a softer role better suited? What about a cool role or perhaps a scary Jason-like, horror movie type? In terms of how one should act in relationships, the choices seem endless. The situation of role abundance is even more confusing for women. What is it like to be a woman? Deciding this issue was one of Sharon's problems. Should one be like Cher, Oprah, Linda Evans, or Dolly Parton? The choices include attractive, sexy, coy, feminist, realist, successful, impish, mature, rebellious, romantic, cold, and so on. Even more than men, women can fall under the bewilderment of multiple-role confusion.

Although the above passage may sound simplistic or a bit extreme, the effects of visual images on personal identity are very powerful. Television serves up a continuous menu of role stereotypes and simplistic solutions (Condry, 1989; Moyers, 1989 [interviews with H. S. Commager and J. Lukacs]). Watching television is a popular activity in the United States that, on the average, for many people occupies over four hours a day. Furthermore, aside from the inane, commercial thrust of a show, with few notable exceptions the standard show is directed toward a person with the intelligence of the average thirteen-year-old. The above data by no means imply that all people watch television for over 50 percent of their waking hours. The figure represents a normative average that includes young children, the old and infirm, and people with very little to do. Nevertheless, even with these adjustments the data on viewing and show quality are frightening.

If one includes all the images presented in magazines, movies, and videos, the number of external images greatly increases. When an image becomes popular, as in the image of Madonna or Rambo, it becomes literally a cultural prescription for identity. In the absence of consistent sources of identity construction from people who should really be influential, for example well-adjusted parents, leaders, families, or friends, people, especially children and adolescents, are forced to turn to externally fabricated channels. With the scarcity of well-adjusted role models, the power of the image becomes entrenched. From the magazine photographs of *Cosmopolitan* and *Playboy* to the televised scenarios of "Dynasty" and "thirtysomething," the influence of the image upon identity increases. The ready-made status of celebrity video heroes becomes a poor but convenient substitute for the real thing. The real thing, of course, can be found only in the total consciousness of an alive, consistent, and psychologically healthy person. Yet, television and video characters increasingly seem to be filling this role. Video heroes, although unidimensional, are at least consistent; they are there every Saturday at ten o'clock and provide remarkably persistent substitutes. In the preceding chapter it became evident that the transitional, postmodern era contains elements of overchoice and identity confusion. This confusion is evident, for example, in the swift alterations in contemporary family structure. In situations where stable internal guidelines for behavior are missing, people must increasingly augment their identity by turning to externally provided behavioral prescriptions. Stable internal guidelines for identity can develop only under consistent and stable psychological conditions. This postulate has been one of the most accepted and tested guidelines for effective psychotherapy.

Despite its occasional bad press, psychotherapy can be a difficult profession. Although the profession is overutilized by well-adjusted neurotics and character disorders, there are still an inordinate number of patients whose pain is genuine and all too terrifyingly real. Work with these people is often a disappointingly slow task of pacification, unification, and support. Patience is a necessary prerequisite for the profession. Yet on occasion one has, usually with a difficult patient, a wonderful, synthesizing session. Such sessions, although rare, for both therapist and patient are a richly rewarding phenomenon. At least for a moment, for the containment of a 45-minute lifetime, things seem to make sense and the pain of living is diminished. On television this event always happens before a show is over. Television is the undisputed champion of wonderful, synthesizing sessions. No matter how severe the problem, a solution—and before the last commercial—is always imminent. If only the world were such a place.

CULTURE, TELEVISION, AND GENERAL SYSTEMS

Desirable psychological conditions conducive to optimal development do not exist in a vacuum; they are very dependent upon the social, economic, and political nature of the culture. There are many reasons to suspect that general cultural conditions in the United States and perhaps many other countries that are less than ideal for healthy human development. This culture is woefully inadequate in terms of conditions that would promote the full and rich development of a complete consciousness capable of affective awareness, empathy, intimacy, and dialogue.

In a general systems analysis of consciousness, all phenomena are both contextual and connected. In a reciprocal manner, systems and structures are related to and dependent upon parts and substructures. At times there is almost a symbiotic relationship. But it must be remembered that although a part or substructure (like a person) might be important and even influentially autonomous, it is nevertheless always expendable. The thought that people are potentially disposable commodities, although upsetting, is unfortunately true. The priority remains that the overall general system must continue to exist. In terms of the cultural system, the more uniform, reliable, and conformist people are, the more the overall system will flourish. The successful continuation of the overall system depends not upon issues of positive or negative individual effects but, rather, only upon continuation of the conditions that allow the system to survive.

The conditions that promote the continuation of the overall system are to be found in the general culture. In a sense, the general culture is the system's attempt to maintain itself. The general system and the overall culture are inseparable. If one were to inquire as to the nature of the general system of the United States, it would be inevitable that one would have to discuss the overall cultural climate. Cultural conditions are, therefore, the elements that first begin to construct consciousness, that is, perspective, focus, values, reality assumptions, and language. Reality, then, especially the realities of personal relationships, are a construction and interaction between individual subsystems and culture. If the culture is ailing, so then is individual consciousness and thus individual reality. Unfortunately, it is not relevant to the survival of the general system if the individual parts might be ill. All that is necessary is that the parts continue to perform functionally.

In systems terms to perform functionally is to survive. Within this postulative framework, what makes visual technologies so potentially destructive is that they provide a unidimensional, ready-made reality. The ready-made construction of reality is true for all forms of visual media, including photography and advertisements. Television, movies, and videos are by far the most powerful reality constructors. Part of their power is contained in the subtlety of their effects. On the surface, visual media provide entertainment, information, news, and passive activity that earn them a tremendous amount of support. Yet the above mentioned appealing qualities must be considered secondary to their systems purposes of (1) promoting consumerism, (2) making a profit, and (3) constructing reality so that the system survives.

This constructive process always involves the constrictive manipulation of consciousness. The intrapersonal and interpersonal dimensions diminish, values and reality assumptions become uniform and stable, perspective and focus remain limited, and language becomes reflective of and partially generated by abstract and impersonal programming. Yet visual technologies accomplish the above in a most paradoxical manner in that the manipulation manifests itself under the pretense of entertainment, news, information, and passive activity. Manipulation is thus accepted as an inherent and valuable cultural pastime. No one involved in this subtle process would call it manipulation, but that is indeed what it is. When a group of men spend their entire weekend watching the sports channel, no one thinks they are being manipulated; rather, one thinks they are being entertained. The issue of free will would not even enter the picture. Each man would simply take it for granted that he was doing as he chose. No one would realize that the sports channel is a form of passive entertainment and that passive entertainment is not quite the same as the direct and active, personal involvement in an activity. In an era of "couch potatoes" such matters have become passé. The same holds true for scores of other video outlets; soap operas, movies, the shopping channel, and Nintendo are all examples of the systematic, video manipulation of consciousness.

With the sophistication of modern electronic media, these so-called techniques of control and manipulation are reaching unprecedented levels where deception is becoming the norm (Moyers, 1989 [interview with B. Tuchman]). Visual technology has taken "the human experience and

redesigned it into a fraudulent event" (Slattery, 1989). The current emphasis on "reality television" is creating an almost surrealistic reality where
image, illusion, and concrete events become indistinguishably entangled
(Barol & Huck, 1988). As Achenbach (1989) states:

Lies have been raised to an art form in this country, information manipulated so delicately,
so craftily, with such unparalleled virtuosity that it is sometimes a challenge to tell the
genuine from the fake, the virtuous from the profane. The technology of falsehood has
greatly outdistanced the progress of judgement. . . . Yes, Congress really did solicit
testimony about the state of the American farm family from three actresses who had
played farm wives in movies [and], yes, thousands of people really did write letters to
the television show Marcus Welby M.D. asking for advice about their medical problems.
(pp. 113–14)

ADVERTISEMENT, ENTERTAINMENT, AND VALUES

The manipulation of consciousness has a long and established history
and is certainly not limited to electronic visual media. Vance Packard
(1957), one of the first to point out the relationship between all forms of
advertising media and control, quotes one public relations person as
saying: "To public relations men must go the most important social
engineering role of them all—the gradual reorganization of society, piece
by piece, structure by structure" (p. 187). Anticipating the corporate
technocrat of the 1980s, Packard likewise states: "Big business, big
government and big unions [will] tend to level people down to a common
denominator where it will be harder for a man to be independent, individualistic [or] his own boss" (p. 185). Finally, Packard quite clearly describes the desire for cultural control, operating on what is called the
second level of change, stating that "the second level was cultural change,
which is where you must operate . . . if you want to influence people's
ideas. . . . If you want to change their ideas you work on the second level
where different psychological pressures, techniques and devices . . . must
be used" (p. 190).

Society in the United States is shifting from a modern industrial base of
product control to a postmodern technological base of information and
mind control involving the engineering of consciousness and consent
(Galbraith, 1967; Montagu & Matson, 1983). In order to adapt to such a
society, all that is really necessary is to conform and consume. Since
external variables are highly predictable and easily manipulated, they
become the principal values of the culture and, therefore, the culture's
principal map of reality.

In a general systems framework, this type of cultural structure has no need for interpersonal or intrapersonal consciousness, *I—Thou* dialogue, or the development and enhancement of the individual perspective and focus. In short, such parts and substructures are eliminated, by atrophy, from the general cultural system.

This type of cultural system need not emphasize values that promote inner growth, expand consciousness, create self-actualizing experiences, or provide alternate perspectives of reality. In doing so, the main cultural values severely restrict the individual's capacity for happiness and self-fulfillment and actually run contrary to basic biological processes. As Avery Weisman (1965) states: "The aim of any biological process is to bring about some form of regulatory equilibrium, but in human activity inner equilibrium is recognized by a feeling of fulfillment, quiescence, mastery or completion. . . . These are internal values not being taught or emphasized in our society" (p. 69).

This society emphasizes the external image, as manifested, for example, by appearance and material wealth, while placing little value on inner experience (Fromm, 1956, 1973, 1976; May, 1953, 1986). The current fashion in Western society is on external "images and looks," as in, for example, the "successful look," the "sexy look," the "intelligent look," or the ever-popular "power look." These "looks" have nothing to do with true power, sex, intelligence, or success, but are, rather, externally manipulated variables designed to provide specific appearances. They are orchestrated illusions created by the animative abilities of the media professions. This reliance on the external image is best illustrated by the 1988 media-orchestrated presidential election of George Bush and the preceding Hollywood presidency of Ronald Reagan. As E. L. Doctorow says, the grammar of politics today appears to be a visual grammar.

People are becoming increasingly dependent upon orchestrated images as a source of information. In an age of information overload, people are likewise becoming used to information packaged as entertainment. Television news has already become prime-time entertainment. As Neil Postman maintains, the transformation of complex issues into theatrical headlines by television networks deprives the viewer of a coherent and contextual understanding of his world. Information entertainment is really disinformation. In this type of system accurate information becomes secondary to lively entertainment and popular ratings. What is created is the clever illusion that information has been provided, yet this information leads people not toward but away from true knowledge. Talk shows have become a major source of psychological information and education in the country today. Within the context of a talk show, illumination becomes secondary to sensationalization. One psychologist, commenting on her appearance on the Oprah Winfrey show, felt her need to educate and inform was completely overshadowed by Oprah's need to be exciting and entertaining (Harkaway, 1989).

Actually, entertainment is really secondary to consumption and manipulation. In a systems sense, television entertainment is a substructure of the general system's mercantile orientation. With the exception of some public access channels, television shows will stay on the air only if they are supported by commercial interests. Big business will sponsor a show only if it is popular and attracts many viewers, thereby providing access to its markets. Again, the principal goal of the televised images becomes the manipulation of identity and consumption. If information is provided, it is only in the most marginal of ways and is completely secondary to the promotion of a certain life-style and image. Sandwiched between the numerous editions of the morning, midday, afternoon, evening, night, and late night news is a plethora of consumptive messages. In the information overload culture of twenty-four-hour irrelevant news, consumption becomes both a divergence and a misplaced antidote.

The predominance of manipulation and illusion has a special affinity for the news industry. This type of manipulated illusion affects all professions but has an extra impact on journalism. Journalism has become a medium for conveying predominant cultural values disguised as news. The press does not act but is acted upon, as most news derives from officially sanctioned sources (Karp, 1989). As Lyndon Johnson once said, "Reporters are puppets." An associate producer for CBS news claims that the prefabricated, entertainment quality of televised news is responsible for the bland homogenization of the American character. Americans have become a nation of made-for-television moments where everyone plays for the sound bite and the little red light of the television camera (Rickenbacker, 1989).

CONSUMERISM AND CONSCIOUSNESS

The world in general is becoming a global, consumeristic culture of wealth, material success, and survival that does not value introspection and views the interpersonal and intrapersonal dimensions as commodities to be bought, sold, and, most of all, manipulated (Chomsky, 1988; Slater, 1976; Wachtel, 1983). Connections among nations seem more dependent upon issues of free trade than upon problems of world peace or ecology. Sociologists now talk of "consumer frenzy" as an outlet for humanity's growing feeling of powerlessness. The sense of meaning or personal identity comes for most people not from who they are but, rather, from what they own and consume. Objects of consumption such as clothes, houses, furnishings, automobiles, and jewelry all become symbols of image and identity. People look to their possessions not just for pleasure but for meaning. Shopping has become the obsession and passion of this culture, a fact that perhaps partially led to *Fortune* magazine's statement that "in the metaphysics of the market, only those who buy and sell truly exist." Lawrence Shames (1989b), commenting on the impoverishment of contemporary culture, states:

What consumer society tended to do . . . was to withhold such basic gratifications as a sense of purpose, of community, of simply being comfortable in one's skin, and to offer up in place of those things the whole glittering panoply of stuff that could be purchased. The impoverishment came from the fact that while feeding one's life on consumer goods might distract one from the more basic hungers, it could never really satisfy them—and the basic hungers didn't go away. (p. 67)

Humanity's basic hungers, of course, have to do with intimacy, love, and the complete and full expression of consciousness to its fullest potentials. Within the restrictive orbit of conspicuous consumption, the joy of expressing one's complete consciousness plays not even a minor role. In fact, being completely conscious is anathema to commercial consumption. In place of *I—Thou* relationships or a spontaneous and alive consciousness, people have their possessions. The fact that possessions are dead and people alive does not seem to make much of a difference. But what do possessions do for people?

IMAGES AND SYMBOLS

The symbolic power of possessions is directly related to their power over people. Symbols are very important to humanity and are therefore an integral part of any discussion concerning consciousness. After all, the parts and subsystems of consciousness are essentially composed of symbols; words are symbols, and values are symbols. In fact, in this complex world just about anything can have symbolic meaning.

Possessions, at best, seem to be a double-edged sword because, paradoxically, American are not a pleasure-oriented culture and do not really gain happiness from their acquisitions. Because their materialism is symbolic, it does not include the aliveness of the intrapersonal and interpersonal dimensions and therefore lacks the true sensuality and eroticism of classic material enjoyment (Brown, 1959; Marcuse, 1955, 1964). As the classic cultural philosopher Allan Watts (1972) observed: "Our pleasures are not material pleasures but symbols of pleasure, attractively packaged but inferior in content" (p. 75).

Modern symbols are predominantly a product of the impersonal dimension of consciousness and are only remotely connected to the interpersonal and intrapersonal dimensions. As a means of representing reality, symbols have become dependent upon the abstractive abilities of people's impersonal, linguistic consciousness. By predominantly conveying an impersonal abstraction, symbols, like consciousness, have become constricted and have lost their aliveness. A friend of mind was once anxious because he did not own a house. For my friend, home ownership was the ultimate symbol of personal success. Now that he owns a home, my friend has become anxious about it. Ownership did nothing to assuage his anxiety. Home ownership has become the ultimate, empty symbol of the American dream.

In order to represent an experience faithfully, an external symbol (like a house) must convey a large amount of information to all dimensions of consciousness. The symbol must be felt within all realms of consciousness. The impersonal dimension alone will never suffice. A symbol's message is usually transmitted in a surreptitious or paradoxical manner that transcends the linear logic of impersonal consciousness. Rituals, myths, and established customs are all symbols that convey information in disguise. Joseph Campbell implies that one of the most crucial things that symbols provide is the rich and mysterious experience of being alive. Healthy symbols provide more than just "having"; they provide "being," an experience that always includes the affective domains of consciousness. If the ritual of a wedding or a wake is to be successful, it must convey a deeply emotional experience.

These emotional experiences of aliveness are crucial. Complete consciousness is experiential and affectively alive; it is likewise potentially chaotic, often irrational, and usually unpredictable. These qualities are what being alive is all about. Intense emotional experiences do not replace order, rationality, and predictability but, rather, complement them and create a complete experience. Symbols, especially visual symbols and images as they have become or are communicated by the commercial mass media, are not complete; they are distorted representations that become only dimly connected to their proxy objects (Solomon, 1989). Visual, electronic technologies maintain a "cool and neutral" position by presenting situations and characters that are symbolic. That is, although they appear to be real, they are not. Such symbols are impersonally constructed entities that reflect the absence or suppression of the qualities of consciousness that contribute to life's wonderful but uncertain nature, that is, intense emotions, irrationality, and unpredictability. This constriction of consciousness is caused not by the technology of television but, rather, by the technology of its use, namely, manipulation and control. Postmodern, symbolic constructions are a far cry from what metaphorical representations should be. They are not even half alive. What electronic symbols convey is too easily distorted into a flat and sterile consumer product. For the experience of consciousness to be complete, both rational and irrational components are necessary. Neither is sufficient without the other. In regard to the irrational qualities, it must be remembered that they are only part of the picture; that is, by themselves they are potentially useless and destructive.

Anyone who has, knows, or works with adolescents is aware that the qualities of chaos, irrationality, and unpredictability can often unconsciously emerge explosively and violently as part of the teenage rebellion process. Some of the reasons for these eruptions will be explored in the next chapter. For now the analogy is provided as a way of showing that, by themselves, the potentially chaotic elements of intrapersonal and interpersonal consciousness are not that productive. One of the basic human goals is to evolve a complete and dynamically expressive consciousness. Rebellious eruptions, in and of themselves, are just another form of limited consciousness.

SUMMARY

The position in this book should not in any way be misunderstood as antitechnological. Technology is capable of a myriad of positive and healthy consequences and in and of itself is definitely not the problem. It is the use, or rather misuse, of technology that needs to be corrected. Consciousness, not television, is what requires healing.

Aside from the beneficial effects of video technologies in science and research, there are likewise the public and educational programs that offer new and healthier perspectives, focuses, and values. Television can be extremely therapeutic and informative. A general educational campaign employing television and advertising has resulted in some decrease in smoking. The public has also been assisted and informed concerning the deleterious effects of certain illnesses or life-styles. Movies, television, and video, if utilized correctly, have proven themselves to have tremendous potential value. There have been some incredibly powerful and purposeful movies of great personal and social importance. Notably, certain documentaries fall in this category.

For approximately six months, a colleague and I had a show on a local, public access, cable television channel. The show, which was called "The

Existential Half-Hour," provided an educational and provocative summary of contemporary psychological and philosophical issues. Because we did not conform to station attitudes and policy, we were eventually taken off the air. Even so, three years after the show was removed, we still run into people, mostly teenagers, who not only watched the program but actually enjoyed it. Most of them said that the program was a little over their heads and that they didn't know what we were talking about but wished the show was still on and wondered why it had been taken off. Many people said that at least we made them think about their lives. Sometimes I wonder just how much could be accomplished if the majority of broadcast time were decommercialized and given its proper perspective and focus toward the healthy and happy evolution of human life and consciousness.

10 *Community in America: The Psychopathology of Everyday Life*

But when you think about what people are actually undergoing in our civilization, you realize it's a very grim thing to be a modern human being.
—Joseph Campbell

A direct contention of this book is that the often-perceived breakdown of human consciousness is directly related to a similar deterioration in community. Each feeds on the other.

There is a common belief that in order to have community, conflict must be present. Many people report that the time they either felt the most alive or felt the greatest sense of community was during a catastrophe or a war. For many veterans the zenith of their life occurred during whatever "great war" they had fought. While having a common enemy does bind people together, it nevertheless creates only an ad hoc community. During a crisis, people are famous for banding together and helping each other. In fact, crises like the California earthquake, Hurricane Hugo, or the east coast blackouts do create a type of communal bonding. The bonding is, however, only temporary, and as the crisis ends, the community dissolves. Real community requires more than the glue of crises to hold it together; it requires a construction of shared values.

Biologists teach that all organic life organizes itself into some variation of community. The essential nature of a community follows the axioms of general systems theory and thus can be considered to have an interrelationship of parts and structures. Each part of a cell is dependent upon what happens within other parts of the cell as well as upon the larger body of which the cell is a member. The eminent biologist Lewis Thomas (1974) makes the astute observation that the planet can be compared to an extremely large cell. Within both a planet and a cell, within a community of algae or a village of people, a very high degree of interdependency exists.

In a systems sense people can be considered parts that need to be mutually dependent upon each other. The conditions of human nature are such that mutual dependence must include a relationship of consciousness. Within this relationship the interpersonal, intrapersonal, and impersonal dimensions must all be expressed. If one dimension predominates, a distorted perception of reality occurs. The dimensions that most often predominate are the intrapersonal and impersonal dimensions. When the intrapersonal sphere dominates, the more easily identifiable process of madness occurs. When the impersonal dimension dominates, the process, which is difficult to identify, of alienation and despair develops because the impersonal dimension operates on an abstract level of symbolization. If the symbols were alive, there would be no problem. Alive symbols would represent relative positive qualities of a healthy and alive consciousness. But, as explained in the previous chapter, having lost their connections to consciousness, symbols have become dead. Not only are people not relating to one another but they are relating to dead symbols as well. Nowhere is this deadness more apparent than in the state of community. The alienation and despair underlying most communities can be considered the breeding ground for psychopathology. If the community is sick, so too must be the individual.

THE YOUNG AND THE OLD

Although this condition in some way affects all people, there are two subgroups that are especially touched: young and old people. *Young* refers to people under eighteen, and *old* refers to senior citizens or the geriatric portion of the population. These two groups, which contain, respectively, approximately 12 percent and 17 percent of the general population, account for an inordinate disproportion of psychological disturbance and suicide. For younger people the psychological distress usually manifests itself as some form of mood disturbance, substance abuse, rebellion, and acting out. In older people apathy and variations of mood disturbance are the most common complaints. Two case studies, as examples, will be explored from a community perspective.

The Case of Jason

Jason is a bright, articulate fifteen-year-old who, because of truancy and drug use, was referred by his high school counselor. Jason believes that the world is becoming a cold and dead place. He has a hard time negotiating reality in a world where "we are forced to eat other live creatures in order to survive." Jason is failing in school although the last books he has read and can articulately discuss are physicist Stephen Hawkings's book on the origins of the universe and philosopher Peter Singer's book on animal liberation. Jason is musically talented, plays with his friends in a band, and has a girlfriend whom he loves and with whom he plans to go to Europe. Jason has no interest in doing well in school. He likes to hang out, play music, smoke marihuana, and ingest mescaline, but basically he is indifferent. Jason and his friends feel that living is worthless, so they often act impulsively self-destructive. My work with Jason focused mainly on changing his self-destructive impulses so that he could enjoy living a long life.

Jason's Community

Jason could be described as a sensitive and creative individual living in an insensitive world that devalues individual expression. Is something wrong with Jason for feeling he doesn't fit in? Many kids like Jason, not quite as bright as he is, have very similar personal struggles. The noted psychoanalyst Alice Miller (1983) eloquently describes the terrible conflicts of gifted and sensitive children trapped in a world of narcissistic authority figures.

Jason lives in one of the richest counties in the United States. Yet in 1988 the county had at least 4,455 homeless people, over 50,000 people who were listed as "at risk for becoming homeless," and according to a 1980 census, 58,896 people who were living in poverty. Because of the affluence of the community, most of these people might just as well have been invisible. Jason knew of them but reported that he hardly ever saw them.* By his sophomore year of high school, most of Jason's neighbors and classmates had their college of choice picked out. Many of them already knew either what they wanted to major in or what profession they would enter.

In his community, Jason's adolescent contemporaries consisted of either kids destroying themselves on drugs and alcohol or kids planning

---

*Statistics are from *Fact sheet: Hunger and homelessness in Westchester County*. The Sharung community, Yonkers, N.Y., 1989.

for an Ivy League career. Jason fit in with neither. The kids who excessively abused drugs were wasting away while the career planners were totally absorbed with competition and achievement. With few exceptions, none of these adolescents had learned to value consciousness, relationships, and moral behavior. What they had learned was to value competition, with extra emphasis on winning. Victories that Jason's companions venerated were, of course, power, money, and status. Although they were learning subjects in school, the content was totally secondary to the rather pervasive, covert message of competitive achievement. Teachers and parents would openly say that the kids were entering a "tough, dog-eat-dog world where only the strong survived." It was no surprise that Jason's peers were very preoccupied with the impersonal dimension of consciousness. This is what they were being taught. Understandably enough, all of Jason's contemporaries were preoccupied with cars, dating, social status, knowing the "right" people, and fashion.

Jason's parents were fairly successful people, both of whom were college graduates. Jason had told me that his parents were "totally preoccupied" with their new house. The family lived in a new, working-class, suburban development of clonelike houses and manicured lawns. When I met his parents, I told them that Jason felt that they were more devoted to the appearance of their house than to their son. Their response was both indifferent and angry. They both felt that they had worked "very hard to get where they were," and they were very proud of their house. They felt it was very important that Jason be inculcated with the same sense of pride and responsibility. Because his parents realized that "[I] valued the American home . . . and probably had kids of my own whom I was concerned about," they thought I should make Jason behave like them. When I explained that this approach might be beside the point and that what was currently important was Jason's personal identity as well as their relationship with him, they did not seem to understand. They were decent, hardworking people who definitely were concerned for their son and certainly meant well, and yet they clearly did not understand what I meant.

THE PLIGHT OF DECENT PEOPLE

The overwhelming majority of people could be described as decent people. The "decent people phenomenon" seems to be a cross-cultural condition. It seems to affect all cultures equally. This decency manifests itself in a rather basic desire of people to act in a good way, be kind to others, provide a safe and healthy world for their children, and try to follow some sort of moral code. Jason's parents are decent people. The plight of decent people has to do with the flight of consciousness into the external dimension of impersonalness. The impersonal dimension of consciousness is by nature external in that it consists principally of the physical universe. In the impersonal dimension, things, not people, are important. One may not know how to relate to another, but he certainly knows his relationship to his house or automobile.

In such a world things and symbols become the monarchs of behavior, and consciousness of alternate points of view or other realities becomes a prisoner. The world does not appear constructed but rather looks like a stable and consistent realm of set laws and objective realities. These set laws become learned, cultural prescriptions of behavior. Perspective, focus, values, reality assumptions, and language become limited by the power of impersonal consciousness. Because consciousness is impersonal and external, it can be constantly transmitted and manipulated. Reality, as Herbert Marcuse said, becomes unidimensional. Furthermore, such unidimensionality leads to an overreliance on assuming a passive posture not only to cultural or political change but to life in general. The growing predominance of passivity is a serious problem that will be discussed more in the final section on the psychopathology of everyday life.

Most people, not just so-called patients, are extremely limited in their understanding of life. They mean well, but they really do not know what to do or how to do it. People want intimacy, love, understanding, justice, and freedom and yet, except in a very limited sense, do not quite understand how to construct such conditions. They can accomplish this goal within their own material and impersonal world of symbolic objects. People, like Jason's parents, can buy a house and work hard to transform that house into a showplace for people to admire. They can put all their energy into that house, and in doing so they make the house a rather powerful symbol for themselves, a structural metaphor of their lives. The same can be done with clothes, cars, jewelry, paintings, and in essence virtually anything. All that is necessary is to consume and then utilize one's consumptions as reflections of oneself. The laws of consumption as well as the images of consumptive strivings are easily taught to people through the media. The technology of electronic media has allowed the image of consumptive success to become the most prominent goal (see chapter 9). If no one cared or no one admired Jason's parents' house, its value as a reflective symbol would be greatly reduced. Its image and what that image symbolized were more important than the house itself.

Awareness of other realities or alternate points of view depends upon the development of comprehensive perspectives and focuses as well as the evolution of a well-integrated value system and the limited use of language. Language has to be limited because the nonlinguistic, emotional, and creative modes of experiencing reality also require free expression. Consciousness becomes a dynamic and active intrapersonal, interpersonal, and impersonal participant of reality. Both the existence and continuation of healthy consciousness depends upon the deliberate creation of conditions that promote its expression and growth. In other words, such consciousness has to be culturally valued and conveyed through education, the media, and other vehicles of cultural edification. Yet when it comes to conditions that would promote healthy consciousness, this culture operates within a double standard. On a linguistic level, the culture says it values individual expression, but in reality, it principally values consumption and conformity.

Jason's clinical example represented the alienation and dissatisfaction of youth. In Jason's community there was no place for free and creative individual expression, nor was there room for the development of a healthy, *I—Thou*, parent-child dialogue. The other end of the spectrum, the geriatric patient, will now be examined.

The Case of Robert

Robert was a healthy and intelligent 68-year-old widower who consulted me for symptoms of depression. He had been seen twice before by psychiatrists and was receiving a steady diet of the antidepressant Prozac. Despite the medication Robert still claimed that he felt depressed. Upon further exploration we discovered that Robert's feeling of depression was mainly characterized by feelings of emptiness. Robert was lonely for someone to relate to. Until his forced retirement, he had been a skilled craftsman who was very well read and well traveled. He had likewise had a very loving relationship with his wife with whom he shared many interests. Unfortunately she had died suddenly of cancer six years earlier. Since his wife's death Robert was unable to find anyone to relate to on anything but what he described as a "superficial level." He claimed that all people talked about was nutrition, illness, and money. Robert had tried living several places, including Florida, but found that he was always being shunted off to either a golf course or a senior citizens center. For over a year I had an enjoyable therapy relationship with Robert. After a year his emptiness was less acute, so psychotherapy was phased out.

Robert's Community

In a culture that worships the image of eternal youth, life for elderly people is quite difficult. In an exploration of the developmental tasks of life, the psychoanalyst Erik Erikson (1963) cites the wisdom of integrity as being the psychological hallmark of successful aging. In the absence of integrity, despair occurs. What Robert discovered is that most of his contemporaries, although lacking in wisdom, were able to conceal their despair behind a facade of recycled youth. Robert's contemporaries place undue emphasis upon external appearance. The image of youth, obtained through either fashion or plastic surgery, was a very sought-after commodity.

Everywhere Robert found extra emphasis being placed on leisure activities that were relatively useless toward viably contributing to any sense of community. He found people "trying very hard to be young again." Like teenagers who are allowed to "play" because they are not yet accepted into the adult world, senior citizens are encouraged to "play" because they no longer fit into or belong in the so-called adult world. Research has clearly indicated that aging is successful only if a person continues to be valued as an integrated and functioning part of a community. Robert wanted to use his skills as an active contributor to the well-being of "something." That "something" was a sense of community, which Robert found increasingly difficult to find.

In a culture that rarely values people separately from their image and income potential, elderly people often find themselves shunted away from active involvement. Little emphasis is placed on understanding the cycles of life, preparing for death, or working on what Erikson calls healthy concern for future generations. Elderly people are increasingly encouraged to exist in a narcissistic fashion in an egotistic world. Under these conditions they often become very concerned with their own welfare and security. Because they felt that they were being taxed unfairly, the lobbying efforts of well-to-do elderly people were responsible for the 1989 congressional removal of Medicare's catastrophic medical coverage, a coverage extremely important to those people with limited income. In a culture that places undue emphasis on the self, the needs of poorer and less politically influential people become forgotten.

THE DEVELOPMENT OF COMMUNITY

Why have communities developed the way they have? This question is connected to the fact that Americans live in a country in which during the last presidential election less than 53 percent of the potential electorate voted (Granverg & Holmberg, 1988;Moyers, 1989). Because the way people live their lives is connected to consciousness and consciousness is intertwined with everything, this question cannot be easily answered. It can, however, be narrowed down.

In the previous chapter the concept of ensembled individualism was introduced. The idea refers to the belief that the fates of both the community and the individual are intimately connected. The experience of a full range of consciousness is necessary for the development of an individual's complete potential. This principle also holds true for a community. For a community to develop and thrive on the parallel development of its members, the experiences of ethos, telos, agape, and pathos must be present. People do not discuss these feelings any longer, though in older, perhaps ancient days, they were quite common. Such affective experiences are important because they emotionally link the individual to a greater context. *Ethos* refers to the customs or characteristics of individuals in relation to their community. The ethos must be communal by nature. An individual does not make his own ethos but rather becomes part of a mutually constructed one. *Telos* represents the end purpose of the community's ethos, that is, the reason for its existence. Every community, like every individual, must have a reason and a purpose for being. Life must be more than just survival. *Agape* means the feeling of altruistic, nonselfish love. It may be love of another person, love of an idea, or love of a community, but the word, which basically implies being struck with such wonder that one's mouth falls open, embraces the Buberian concept of *I—Thou* relatedness. *Pathos* means suffering. Yet, pathos goes beyond the narcissistic feelings of depression or personal sadness. Pathos places human suffering within a teleological perspective so that suffering becomes both meaningful and purposeful. Pathos is always contextual and is representative of ensembled or allocentric individualism.

All these experiences are more than just emotional. They are an expression of what total and complete human consciousness can be and in that sense are transcendent. Their expression, therefore, allows both the individual and the community to survive and flourish (Moyers, 1989 [interview with S. L. Lightfoot]). Ensembled individualism and conditions that would freely allow the expression of these experiences do not describe the state of community today. People like Joseph Campbell have said that it is the absence of these four classic, experiential factors that causes the loss of the spiritual dimension of community. The spiritual dimension of an active community is the breeding ground for *I—Thou* relationships. For Joseph Campbell this loss was profoundly disturbing.

CONSCIOUSNESS AND ECONOMIC SYSTEMS

A multitude of factors contributes to the development of community. Perhaps the ways and means of people's sustenance are the most important. The way people live their lives is very dependent upon economic factors. The philosopher Michael Polanyi (1961) felt that matters of economy were submerged in social relationships and that any economic system could run on noneconomic factors. In the United States the noneconomic factors are mainly consumption and competition, and the economic system is capitalism.

In order for a capitalistic system to do well, the constant and continuing consumption of goods and services must flourish. What is important is that there always has to be a market for the exchange of goods. In such a system the relationships between people, except for economic reasons, are really not that important. Norman O. Brown (1959) repeatedly makes this point in his classic work *Life Against Death* and quotes the economist F. H. Knight as saying: "It is the market, the exchange opportunity, which is functionally real, not the other human beings; these are not even means to action. The relationship is neither one of cooperation nor one of mutual exploitation, but is completely non-moral, non-human" (p. 282).

An economic system in which, with the exception of exchange, consumption, and profit, human relations are irrelevant is not the breeding ground for developing healthy community life (Moyers, 1989 [interview with M. Nussbaum]). The product of the crippled communities that the United States brand of capitalism has created is an impersonal, constructed consciousness in which human relations are not really important. In this type of system competition is taken for granted, and what becomes valued is winning. Winning is further associated with a consciousness concerned with power, success, control, acquisition, and an overall style of emotional detachment and one-upmanship. Ralph Waldo Emerson said of American culture in 1847 that "if there is one test of national genius universally accepted, it is success."

Today is, perhaps, a rather difficult historical time to focus on the pitfalls of capitalism. Current changes in the communist, totalitarian societies of Eastern Europe and, to some extent, the Soviet Union itself have empowered, it seems, numerous politicians and scholars to glorify what has been called the "victory of capitalism over socialism." For several reasons such a perspective is, first, ultimately erroneous and, second, irrelevant to the thrust of this book. The mistake is to confuse socialism with totalitarianism. They are not the same thing. Totalitarianism, especially as communism has presented itself, is an openly deceptive and repressive political system in which human rights are directly and blatantly violated. Socialism, in contrast, especially modified or democratic socialism, is an economic system in which the community or state maintains some control over the production and distribution of goods and services. Failure of the system in communist countries is really a failure of totalitarianism, a system under which any economic system would falter.

Moreover, the reason these changes are not directly related to this book is that its intention is not to discuss the replacement of the capitalist system. Rather, in exploring the relationship of capitalism to consciousness, this book wants to expose the negative effects of capitalism. There is a common adage that capitalism doesn't have a conscience. To a large extent this adage is true. Although this book will not discuss possible solutions, a more balanced blending of socialistic thought within a capitalistic framework is not at all beyond the realm of possibility—difficult, perhaps, but not impossible.

But is it possible to have capitalism maintain a cooperative mode of operation? The answer is probably yes. Within a systems perspective, just as it is not technology itself that is the problem, it is not capitalism per se that is at fault. The intention in the last two chapters was to highlight some additional contributory factors, the basic one being the constriction, externalization, and manipulation of consciousness. In the United States, people are dealing with capitalism run amok. Values of competition and greed have become entrenched. This is a nation in which Richard Nixon proclaims that "greed is good" and the Donald Trumps assume deity status.

If consciousness is directly controlled in communist societies, it is subtly and covertly controlled here. The manipulation and restriction of consciousness seem potentially ubiquitous, but the methods used differ. It becomes necessary, then, to understand thoroughly what the negative ramifications of capitalism are on both the individual and the community level of consciousness.

COMMUNITY AND CONSCIOUSNESS

Community in the United States is characterized by people living in personal dwellings among other groups of people living in personal dwellings among other groups of people who basically provide services and sell goods. Some of the people who provide goods or services actually live in the community while others are only transient. When the community is large, as in urban centers, the number of transient people that a community member encounters in order to obtain goods or services is astronomical. The affairs of these groups of people are basically managed and administrated by another group of elected political officials who may or may not live in the community they administrate. Within this type of system people are expendable and replaceable. Because their purpose becomes impersonal and removed from any context of intrapersonal expression or interpersonal dialogue, anyone can be easily replaced. The raison d'être of the community is to thrive through the efficient workings of a market. The possibilities of community relationships within this system are

1. community member to community member
2. community member to provider of goods or services
3. community member to political administrator
4. provider of goods or services to provider of goods or services
5. provider of goods or services to political administrator
6. political administrator to political administrator

Of these six choices only relationship 1 contains possibilities outside the impersonal dimension of consciousness. In a Buberian sense, relationships 2 through 6, because they are limited and predetermined, have to be of an *I—It* or an *It—It* nature. The only chance for an *I—Thou* encounter is contained within relationship 1. Yet for various reasons this culture does not encourage *I—Thou* intimacy.

In a capitalistic system each person is encouraged to consume as much as possible. Because ownership is individual and exclusive, there is very little room for cooperative sharing. Actually there is not really any reason for relationship 1 to exist. The effective workings of the system (the marketplace) do not require that individuals relate to one another. A common and unfortunately true aphorism in the United States is that divorce is good for the economy because it inevitably generates more consumption.

PROFIT, GREED, AND CONSCIOUSNESS

What is especially distressing about a competitive market economy is that hunger for profit can masquerade as altruistic concern for the individual. The decades have generated an unfortunate litany of those who have made money from other people's suffering. When someone commits a crime or an ethical atrocity, even before the dust settles, book and movie rights are secured.

Recently this country has witnessed the marketing of fire walking, channeling, EST, and spiritual advisers. The consumer in search of a seminar or workshop on relationships, for example, on women who love too much or men who love too little, will not find the marketplace vacant. A recent entry has been Justin Sterling's $500-weekend workshop on "Women, Sex and Power" in which he teaches women to be more passive and traditional. He already has over 20,000 graduates and grosses over $1.5 million a year.

Greed for profit is not limited to providers of unusual services but affects mainstream science as well. Barry Schwartz (1990) calls this commercialization phenomenon economic imperialism, a process that he describes as

the spread of economic calculations of "interest" to domains that were once regarded as noneconomic. It is the infusion of a practice with the pursuit of *external goods*. This pursuit pushes a practice in directions it would not otherwise take and in doing so undercuts the traditions that comprise it. . . . It is not good science to decide what to study on the basis of what people are willing to pay for. Yet government agencies are able to manipulate fields of inquiry by shifting funding from one domain to another [emphasis added]. (p. 13)

Economic imperialism promotes the practice of utility maximization and changes the definition of what is good from a moral to an economic base.

It is usually always forgotten that the numerous, traditional providers of services such as rehabilitation, counseling, or psychotherapy are out not only to earn a living but to make a rather large profit as well. The average fee for psychotherapy in the New York City area is well over $100 a session. The profit factor affects not only the availability of services but the length of treatment as well. A patient's fee can often be a nonclinical indicator of how long his therapy lasts. The availability of money has widened the gap in the delivery of psychotherapeutic services between the public and the private sectors. A recent study indicated that the average time spent by psychiatrists with patients in a public mental health center was 6 minutes in comparison to 45 minutes for the same practitioner's private practice (DeBerry & Baskin, 1989). An employee assistance program's main reason for existence is the maximization of profit and the ending of lost income. Most people are lulled into believing that employee programs serve the well-being of the individual. Yet, in a market economy the individual's welfare is totally secondary to business success. The following excerpts are from a journal devoted to the employee assistance business (*EAP Digest*, October 1989):

Increasingly, small businesses are adopting drug policies and many are developing procedures for directing impaired workers to treatment facilities. These efforts . . . have created an environment conducive to EAP development within the small business community. This window of opportunity will be open only for a short period (p. 6). The low productivity and poor morale of troubled employees have a way of sweeping through a company, making other workers and profits suffer (p. 9). Illegal drug use cost employers over 60 billion dollars last year, with lost worker productivity accounting for 33 billion

(p. 12). Every employee with an alcohol or drug-related problem costs you 25 percent of his salary each year. . . . [P]roviding treatment is a sound business decision as well. (p. 34)

H. L. Mencken once said that this is the only society in which virtue is synonymous with money. Although a market economy can survive on an impersonal level, human relationships cannot. Consciousness of relationships remains outside the orbit of financial success and must be valued intrinsically for itself. Ultimately, relationships are the glue that holds human life together. Speaking of the importance of community for relationships, the Kentucky farmer-philosopher Wendell Berry (1989) stated: "A human community, if it is to last long, must exert a sort of centripetal force, holding local soil and local memory in place. . . . Country people more and more live like city people, and so connive in their own ruin. More and more country people, like city people, allow their economic and social standards to be set by television" (p. 31).

The basis for community in the United States closely follows several of the principles that sociologist Todd Gitlin (1989) proposes as an explanation for postmodernism (see chapter 8). The most relevant proposals describe postmodern life as a huge, global shopping center and as an anesthetized, unidimensional television generation. Other reasons discussed in previous chapters include

1. The increased mobility and transience of the postmodern culture.
2. The manipulated decline in individual consciousness. Although there has been an increase in information, there has been a decrease in awareness.
3. The irrelevancy of intimacy. Relationships of an *I—Thou*, Buberian nature are definitely not essential to the American political-economic cultural system.
4. The growth of the impersonal dimension.

CAPITALISM, COMPETITION, AND CONSCIOUSNESS

Albert Einstein and Karl Marx are two of capitalism's most prominent critics. Both of them believed that the incessant competition promoted by capitalistic values leads to a pathological breakdown of both the individual and community. Einstein stated that

The profit motive in conjunction with competition among capitalists, is responsible for an instability in the accumulation and utilization of capital which leads to increasingly severe depressions. Unlimited competition leads to a huge waste of labor and to a crippling of the social consciousness of individuals. The crippling of individuals I consider the worst evil of capitalism. Our whole educational system suffers from this evil. An exaggerated competitive attitude is inculcated into the student who is trained to worship acquisitive success as a preparation for his future career. (Schwartz & McGuinness, 1979, p. 169)

Marx's position concerning the ill effects of capitalism is, of course, more well known and has been thoroughly analyzed. His work, much of it in collaboration with Friedrich Engels, was heavily indebted to the philosopher. G. W. F. Hegel. Essentially, Marx associated the competitive values of capitalism with greed, hoarding, and power over other people (Brown, 1959; Marx & Engels, 1967). However, it is not capitalism per se but the distorted predominance of a competitive ethos that is the source of the problem. Both Einstein and Marx recognized the deleterious effects of exaggerated competition. Competition runs deep within the veins of society and, indeed, may be considered the ethical marrow of Western civilization. One may say that its universal acceptance as a way of life has been growing since the Renaissance. As R. H. Tawney (1960) points out: "The rationale for modern industrialism and capitalism was given by the emphasis on the 'right' of the individual to amass wealth and employ it as power. Men were free to follow their own interests or ambitions or appetites untrammeled by subordination to any common center of allegiance" (p. 23).

Competition became the ethical basis for such an individual, acquisitively oriented society. The dominant goal of competition, winning, and becoming number 1 at the expense of others has profound and pervasive effects on all aspects of human development and relationships. The ethicist Michael Josephson claims that winning itself is more important than money, stating: "It's the need to win, to be clever and successful in other people's eyes that sometimes causes people to sacrifice the fundamental ideals that motivated them to the enterprise in the first place" (Moyers, 1989, p. 245).

The need to win affects relationships between people. In reference to competition's effect on relationships, Karen Horney was one of several theorists to explore its destructive tendencies. She clearly perceived competition as being anathema to intimacy, stating: "All these destructive impulses involved in the neurotic striving for power, prestige and possession enter into the competitive struggle. . . . The ability to humiliate or exploit or cheat other people becomes . . . a triumph of superiority. . . . If an individualistic competitive spirit prevails in any society it is bound to impair the relations between the sexes" (1973, p. 197).

These sentiments are well backed by numerous and respected theorists such as ethnologists, who stress the rarity of competition in the nonhuman domain. Animal ethnologists and sociobiologists stress the importance of altruism and cooperation as being essential to the survival and development of all living systems (Alle, 1951; Gould, 1978; Montagu, 1952). Kropotkin (1955), for example states: "Competition . . . is limited among animals to exceptional periods. . . . Better conditions are created by the elimination of competition by means of mutual aid and support. . . . Don't compete! Competition is always injurious to the species and you have plenty of resources to avoid it" (p. 89).

The debilitating effects of competition on human consciousness and relationships have been well documented experimentally (DeBerry, 1989a). It is clear that competitive values as well as the values of rampant capitalism have created conditions that lead to both crippled communities and psychologically damaged individuals (Wachtel, 1988). What isn't exactly clear is why the cultural/political/economic system doesn't change. Why doesn't capitalism develop more of a cooperative ethos? These are very important questions, to be discussed later in this chapter.

In chapter 8's case of Joseph, he wondered why no one in his community ever shared his lawn mower. There was no community lawn mower. Joseph and I wondered why this was so. We especially wondered why, if Joseph tried to discuss this issue with a neighbor, all he received were puzzled expressions or explanations on why it was important to have "one's own lawn mower." This process of individual possession and competition holds true for just about everything but becomes especially apparent for cars and houses.

HOUSES, AUTOMOBILES, AND
THE POSTMODERN FEUDAL LORD

Two cultural entities, one the product of modern technology and the other a traditional and ideal value more than anything else, are directly responsible for the breakdown of community and the isolation of the individual. These are the American (United States version) house and automobile. The construction and utilization of single-family homes in this country have far exceeded any practical utilitarian background. Houses have become far more than simply places to live or to raise a family; they have become symbols and status symbols. In this capacity they have become structural reflections of money, power, and success. An unwritten cultural law states that wealth should translate into (1) a more expensive, opulent, and extensive house, (2) the possession of multiple dwellings even if they are not always utilized, (3) furnishings and decorations that reflect one's income, and (4) a house that is isolated from the public.

Owning a home, a "castle of one's own," as the great American dream has exceeded all possible expectations. It is perhaps a number 1 priority of all new immigrants as well as the capitalistic dream fuel that keeps the engines of this economy perpetually running. Owning a home represents success and acceptance. Fixing one's home in a certain style has become symbolic of the ultimate expression of individual taste.

Yet obsession with perpetuating individual home ownership has contributed not only to individual isolation but to the breakdown of community living as well. Not only are people expected to live alone but they are required to be self-sufficient. Community openness or easy access to neighbors is not encouraged. The very structure and nature of people's singular dwelling places preclude such involvement. Most people go to work only to return home, close their doors to the world, and immerse themselves in television or isolated individual activity. Even those who avoid such a pattern find it difficult to develop community camaraderie with neighbors. In many ways this concept of community home ownership is a type of postmodern feudalism. Instead of evolving into a type of postmodern community tribe, people seem to be partially devolving into a postmodern feudal system.

The conventional adage "Every man is a king when he is in his own castle" certainly bears testimony to this possibility. Each individual unit is encouraged to be as independent and self-sufficient as possible. It is the covert goal of each household to be independent consumers who consume as much as possible. From food to lawn mowers and eventually weapons and fallout shelters, each successful homeowner attempts to insulate himself in an independent and protective cocoon of social isolation. The medieval illusion of an independent lord and master is, unfortunately, a value that remains tenaciously entrenched. Aside from one's home, nowhere else does this territoriality become as obvious as it does with automobiles.

Next to a lavish home the automobile is probably the second most valuable symbol of status. Power, sex, and other culturally prized values are endlessly linked by the media with car ownership. On a symbolic and perhaps adolescent level, an indescribable difference exists between a Hyundai and a Mercedes. The technology of the automobile as well as its resultant behaviors has certainly not been conducive to the development of community. Interestingly enough, cars contributed to the isolation of the suburban household. Almost all post–World War II, suburban communities were constructed with the automobile in mind. Walking around wasn't really given any thought. Communities were designed for people to come out of their houses, get in their cars, and drive. Some houses have attached garages, so no outside appearance is necessary. As the modern mall replaced the town square, it became the fundamental location to which people had to drive. Outside of traditional religion, central meeting places in which people in need of camaraderie, meaningful dialogue, or simply the need to happily commiserate vanished. The concept of separation between the church and the state became complete, and while churches have at least a purported sense of community, the state has none. The state's only virtue is to continue to exist efficiently.

The problem is "that we have thrown the baby out with the bath water." What started out as a division between dogma and human rights became instead a travesty of intimacy and dialogue. This is not what separation of church and state is all about. All that was supposed to be excised was the repressive nonsense of theological precepts, not the need for people to talk to each other. The need for people not to talk to each other is clearly a need of the state.

One way in which a state can accomplish this goal is through inadvertent, manipulated consumption. If a person can buy a car, television, VCR, speedboat, or any other of the mindless but endless products available, then why in the world would he have a need to talk with anyone? Not only will he soon forget others, but he will also forget the need for them as well. Only in the remotest sense does any kind of human need for each other become manifest, and, unfortunately, this occurs at the mall. The mall, unlike the traditional community center, central meeting place, or town square, does not require personal involvement, dialogue, or personal interaction; all the mall requires is consumption. (Since they usually have nowhere else to go, adolescents are the one exception to this rule.)

Although there has been some attempt, especially in crowded urban areas, to modify reliance on the car, most major financial commitments still go into highways as opposed to mass transit or public transportation. After all, one of the ultimate signs of success remains driving to work in a self-contained, chauffeured limousine. People act differently when they are in cars. Even the most mild-mannered person can become hot-tempered, violent, and potentially dangerous. Driving is usually not a cooperative venture. Along with sports, driving is one of America's most dangerously competitive social behaviors. Once a person is ensconced in his protective bubble, all sorts of primitive behavior may occur. The individual becomes like a reptile. The brain scientist Paul MacLean (1969) developed a triune brain theory that describes the brain as being composed of at least three structural parts. According to the triune theory, humans possess an atavistic reptile brain surrounded by a paleomammalian brain, both of which are surrounded by the more recent and civilized neocortex. Although the neocortex is usually dominant, all three of these structures play an active role in daily affairs. The primitive reptile brain, as in most snakes and lizards, is territorial, aggressive, compulsive, ritualistic, and paranoid. This sounds like a contemporary description of driving behavior.

THE PSYCHOPATHOLOGY OF EVERYDAY LIFE

Is the idea of what it is to be human disappearing, along with so many other
ideas, through the modern skylight?

—O. B. Hardison

Although Herbert Marcuse noted that this is an age noted more by happy conformism than by anxiety, he failed to take into account an important clinical shift in contemporary psychopathology. If one eliminates genetically mediated syndromes such as schizophrenia and major affective disorders, increasingly typical psychotherapy patients manifest two forms of character pathology known as narcissistic and borderline personality disorders (Masterson, 1985). Such patients typically present not with complaints of anxiety but rather with complaints of inner emptiness, alienation, feelings of being misunderstood, identity confusion, difficulties with intimacy and relationships, chronic depression, poor frustration tolerance, poor impulse control, contradictory polar states of grandiosity and devaluation, unhappiness, and loneliness. This shift in psychological distress appears in my clinical practice, my collegial relationships, and my personal life. The temper of psychological disturbance has been transformed, and though in some ways the alteration has been subtle, it is also both insidious and profound.

A change in the nature of psychopathology itself is occurring, which is very prominent and can be compared to a paradigm shift in that the focus of the behavioral sciences has migrated from the treatment of sexual and aggressive types of hysterical and obsessive neurosis to general character pathologies of identity and relationship confusion. Since individual pathology is always linked to the cultural climate, one could easily say that since the inception of formalized psychotherapeutic treatments, the general culture has significantly changed. For example, the difference between the repressed neuroses of Sigmund Freud's day in comparison to the present period is rather outstanding.

The cultural climate of the Victorian era, during which psychoanalytic theory originally began, was both a limited phenomenon contained within the boundaries of Euro-American culture and a phenomenon representative of a new transition period, that is, a time when Western societies were still immersed in the beginning of the shift from a nineteenth-century premodern-to-modern industrialized state to a modern-to-postmodern postindustrialized, technological state.

Today, in contrast, clinicians, with the exception of those working in Third World, technology-poor areas of the world, rarely if ever see cases of repressed sexual or aggressive impulses or hysterical/obsessive neurosis. The expression of psychological distress in such a fashion has literally vanished and has been replaced by borderline and narcissistic character pathology. Thus, the data themselves have changed.

This psychopathology is partially a product of cultures exposed to the accelerated, value-bereft, postmodern technologies of the consumeristic and media-saturated global village. Because a global village is becoming an ever-increasing reality, disturbances in consciousness will no longer be local phenomena. A pathology of consciousness will be a global pathology. This type of psychopathology may be representative not of a transition phase but rather of a permanent alteration of consciousness and, hence, what it is like to be human. The impersonal dimension of consciousness may predominate and permanently alter what it is like to be human. The experiential criteria for being alive are changing. The poet Rainer Maria Rilke (1975) said, as early as 1925, that "animated things, things experienced by us, and that know us, are on the decline and cannot be replaced anymore. We are perhaps the last still to have known such things" (p. 141).

Within a general systems framework, it is not difficult to conceptualize how psychopathology on the molecular level of the individual affects and is affected by psychopathology on the molar level of the community, nation, and world, as these are all interacting parts and substructures of the same general system. The parallels are legion. For example, on an international level there are the "identity crises" of the United States and other nations, the feelings of mutual mistrust among nations, the inability of nations to act rationally on issues of global ecology and human welfare, and the impulse to use military force. On a national level there are the breakdown of the traditional nuclear family, drug abuse, the loss of a true political dialogue of issues, and the increase of divorce. Identical problems exist on the community level, where meaningful relationships between neighbors is becoming a thing of the past. The individual and the world community are interlocked in a mutually dependent system of consciousness, ideas, values, and reality. What happens to one part of this system happens to the whole system.

THE MANUFACTURE OF CONSCIOUSNESS

Consciousness is not a static entity. Rather, it is a dynamic and fluid process that is always in flux. While one may learn to perceive his personal identity as constant, his consciousness is not (see figures in chapter 4). The question then arises, Can consciousness be manufactured? The answer, of course, is yes. If one agrees that consciousness can be altered and manipulated and that it can be treated as an object or commodity, then one is faced with the rather discomforting notion that it can be manufactured. Consciousness is limited by two basic factors: neurological "hard wiring" and the component substructures of consciousness, namely, perspective, focus, values, reality assumptions, and language. Such substructures have to be learned. Or, to say it differently, they must be taught. People can be conscious only of what is in the system; that is what they affectively and cognitively know. If all that people are taught is to consume and compete, then consumption and competition will be all they know, and all that they are conscious of will be contained therein.

What is so frightening is that people have the capacity to believe that what they are conscious of is what they are supposed to be conscious of. There will be no alternatives. Recently I had the opportunity to visit people I had not seen for a while. Sitting in their new house, I listened to them talk about how happy they were. They were both making considerable money and could finally afford all the things they had always wanted—a new condo with color-matched interior design, tasteful works of art, matching fur coats, and countless other commodities. As I sat there listening to them, what amazed me was that their happiness was real. What they were conscious of was what they were supposed to be conscious of. In their minds they had "made it"; they were complete.

Soon the impact of postmodern technology will become so invasive and yet so subtle and insidious that what people think and feel will be in danger of becoming mass-produced.

SYMPTOMS AND FUTURE DIRECTIONS

As long as these complaints are treated as symptoms, one will miss the general point that what happens on an individual level (to "patients") happens to all people in a different manner. The fact that because of psychobiological vulnerabilities some people will develop symptoms and "illnesses" should not always negate the validity of their perceptions, that is, consciousness. Historically some of the most sensitive and profound observations regarding humanity have coexisted with severe psychopathology, Nietzsche and Kierkegaard being two of the most famous examples.

Critical thinkers seem divided over these issues. People like Eric Fromm, Rollo May, Christopher Lasch, and Ashley Montagu believe that humans have become a "damaged race" producing "damaged offspring." This school perceives borderline and narcissistic personalities as becoming entrenched. Others, like Fritjof Capra and O. B. Hardison, are more optimistic and feel that people are in a positive period of transition, one that is moving toward an improved and enlightened consciousness. Deciding in which direction people are moving should be the first priority. If people cannot agree upon what is happening and where they are going, there is little point in offering solutions for improvement.

"The only evolution remains the evolution of consciousness, and the material evolution of the world is a consequence of this." Unless people recognize that they are all victims of a general externalization of human consciousness, the entire mental health profession will continue to be acting in what the philosopher-psychoanalyst Richard Chessick calls "bad faith." Such bad faith manifest itself in the frantic retreat from understanding what is happening to the human mind, to the theoretical sanctuary of behavioral and biological reductionism. Clinicians "treat" symptoms, modify behavior, and tranquilize despair, continue to construct theories, and escape into transpersonal and occult metatheory only to find themselves standing still and, in a most fundamental way, unable to change anything.

Perhaps the most critical implication of the present model of consciousness is that in a general systems framework, a part or substructure that is no longer utilized is painlessly eliminated. The overall system continues operating as before, simply minus the missing part, as, for example, with the human organism after removal of the spleen. As intrapersonal and interpersonal consciousness, especially affective and intuitive awareness, constricts, people become in danger of losing it altogether. With this loss goes the true ability to experience aliveness on anything but the most cerebral, superficial, and symbolic of planes. As Joseph Campbell (1988) states: "People say that what we're all seeking is a meaning for life. I don't think that's what we're really seeking. I think that what we're seeking is an experience of being alive, so that our life experiences on the purely physical plane will have resonances within our innermost being and reality, so that we actually feel the rapture of being alive" (p. 3).

Joseph Campbell's explanation partially answers the question raised earlier asking why both the cultural system and human consciousness are so difficult to change. Partially, effective and lasting change is so difficult to achieve because people have confused having with being. The image of anything, the illusion of almost any possibility has become more important than the experience of being, the experience that makes people alive. Eric Fromm has been the main proponent of this position, a position that says that people allow themselves to be manipulated and deceived into submissive behavior because they are afraid to be alive (Moyers, 1989 [interview with S. Bok]). They have become victims of what back in the 1920s Walter Lippmann called the "manufacture of consent." Noam

Chomsky (1988, 1989) calls this process "marginalizing," stating that it reduces the participation of people in the political system to that of obedient consumers, rather than true participants.

PASSIVITY AND THE INSULATION OF WEALTH

Eric Fromm believed that people accept these regressive solutions because a truly human society has not yet evolved. People are too passive; they are afraid to express themselves. The historian John Lukacs (1989) claims that consciousness has evolved to the point where people have become unwilling to think, unwilling in any sense of the word to evaluate quality and truth. Most people have truly become postmodern sheep. Furthermore, enough people in the United States today still have the potential of accumulating enough material wealth to make themselves comfortable. As Noam Chomsky says, there is only one political party, and it's called the business party. This excess wealth insulates people from each other and only exacerbates the problems already described.

The protective encasement of wealth, along with the lingering values of a postmodern feudal culture and in combination with the entire externalization process, has elevated passivity to a new height. The problem of passivity is directly related to the plight of decent people. An earlier part of this chapter introduced the idea that decent people are in trouble and that the manipulation of consciousness and the tyranny of the image have allowed people to withdraw and cultivate a passive approach to life. The ability to withdraw from political change and still maintain some degree of comfort is increasingly becoming dependent upon money.

In the United States people utilize money as a means of developing a comfortable life-style. Everything they need, or think they need, can be stored away in their postmodern castle. They feel they have become independent and do not need anyone to survive. But in doing so they become isolated. This state is not really a true self-sufficiency and thus cannot be compared to the reasons that medieval feudal towns originally developed. They had to develop; the difference is that people do not. Many people have learned, then, to protect what they have. In relation to personal and cultural problems they combine a passive stance with a half-hearted, pseudo-communal involvement. One of the reasons there has been no significant change in consciousness in the United States is that as a nation, Americans have become too comfortable. They have too comfortable a middle class. The placid middle class can buy goods from the Greenpeace catalogue, charge items with an environmental credit card, and donate money toward saving trees in the Amazon. Yet, they can continue to engage in alienated work, compete, profit, buy houses, cars, and entertainment technologies, and continue to become estranged not only from themselves but from each other. This approach is passive and ambivalent, a bit like standing up and sitting down at the same time. It is reflective of a true loss of an active political consciousness, a loss that seems endemic to middle-class culture. Thus, a vicious cycle ensues in which people who are aware of what is going on resign themselves into retreating into their comfortable and safe, postmodern feudal castle. As Eric Fromm (1955) said: "The subjective function of character for the normal person is to lead him to act according to what is necessary for him from a practical standpoint," resulting in people wanting to act as they have to act (p. 71).

People who desire *I—Thou* commitments to the world have retreated into the intellectual and material sanctuary of postmodern feudalism. The critical question, a question well beyond the intent of this book is, Does this state of affairs have to be accepted?

THE ROLE OF THE BEHAVIORAL SCIENCES

The first step toward improving the present situation is to augment present theories and techniques of treatment with general constructs based on the human mind and human consciousness. It was only about a century ago that philosophy, psychology, and theology were all taught in one department. Just as at one time separation of these disciplines was necessary, so now is reconciliation warranted. In a historical, perhaps evolutionary, way the science of psychology must begin to reincorporate consciousness into its epistemological and methodological framework. A true science of psychology (and psychotherapy) must include the empirical and intuitive in a general scientific framework where inner states, as much as possible, can be both operationally and intuitively understood and explained. In doing so, psychology will be a more comprehensive science, closer allied with its revered elder brother, physics. The present model of consciousness, by avoiding inferences to the unconscious and thus metapsychological speculation, is a step in this direction. The rather enigmatic questions concerning what happens to intrapersonal and interpersonal affective awareness as it constricts (e.g., is it repressed, denied, split off, or placed in a nonlinguistic cerebral module?) are a subject for additional research. Psychology, however, has devoted a disproportionate amount of time to these questions, and attention must now return to ordinary consciousness.

People must not be content with atomistic observation; rather, they must realize that existence is part of a general ecological framework and is in need of an ecological understanding. History, communication and political sciences, sociology, and, perhaps most important, cultural anthropology must be reintegrated within psychological theory and research (Bateson, 1975; Prilleltensky, 1989). Psychology must learn that its methods and paradigms are, likewise, results of historical and evolutionary forces and trends. The help of psychology, not only on an individual level but on a community and global scale, as a restitutive force for understanding and well-being is sorely required. However, in order to "fix" the world, it is first necessary to abandon the piecemeal approach and understand how consciousness has changed. In the words of Charles Hampden-Turner (1982): "Such is the modern world that it accelerates our separateness, whether or not we experience this as freedom. We must learn to unify ourselves by developing that which is uniquely human, our reason and love" (p. 48).

SUMMARY AND CONCLUSION

This book has proceeded from a systems description of the elemental structures of individual consciousness to the general cultural structures in which they are embedded. General cultural structures are critical because they influence the development of the substructures of consciousness, namely, perspective, focus, values, reality assumptions, and language. In essence, the text has explored the rich and complex inner world of intrapersonal, interpersonal, and impersonal consciousness and demonstrated how this world is becoming both constricted and externalized to the impersonal dimension.

The importance of this chapter partially lies in the fact that it touches people's daily lives in a very existential way. It is not a theoretical chapter and does not begin with the exploration of a postulate but instead is comprised mainly of observations and subsequent discussions of the observations.

Experience, unlike theory, is not subject to a verification process. Experience simply is; it happens; it occurs; it exists. Experience is not a passive process. Through the operations of the consciousness structure, experience is interpreted. The process of interpretation assigns descriptive meaning to experience. Only qualities of mysticism, sainthood, and lunacy are powerful enough to deter the interpretive function of the mind. As a rule people tend to defend their interpretations zealously. Being wrong or making a mistake is not exactly postmodern fashion. Interpretation depends upon perspective and focus and is greatly influenced not only by temporal and spatial factors but by values, reality assumptions, and language itself. Endless permutations of these factors (as illustrated in the figures in chapter 4) determine consciousness, and consciousness itself determines personal identity or self. Since people are usually not aware of all the operations of consciousness, it seems that their personal identity interprets reality.

Sometimes individual interpretations hold a common cultural thread, and at times they are idiopathic. This book's ideas concerning consciousness and its relationship to community will undoubtedly be interpreted along countless lines. But whether these ideas or someone's interpretation of them is right or wrong does not really matter. Based upon one's individual history, interpretations of these ideas can be endless. What does matter, however, is that these ideas not be considered in isolation but that they be analyzed in terms of how they affect people's daily lives. Ideally, they can modify and improve people's construction of reality.

Interpretation is not identical to construction. An interpretive universe is quite different from a constructed universe. Interpretation, although a valid process, represents an act by a subjective observer upon an objective observed. In an interpretive universe a real and tangible reality exists. This real and tangible outside reality is always begging for subjective interpretation. Thus *I*, the person, represents an entity that is always gazing out at *Thou*, the universe.

In a constructed universe "I" and "you" are one. There are no "objective" external realities but only interrelationships, patterns of relative possibilities and reciprocal constructions. The constructed universe is clearly a quantum entity. A universe of such probable realities can be accepted and understood only within the framework of epistemic dualism, which distinguishes between what ought to be and what is. By one's acknowledging that the universe is his reality and that his actions and experiences and interpretations within his reality do indeed make a difference, then he will make a difference. As Lawrence LeShan (1976) states: "At least if we cannot answer these questions we have to come to agreement on one thing: We can learn to perceive the world differently, and then to act differently in this new world. This is a great step. It is not just that we must learn what is 'out there' and react to it. We must learn that there is a constant interplay between our consciousness and outside 'reality' wherein each affects the other" (p. 10).

The principles of constructionism demand that from ideas a physical model must be built. In other words, since a tangible reality does exist, ideas must be transformed into models that can affect that reality. If the postulates in this book are correct, then the ideas and observations are certainly worth testing. To paraphrase Heinz Pagels, nothing kills a good idea more than the lack of a constructed physical model.

Ideally, a model community needs to be constructed. Within a holistic and ecological community framework, people will be able to construct and experientially validate conditions best suited for the development and evolution of each individual's full potential. Systems, however, are very resistant to change, and the overall cultural system has become incredibly powerful and recalcitrant to modification. Furthermore, although the theoretical language in this book is new, the ideas are not. Countless books have been written about how people are entering a new age of humanity and a new age of consciousness.

This evolution will probably not occur; it ought to, but it isn't. But things are at least potentially changeable. Perhaps the overall cultural system is not as strong as feared. Perhaps the threat of ecological destruction will propel people into a new way of relating not only to the environment, but to themselves as well. Maybe the existing mental health system will crumble beneath the weight of its burgeoning inauthenticity. There might, after all, be a chance to start over. Although there is no one reality of what it is like to be human, there is, nevertheless, an approximate best reality. The approximate best reality is the closest people can come to creating ideal conditions for life on this planet.

The planetary reality may be arbitrary, but the conditions for an ideal human consciousness are not. No one is immune to the transformation of consciousness. Everyone is in the same boat. The conditions of consciousness that can lead to a world where the optimal potential of each person and community are realized are definable. Furthermore, they are physically testable. It is only through the construction of conditions that could encourage the development of an ideal consciousness that the world can change. Certainly, the effort seems worth the trouble.

References

Achenbach, J. (1989, November/December). Creeping surrealism: Does anybody really know what's real anymore? *Utne Reader, 36.*

Adler, A. (1931). *What life should mean to you.* A. Porter (Ed.). Boston, Little, Brown.

Alioto, A. M. (1987). *A history of Western science.* Englewood Cliffs, N.J.: Prentice-Hall.

Alle, N. C. (1951). *Cooperation among animals: With human implications.* New York: Schuman.

Andrews, J. D. W. (1989). Visions of reality. *American Psychologist, 44,* 802–17.

Baars, B. J. (1988). *A cognitive theory of consciousness.* Cambridge: Cambridge University Press.

Barol, B., & Huck, J. (1988, October 17). At long last. Television gets real. *Newsweek.*

Bateson, G. (1975). *Steps to an ecology of the mind.* New York: Ballantine Books.

Beaumont, J. G. (1981). Split brain studies. In G. Underwood & R. Stevens (Eds.), *Aspects of consciousness.* New York: Academic Press.

Becker, E. (1973). *The denial of death.* New York: Free Press.

Bellah, R. (1987). *Individualism and commitment.* New York: Harper & Row.

Berger, P. L., & Luckman, T. (1966). *The social construction of reality.* New York: Doubleday.

Berry, W. (1989, October 9). A tapestry of prairie life. *Time.*

Blackburn, T. R. (1973). Sensuous-intellectual complementarity in science. In R. E. Ornstein (Ed.), *The nature of human consciousness.* New York: Viking Press.

Bloom, A. (1988). *The closing of the American mind.* New York: Simon & Schuster.

Bloom, F. E., & Lazerson, A. (1988). *Brain, mind and behavior. 2d ed.* Salt Lake City: W. H. Freeman.

Bohm, D. (1980). *Wholeness and the implicit order.* London: Routledge & Kegan.

Bohr, N. (1958). *Atomic physics and human knowledge.* New York: Wiley.

Boorstein, D. J. (1964). *The image: A guide to pseudo events in America.* New York: Harper.

Bornstein, R. F. (1988). Radical behaviorism, internal states, and the science of psychology: A reply to Skinner. *American Psychologist, 43,* 819–21.

Briggs, J. P., & Peat, F. D. (1984). *The looking glass universe.* New York: Simon & Schuster.

Brown, N. O. (1959). *Life against death.* Middletown, Conn.: Wesleyan University Press.

Brown, R. (1988). The development of language and language research. In F. S. Kessel (Ed.), *Essays in honor of Roger Brown.* Hillsdale, N.J.: L. Erlbaum.

Buber, M. (1970). *I and Thou.* (W. Kaufman, Trans.) New York: Scribner.

Campbell, J. (1988). *The power of myth.* New York: Doubleday.

Capra, F. (1988). *Uncommon wisdom.* New York: Bantam Books.

――――. (1982). *The turning point.* New York: Bantam Books.

――――. (1977). *The tao of physics.* New York: Bantam Books.

Chapple, E. D. (1970). *Culture and biologic man.* New York: Holt, Rinehart & Winston.

Chessick, R. (1985). The frantic retreat from the mind to the brain: American psychiatry in *mauvaise foi. Psychoanalytic Inquiry, 5,* 369–403.

Chomsky, N. (1989). *Necessary illusions: Thought control in a democratic society.* Boston: South End Press.

――――. (1988). *The Chomsky reader.* New York: Pantheon.

――――. (1968). *Language and mind.* New York: Harcourt Brace Jovanovich.

Churchland, P. M., & Churchland, P. S. (1990). Could machines think? *Scientific American, 262,* 32–40.

Condry, J. C. (1989). *The psychology of television.* Hillsdale, N.J.: L. Erlbaum.

Dapkus, M. A. (1985). A thematic analysis of the experience of time. *Journal of Personality and Social Psychology, 49.*

Davies, P. (1983). *God and the new physics.* New York: Touchstone Books.

DeBerry, S. (1989a). The effect of competitive tasks on liking of self and other. *Social Behavior and Personality, 17,* 61–81.

――――. (1989b). Schizoid phenomena, object-relations theory and psychobiology: A proposed model. *Contemporary Psychotherapy, 19,* 81–109.

――――. (1987). Necessary and sufficient factors in psychotherapy: A model for understanding iatrogenic disorders. *Contemporary Psychotherapy, 17,* 235–50.

DeBerry, S., & Baskin, D. (1989). Termination criteria in psychotherapy: A comparison of public and private factors. *American Journal of Psychotherapy, 43,* 43–53.

Deikman, A. J. (1971). Bimodal consciousness. *Archives of General Psychiatry, 25,* 481–89.

Derrida, J. (1981). *Dissemination.* Chicago: University of Chicago Press.

Engels, G. L. (1987). Physician-scientists and scientific physicians. Resolving the humanism-science dichotomy. *American Journal of Medicine, 82,* 107–11.

Engels, M. (1984). *The language trap.* Englewood Cliffs, N.J.: Prentice-Hall.

Erikson, E. (1963). *Childhood and society. Rev. ed.* New York: Norton.

Ewen, S. (1989). *Consuming images: The politics of style in contemporary culture.* New York: Basic Books.

Fairbairn, W. R. D. (1952). *An object-relations theory of personality.* New York: Basic Books.

Farb, P., & Armelagos, G. (1980). *Consuming passions.* New York: Simon and Schuster.

Fawcett, B. (1989). *Cambodia: A book for people who find television too slow.* New York: Grove Press.

Feffer, M. (1988). *Radical constructivism.* New York: New York University Press.

Feldstein, L. C. (1978). *Homo quaerens.* New York: Fordham University Press.

Felman, S. (1985). *Writing and madness.* Ithaca, N.Y.: Cornell University Press.

Festinger, L. (1957). *A theory of cognitive dissonance.* Stanford, Calif.: Stanford University Press.

Foucault, M. (1973). *Madness and civilization.* New York: Vintage.

Fraisse, P. (1963). *The psychology of time.* New York: Harper & Row.

Frank, J. D. (1978). *Psychotherapy and the human predicament.* New York: Schocken.

Freud, S. (1978). *Basic works* (J. Strachey, Trans.) Franklin, Pa.: Franklin Library.

———. (1921). Psychoanalysis and telepathy. In J. Strachey (ed.), *Standard edition of the complete works of Sigmund Freud.* Vol. 18. New York: Hogarth Press.

Fromm, E. (1976). *To have or to be.* New York: Bantam Books.

———. (1973). *The anatomy of human destructiveness.* New York: Fawcett.

———. (1956). *The art of loving.* New York: Harper & Row.

———. (1955). *The sane society.* Greenwich, Conn.: Fawcett.

Galbraith, J. K. (1967). *The new industrial state.* Boston: Houghton Mifflin.

Gazzaniga, M. (1985). *The social brain.* New York: Basic Books.

Gibran, K. (1926). *Sand and foam.* New York: A. Knopf.

Gitlin, T. (1989). Postmodernism defined at last. *Utne Reader, 34.*

Gleick, J. (1987). *Chaos: Making a new science.* New York: Viking Press.

Goldsen, R. K. (1975). *The show and tell machine.* New York: Dial Press.

Goleman, D., & Davidson, R. J. (Eds.) (1979). *Consciousness: The brain, states of awareness and alternate realities.* New York: Irvington.

Gorman, B. S., & Weissman, A. E. (Eds.) (1977). *The personal experience of time.* New York: Plenum Press.

Gould, S. J. (1978). Biological potential vs. biological determinism. In A. L. Caplan (Ed.), *The sociobiology debate.* New York: Harper & Row.

Granverg, D., & Holmberg, S. (1988). *The political system matters.* New York: Cambridge University Press.

Grinker, R. R., Sr. (1974). Preface to general systems theory. In W. Gray, F. Duhl, & N. D. Rizzo (Eds.), *General systems theory.* Boston: Little, Brown.

Guidano, V. F. (1987). *Complexity of the self.* London: Guilford Press.

Hampden-Turner, C. (1982). *Maps of the mind.* New York: Collier Books.

Handy, R. (1969). *Value theory and the behavioral sciences.* Springfield, Ill.: Charles Thomas.

Hardison, O. B. (1989). *Disappearing through the skylight: Culture and technology in the twentieth century.* New York: Viking.

Harkaway, J. (1989, March/April). *Family Therapy Network.*

Harrison, E. R. (1981). *Cosmology.* New York: Cambridge University Press.

Heaney, P. B., & Heaney, J. J. (1973). Martin Buber's meditation on the I—thou relationship. In J. J. Heaney (Ed.), *Psyche and spirit.* New York: Paulist Press.

Heidegger, M. (1962). *On time and being* (Joan Stambaugh, Trans.). New York: Harper & Row.

Herbert, N. (1987). *Quantum reality.* New York: Doubleday.

Herrick, C. J. (1949). *George Ellett Coghill.* Chicago: University of Chicago Press.

Hofstadter, D. R. (1979). *Godel, Escher and Bach.* New York: Basic Books.

Holbrock, B. (1981). *The stone monkey.* New York: William Morrow.

Hooper, J., & Teresi, D. (1986). *The three-pound universe.* New York: Macmillan.

Horney, K. (1973). *The neurotic personality of our time.* New York: W. W. Norton.

Husserl, E. (1931). *Ideas: General introduction to pure phenomenology* (W. R. B. Gibson, Trans.). New York: Macmillan.

Huxley, A. (1954). *The doors of perception and heaven and hell.* New York: Harper & Row.

James. W. [1896] (1950). *The principles of psychology.* Reprint. Dover, Eng.: Constable.

Jaspers, K. (1963). *General psychopathology* (H. J. Hamilton, Trans.). Chicago: University of Chicago Press.

Jaynes, J. (1976). *The origins of consciousness in the breakdown of the bicameral mind.* Boston: Houghton Mifflin.

Karp, W. (1989). Who decides what is news? *Utne Reader, 36.*

Kaufmann, W. (1975). *Existentialism from Dostoevsky to Sartre.* New York: New American Library.

Kierkegaard, S. (1954). *The sickness unto death* (W. Lowrie, Trans.). New York: Doubleday.

Koestler, A. (1978). *Janus.* London: Hutchinson.

———. (1967). *The act of creation.* New York: Basic Books.

Kohlberg, L. (1976). Moral stages and moralization. In T. Lickona (Ed.), *Moral development and behavior.* New York: Holt, Rinehart & Winston.

———. (1973). The claim to moral adequacy of a highest state of moral judgement. *Journal of Philosophy, 70,* 630–46.

———. (1971). From is to ought: How to commit the naturalistic fallacy and get away with it in the study of moral development. In T. Mischel (Ed.), *Cognitive development and epistemology.* New York: Academic Press.

Knight, F. H. (1935). *The ethics of competition.* New York: Harper & Row.

Kohler, W. (1947/1975). *Gestalt psychology.* New York: Mentor Books.

Kropotkin, P. [1902] (1955). *Mutual aid: A factor of evolution.* Reprint. Boston: Extending Horizons Books.

Kuhn, T. S. (1970). *The structure of scientific revolutions.* Chicago: University of Chicago Press.

Laing, R. D. (1965a). *The divided self.* Harmondsworth, Eng.: Penguin.

———. (1965b). *Self and others.* Harmondsworth, Eng.: Penguin.

Lakatos, I. (1974). Falsification and the methodology of scientific research programs. In I. Lakatos & A. Musgrave (Eds.), *Criticism and the growth of knowledge.* London: Cambridge University Press.

Landers, S. (1989a). Senate eyes limiting TV hard sell. *APA Monitor, 20.*

———. (1989b). Watching television violence shapes people's values. *APA Monitor,* #21.

Langer, S. (1967). *Mind: An essay on human feeling. Vol. 1.* Baltimore: Johns Hopkins University Press.

Lasch, C. (1987). Spiritual transformations. *OMNI.*

———. (1984). *The minimal self.* New York: Norton.

———. (1979). *The culture of narcissism.* New York: Norton.

Laszlo, E. (1971). Reverence for natural systems. In E. Laszlo & E. Stulman (Eds.), *Emergent man.* New York: Gordon & Breach.

Lazarus, A. (1972). *Behavior therapy and beyond.* New York: McGraw-Hill.

Lee, D. (1950). Codifications of reality. *Psychosomatic Medicine, 12.*

LeShan, L. (1976). *Alternate realities.* New York: M. Evans.

Lieberman, P. (1981). *The biology and evolution of language.* Cambridge, Mass.: Harvard University Press.

Lorenz, K. (1950). The comparative method in studying innate behavior patterns. In Symposia of the Society for Experimental Biology, no. 4, *Physiological mechanisms in animal behavior.* Cambridge: Cambridge University Press.

Lutz, W. (1989). *Doublespeak.* New York: Harper & Row.

MacIntyre, A. (1981). *After virtue.* South Bend, Ind.: University of Notre Dame Press.

MacLean, P. D. (1969). The paranoid streak in man. In A. Koestler & J. R. Smythies, *Beyond reductionism*. Boston: Beacon Press.

McLuhan, M. (1964). *Understanding media: The extensions of man*. New York: McGraw-Hill.

McQuail, D. (1985). Sociology of mass communication. *Annual Review of Sociology, 11*.

Marcuse, H. (1964). *One dimensional man*. Boston: Beacon Press.

———. (1955). *Eros and civilization*. New York: Vintage Books.

Margulis, L. (1989, October 12). Rethinking evolution. *Newsweek*.

Marmor, J. (1985). Biologic psychiatry and the psychosomatic approach. *Psychosomatics, 26*.

———. (1983). Systems thinking in psychiatry. *American Journal of Psychiatry, 140*, 833–38.

Marx, K., & Engels, F. (1967). *The communist manifesto*. Harmondsworth, Eng.: Penguin.

Masterson, J. F. (1985). *The real self*. New York: Brunner/Mazel.

Mathes, E. W. (1981). *From survival to the universe*. Chicago: Nelson Hall.

Matson. F. (1974). *The idea of man*. New York: Delta.

May, R. (1986). *The discovery of being*. New York: Norton.

———. (1953). *Man's search for himself*. New York: Delta.

Meichenbaum, D. H. (1974). *Cognitive behavior modification*. Morristown, N.J.: General Learning Press.

Merleau-Ponty, M. (1962). *The phenomenology of perception*. London: Routledge & Kegan Paul.

Merton, T. (1972). *New seeds of contemplation*. New York: New Directions.

Miller, A. (1983). *The drama of the gifted child*. New York: Basic Books.

Miller, J. G., and Miller, J. L. (1985). General living systems theory. In H. I. Kaplann & B. J. Sadock (Eds.), *Comprehensive textbook of psychiatry*. Vol. 1, 4th ed., 13–24. Baltimore: Williams and Wilkins.

Mohl, P. C. (1987). Should psychotherapy be considered a biological treatment? *Psychosomatics, 28*.

Montagu, A. (1952). *Darwin, competition and cooperation*. Reprint. Westport, Conn.: Greenwood Press.

Montagu, A., & Matson, F. (1983). *The dehumanization of man*. New York: Simon & Schuster.

Moyers, B. (1989). *A world of ideas*. New York: Doubleday.

Needleman, J. (1979). *On the way to self knowledge*. San Francisco: University of San Francisco Press.

Ornstein, R. (1987). *Multi-mind*. New York: Houghton Mifflin.

———. (1977). *The psychology of consciousness*. 2nd ed. New York: Harcourt Brace Jovanovich.

———. (1973). *The nature of human consciousness*. New York: Viking.

———. (1969). *On the experience of time*. Harmondsworth, Eng.: Penguin.

Ornstein, R., & Erlich, P. (1989). *New world—new mind*. New York: Doubleday.

Oskamp, P. (Ed.) (1988). *Television as a social issue*. Newberry Park, Calif.: Sage.

Packard, V. (1957). *The hidden persuaders*. New York: Simon & Schuster.

Packer, M. J. (1985). The structure of moral action: A hermeneutic study of moral conduct. *Contribution to Human Development, 13* (entire issue).

Pagels, H. (1989). *Dreams of reason*. New York: Bantam Books.

Pearce, J. C. (1974). *Exploring the crack in the cosmic egg*. New York: Washington Square Press.

Piaget, J. (1974). *La prise de conscience*. Paris: Presses Universitaires de France. Eng. trans.: *The grasp of consciousness*. (1980). Cambridge: Harvard University Press.

———. Piaget, J. (1965). *The moral judgement of the child* (M. Gabain, Trans.). New York: Free Press.

———. Piaget, J. (1932). *The moral development of the child* (M. Gabain, Trans.). London: Kegan.

Pivcevic, E. (1986). *The concept of reality*. New York: St. Martin's Press.

Polanyi, M. (1969). The structure of consciousness. In M. Green (Ed.), *Knowing and being*. Chicago: University of Chicago Press.

———. (1961). *The study of man*. Chicago: University of Chicago Press.

Pollio, H. (1990). The stream of consciousness since James. In M. Johnson & T. Healy (Eds.), *The principles at 100*. Hillsdale, N.J.: L. Erlbaum.

———. (1982). *Behavior and existence*. Monterey: Brooks/Cole.

———. (1977). *Psychology and the poetics of growth*. Hillsdale, N.J.: L. Erlbaum.

Popper, K. R. (1972). *Objective knowledge: An evolutionary approach*. London: Oxford University Press.

———. (1959). *The logic of scientific discovery*. London: Oxford University Press.

Pribram, K. H. (1986). The cognitive revolution and mind/brain issues. *American Psychologist, 41*, 507–20.

———. (1977). Some comments on the nature of the perceived universe. In R. Shaw & J. D. Bransford (Eds.), *Perceiving, acting and knowing*. Hillsdale, N.J.: L. Erlbaum.

Prigogine, I. (1980). *From being to becoming: Time and consciousness in the physical sciences*. San Francisco: W. H. Freeman.

———. (1978). Time, structure and fluctuations. *Science, 201*, 777–85.

Prilleltensky, I. (1989). Psychology and the status quo. *American Psychologist, 44*, 795–801.

Pugh, G. E. (1977). *The biological origin of human values*. New York: Basic Books.

Rapoport, A. (1974). Mathematics and cybernetics. In S. Arieti (Ed.), *American handbook of psychiatry*. Vol. 1, 2d ed. New York: Basic Books, 1074–94.

Razran, G. (1971). *Mind in evolution*. New York: Houghton Mifflin.

Rickenbacker, K. (1989, May 1). Where is the goober? *Newsweek*.

Ricoeur, P. (1981). *Hermeneutics and the human sciences: Essays on language, action and interpretation*. (J. Thompson, Trans. and Ed.). Cambridge: Cambridge University Press.

Rilke, R. M. (1975). The notes of Malte Laurids Brigge. In W. Kaufmann (Ed.), *Existentialism from Dostoevsky to Sartre*. New York: New American Library.

Rokeach, M. (1968). *Beliefs, attitudes and values*. San Francisco: Jossey-Bass.

Rokeach, M., & Ball-Rokeach, S. J. (1989). Stability and change in American value priorities: 1968–1981. *American Psychologist, 44*.

Ronat, M. (1979). *Language and responsibility*. New York: Pantheon.

Rose, P. (1973). *The conscious brain*. New York: Alfred Knopf.

Rucker, R. (1982). *Infinity and the mind*. New York: Bantam Books.

Sampson, E. E. (1989). The challenge of social change for psychology. *American Psychologist, 44*.

————. (1988). The debate on individualism. *American Psychologist, 43.*

Sapir, E. (1921). *Language: An introduction to the study of speech.* New York: Harcourt Brace.

Sartre, J. P. (1957). *Existentialism and human emotions.* New York: Philosophical Library.

Schallow, J. R., & McIlwraith, R. D. (1986–87). Is television viewing really bad for your imagination? *Imagination, Cognition and Personality, 6,* 25–41.

Schor, D. (1977). *Clearing the air.* Boston: Houghton Mifflin.

Schwartz, B. (1990). The creation and destruction of values. *American Psychologist, 45,* 7–16.

Schwartz, J., & McGuinness, M. (Eds.) (1979). *Einstein for beginners.* New York: Pantheon Books.

Schwartz, M. A., & Osborne, P. W. (1986). Systems and the structure of meaning. *American Journal of Psychiatry, 143,* 1213–21.

Sennet, R. (1978). *The fall of public man.* New York: Vintage.

Shames, L. (1989a). *The hunger for more: Searching for values in the land of greed.* New York: Time Books.

————. (1989b). Post-modernism defined, at last! *Utne Reader, 35.*

Singer, P. (1975). *Animal liberation.* New York: Avon Books.

Skinner, B. F. (1987). Whatever happened to psychology as the science of behavior? *American Psychologist, 42,* 780–87.

Slater, P. (1976). *The pursuit of loneliness.* Rev. ed. Boston: Beacon Press.

Slattery, D. P. (1989, November 13). An Orwellian wedding. *Newsweek.*

Smith, H. (1976). *Forgotten truth: The primordial tradition.* New York: Harper & Row.

Smith, R. A. (1984). Passport to evolutionary awareness. In J. White (Ed.), *Frontiers of consciousness.* New York: Julian Press.

Solomon, J. (1989). *Symbols, the signs of our time.* New York: J. P. Tarcher.

Sontag, S. (1977). *On photography.* New York: Farrar, Straus & Giroux.

Sperry, R. W. (1988). Psychology's mentalist tradition and the religion/science tension. *American Psychologist, 43,* 607–14.

————. (1987). *Consciousness.* In R. L. Gregory (Ed.), *The Oxford companion to the mind.* New York: Oxford University Press.

————. (1976). Mental phenomena as causal determinants in brain function. In G. G. Globus, G. Maxwell, & I. Savodnik (Eds.), *Consciousness and the brain: A scientific and philosophic inquiry.* New York: Plenum Press.

Stillito, A. M. (1987). Visual system organization. In R. L. Gregory (Ed.), *The Oxford companion to the mind.* New York: Oxford University Press.

Sullivan, H. S. (1953). *The interpersonal theory of psychiatry.* New York: Norton.

Tart, C. T. (1983). *States of consciousness.* Novato, Calif.: Psychological Products.

————. (1975). *States of consciousness.* New York: E. P. Dutton.

Tawney, R. H. (1960). *The acquisitive society.* New York: Mentor Books.

Thomas, H. (1979). *History of the world.* New York: Harper & Row.

Thomas, L. (1974). *The lives of a cell.* New York: Bantam Books.

Triandis, H. C., Bontempo, R., Villareal, M. J., Asai, M., & Lucca, N. (1988). Individualism and collectivism: Cross-cultural perspectives on self-ingroup relationships. *Journal of Personality and Social Psychology, 54,* 323–38.

Tuchman, B. (1978). *A distant mirror.* Philadelphia, Pa.: Franklin Library.

Turiel, E. (1979). Social regulations and the domains of social concepts. In W. Damon (Ed.), *Social cognition: New directions for child development.* San Francisco: Jossey-Bass.

———. (1972). Stage transition in moral development. In R. M. Travers (Ed.), *Second handbook of research on teaching.* Chicago: Rand McNally.

Udell, B., & Hornstra, R. K. (1977). The unevenness of psychiatric care. *Comprehensive Psychiatry, 18,* 1–9.

Veblen, T. (1979). *The theory of the leisure class.* Harmondsworth, Eng.: Penguin.

Von Bertalanaffy, L. (1974). General systems theory and psychiatry. In S. Arieti (Ed.), *American Handbook of Psychiatry.* Vol. 1, 2d ed. New York: Basic Books, 1095–1120.

———. (1973). *General systems theory: Foundations, development, applications.* Rev. ed. New York: G. Braziller.

Wachtel, H. (1988). *The money mandarins: The making of a supranational economic order.* New York: Pantheon.

Wachtel, P. (1983). *The poverty of affluence.* New York: Free Press.

Watts, A. (1972). *The book on the taboo against knowing who you are.* New York: Vintage.

Watzlawick, P. (Ed.) (1984). *The invented reality: Contributions to constructivism.* New York: Norton.

Weimer, W. B. (1982). Hayek's approach to the problems of complex phenomena: An introduction to the theoretical psychology of the sensory order. In W. B. Weimer & D. S. Palermo (Eds.), *Cognition and the symbolic process.* Vol. 2. Hillsdale, N.J.: L. Erlbaum.

Weisman, A. D. (1965). *The existential core of psychoanalysis.* Boston: Little, Brown.

White, L. A. (1949). *The science of culture.* New York: Farrar, Strauss & Young.

White, P. (1982). Belief about conscious experience. In G. Underwood (Ed.), *Aspects of consciousness.* Vol. 3. New York: Academic Press.

Whitehead, A. N. (1925). *Science and the modern world.* New York: Macmillan.

Whorf, B. L. (1957). *Language, thought and reality.* New York: Wiley.

———. (1941). The relation of habitual thought and behavior to language. In L. Spier (Ed.), *Language, culture and personality.* Menasha, Wis.: Banta Press.

Wigner, E. P. (1972). The place of consciousness in modern physics. In C. Muses & A. M. Young (Eds.), *Consciousness and reality.* New York: Dutton.

Wilson, E. O. (1975). *Sociobiology: The new synthesis.* Cambridge: Harvard University Press.

Winnicott, D. W. *Human nature.* New York: Schocken Books.

Winokur, G., & Clayton, P. (1986). *The medical basis of psychiatry.* Philadelphia: W. B. Saunders.

Wolf, F. A. (1989). *Parallel universes.* New York: Bantam Books.

———. (1982). *Space, time and beyond.* New York: Bantam Books.

Youngdale, J. M. (1988). *Habits of thought.* Minneapolis: CLIO Books.

Index

About the Author

STEPHEN T. DEBERRY is an Assistant Clinical Professor at the Albert Einstein College of Medicine and is also in private practice in Westchester County, New York. He has also authored several articles that have appeared in the *American Journal of Psychotherapy*, the *Journal of Geriatric Psychology*, and the *Journal of Contemporary Psychotherapy*.